INTO THE
MINEFIELDS

By the same author

NAVAL

Action Imminent

Battle of Midway

Battleship Royal Sovereign

Cruisers in Action

Destroyer Leader

Fighting Flotilla

Heritage of the Sea

H.M.S. Wild Swan

Into the Minefields

Royal Navy Ships' Badges

War in the Aegean

Task Force 57

Arctic Victory

Battles of the Malta Striking Forces

British Battle Cruisers

Destroyer Action

Eagle's War

Hard Lying

Hit First, Hit Hard

Hold the Narrow Sea

Pedestal

Sailors in Dock

The Great Ships Pass

DIVE BOMBERS

Aichi D3A1/2 Val

Dive Bomber

Douglas SBD Dauntless

Into the Assault

Junkers Ju.87 Stuka

Straight Down!

Stukas over the Mediterranean

Stuka Spearhead

Curtiss SB2C Helldiver

Dive Bombers in Action

Impact!

Jungle Dive Bombers at War

Petalyakov Pe-2 Peshka

Stuka War

Stukas over the Steppe

Stuka Squadron

AVIATION

Close Air Support

Fairchild-Republic
  A-10A Thunderbolt-II

Lockheed C-130 Hercules

RAF Squadron Badges

The Sea Eagles

Vengeance!

Douglas AD Skyraider

North American T-6, SNJ,
Harvard and Wirraway

Ship Strike

T-6; the Harvard, Texanand Wirraway

The Story of the Torpedo Bomber

MILITARY

Massacre at Tobruk

The Royal Marines; A Pictorial History

Per Mare, Per Terram

Victoria's Victories

INTO THE MINEFIELDS

British Destroyer Minelaying
1916–1960

by

PETER C. SMITH

Pen & Sword
MARITIME

First published in Great Britain in 2005 by
Pen & Sword Maritime
an imprint of
Pen & Sword Books Ltd
47 Church Street
Barnsley
South Yorkshire
S70 2AS

ISBN 1 84415 271 5

A CIP catalogue record for this book is
available from the British Library

Typeset in 11/13 Meridien by
Phoenix Typesetting, Auldgirth, Dumfriesshire

Printed and bound in England by
CPI UK

See all previous books by Peter C. Smith at:
www.dive-bombers.co.uk

Pen & Sword Books Ltd incorporates the imprints of Pen & Sword
Aviation, Pen & Sword Maritime, Pen & Sword Military, Wharncliffe Local
History, Pen & Sword Select, Pen & Sword Military Classics and Leo Cooper.

For a complete list of Pen & Sword titles please contact
PEN & SWORD BOOKS LIMITED
47 Church Street, Barnsley, South Yorkshire, S70 2AS, England
E-mail: enquiries@pen-and-sword.co.uk
Website: www.pen-and-sword.co.uk

To the Memory of the officers and men
of the 20th (Minelaying) Flotilla
in both World Wars.

THE PERFECT MINE

Is easy to produce.

Can be stored anywhere without danger or deterioration.

Can be transported by road, rail, sea or air without detriment to its mechanism.

Is capable of being prepared and tested by relatively unskilled personnel.

Is 100 per cent safe before laying or when adrift, and 100 per cent certain in operation when laid.

Can be laid from any height, at any speed in any depth of water from any type of ship or aircraft by anybody of average intelligence.

Cannot be swept or rendered innocuous by the enemy.

Can distinguish between friend and foe.

N.B. There is *no* perfect mine (yet).

(Courtesy of HMS Vernon, Portsmouth.)

CONTENTS

1	Mines – The Neglected Weapon	1
2	A Reappraisal	13
3	The Momentum Gathers	27
4	The Formation of the 20th Flotilla	38
5	Alarms, Excursions and Accidents	50
6	Summer in the Heligoland Bight	61
7	Disaster!	73
8	Sowing the Dragon's Teeth	86
9	The Locust Years	98
10	A New Beginning	111
11	Back to the Heligoland Bight	124
12	Long Odds	136
13	A Tragedy Re-enacted	152
14	Lost Opportunities	166
15	Destroyer Minelayers in the Far East	179
16	Final Days	192
	Index	206

Maps

1   Tracing of Most Secret Chart Z2, showing track
of HMS *Abdiel* and 20th Flotilla, 26/27 June 1918   69

2   Tracing of Most Secret Chart Z2, showing track
of HMS *Venturous* and 20th Flotilla 8/9 July 1918   71

3   Tracing of Most Secret Chart Z2, showing track
of HMS *Abdiel* and 20th Flotilla on 1 October 1918
in British Notified Area   92

4   Humber to the Heligoland Bight – Areas of 20th
Flotilla's main activities 1918 and 1939–40   97

5   British and German declared mine areas 1939–40
and 20th Flotilla's bases and areas of operation   129

6   Operation Wilfred – the Vestfiord Area, Norway,
8 April 1940   138

Figures

1   Layout of a typical flotilla minefield 1918   30

2   Schematic layout of minefield A33 February 1918   45

Tables

1   British flotilla leaders and destroyers
converted for minelaying 1916–18   26

2   Forces involved in laying shallow minefields,
Operations A16, A27, A28 and A29,
February 1918   33

3   Original composition of the 20th (Minelaying)
Flotilla, February 1918   39

4   Pendant number changes in the 20th Flotilla
during 1918   64

5   Individual totals of mines laid by British
destroyer minelayers 1916–18   95

6   Fates of destroyer minelayers 1919–39   101

7   Destroyer minelaying potential on outbreak of
Second World War, 3 September 1939   115

8   British destroyers converted for minelaying
or built with minelaying conversion capability
and actually so utilised 1939–45   122

9   Operation *Wilfred*. Area mined by Force
'WV' 8 April 1940   135

10   20th Flotilla – Casualty figures for 1 September
1940   165

11   Typical record of mines embarked –
        HMS *Intrepid* 8 February 1941   171

12   Typical mining report of operation,
        HMS *Icarus*, 20 February 1941   175

13   HMS *Stronghold* minelaying record off
        Singapore, January–March 1941   185

14:     Individual totals of mines laid by British
        destroyer minelayers 1939–45   201

15   British destroyers equipped as minelayers
        1945–60   203

1

MINES –
THE NEGLECTED WEAPON

On the outbreak of the First World War in August 1914, the Royal Navy was the supreme maritime defence force of the world. Although under challenge from the growth of the German Navy in the decade before, it remained in a position of absolute superiority in all arms. It is true that the numbers of battleships, battle-cruisers, light cruisers and destroyers were never sufficient for all the tasks that presented themselves, and that a critical situation in terms of the first two categories prevailed in the winter of 1914/15. However, in overall terms of size, expertise and tradition, the Royal Navy justified the title of the major fleet of the world. In all respects that is, save one. The exception was the mine.

The deficiency was not because the mine was a relatively new and unknown weapon of war whose potential was untried. That it featured so low in British naval interest was not historical. Such an argument might be considered for the comparative neglect of such new weapons as the submarine or the aircraft, in which fields the Admiralty was to be among the pioneers, but not the mine. In 1914, the mine as a weapon of war was already a century old and its power, effectiveness and limitations had been well demonstrated over the intervening years. If the Royal Navy had needed reminding of the power of this weapon, the humiliating loss of one of its most powerful warships, the new battleship *Audacious*, in the first weeks of the conflict, provided such a lesson early on[1].

[1] See footnote on page 2.

Background

Although various devices that destroyed their target ships by explosion below the waterline (a ship's most vulnerable point), had, at one time or another, been classified as 'mines', the definition suited for this book of a 'mine', in modern naval parlance, is a container of explosives laid in the sea and moored there in the form of a barrier, or fields. Such mines were designed to remain more or less in the position they had been placed. They detonated by 'contact', and there are several kinds: physical, both magnetic and acoustic. There are also mines that are remotely detonated from ashore, known as 'controlled' mines. Their prime function was to destroy or cripple hostile ships. However, they were also used strategically, creating 'no-go' areas, by forming an artificial barrier either for defensive or offensive purposes. They were used to guard entrances to ports and harbours, to protect vulnerable areas of coastline, to deny areas of the sea to the enemy, or to bottle up or threaten enemy sea lanes.

The first practical example of this type of device to go into action is often credited to the American inventor Robert Fulton. After many years of experimentation with other types of underwater and semi-submersible weapons, he came up with an effective device. In 1810, after long years spent on such projects in both Europe and America, the remarkable Fulton was granted a committee by the United States Government to look into his current ideas. Among his portfolio they were particularly impressed by the grandfather of the modern moored contact mine, which offered the prospect of a cheap defence against the overwhelming might of the Royal Navy in any future conflict.

Fulton's contraption was very far-sighted in its design and construction. The device comprised a charge of 100 lb of

[1] It is an interesting point of similarity, that the Royal Navy, in 1914 the supreme naval power, relegated the mine to a very inferior priority. When, almost a century later, the United States Navy had, in turn, become the overwhelmingly superior force, they too had a similar blind spot, and had to turn to the Royal Navy for this expertise during operations in the Persian Gulf.

powder enclosed in a copper casing which had a brass box fitted atop it with a projecting firing lever. The combined casing was given additional buoyancy by having a large deal box tied to it, and the whole assembly was moored to the seabed with a large weight and an anchor. On the firing pin being struck by a passing vessel, the gun-lock was actuated and a musket charge was fired into the powder, resulting in detonation. Fulton was enough of a visionary to include in his mine a timing device, which enabled the period the mine was held below water level to be varied. This gave it the scope to be laid and then lifted at will by the employing force as circumstances changed.

These concepts, much refined down the years, formed the basis of most future fixed mine designs. As this book is not a book on the mine itself, but on one particular method of delivery of that weapon, the reader is recommended to turn to the excellent little volume by Captain J S Cowie, CBE, Royal Navy, for a basic primer on the subject.[2] Suffice it to say that, during the last decades of the 19th and the early years of the 20th century, numerous developments were made that increased both the effectiveness and power of the sea mine. However, as with the submarine, this weapon took very much a back-seat in Admiralty priorities, even as a purely defensive measure. The strictly offensive potential of the weapon received even less prominence.

Of course, there were notable exceptions to this overall under-valuing of the sea mine, notably by Admiral Sir John Fisher during his tenure as Commander-in-Chief, Mediterranean in the years 1899–1902. In the main, the sea mine was principally regarded as a cheap means of defending both established and temporary harbours and anchorages. It would be unfair to claim that most senior officers in the service still regarded the mine in the same light as the Earl St. Vincent who, in 1804, stated that: 'Pitt was the greatest fool that ever existed to encourage a mode of warfare which those who commanded the seas did not want, and if successful would

[2] Cowie, Captain J S, CBE, RN, *Mines, Minelayers and Minelaying*, Oxford University Press, 1949.

deprive them of it.' This stricture could equally be applied to the submarine a century later. But the mine lacked glamour and was still regarded with some suspicion as an equally underhanded infernal device of limited value and totally alien to the long-established offensive doctrine of the Royal Navy in battle. The long and weary years of blockade during the Napoleonic era were forgotten; the few vivid and dramatic main fleet or frigate encounters dominated the memory, as was only natural.

Then again, as ever, the equally long-established tradition of successive British Governments failing to provide the necessary funding to give the necessary range of equipment and research in times of peace, necessitated priorities. That only enough money was granted, and that reluctantly, to maintain little more than a shell of essential defence, was as much a fact of life in the 1900s as it is today. What little money that was wrung out of theGovernment, usually to howls of protest from the opposition and the press, found many uses far more spectacular than the expansion of mine warfare. A whole class of great battleships or a flotilla of dashing destroyers was something tangible to show to the taxpayer when he demanded to know where his money had gone; a depot full of mines was not! Finally, mines and mining was very much a pedestrian and mechanical occupation. By its very nature, it did not grant opportunities to display eye-catching flair, or to otherwise advance the naval officer's career in a highly competitive service.

Nonetheless, the successes achieved by foreign naval forces in the employment of mines in real combat conditions (as with the Russians during the Crimean War in the 1850s, the Americans during their Civil War a decade later and the spectacular loss of battleships to the mine during the more recent Russo-Japanese conflict of 1904–5), could not be totally ignored. The Royal Navy therefore maintained a small nucleus of mine warfare technology and manpower in 1914. Limited development had also been continued with the work of HMS *Vernon,* which became the mining school, a shore establishment at Portsmouth.

What this amounted to on the outbreak of the First World War was as follows:

Stocks of mines on hand

Four thousand spherical moored mines, the BE (BE = British Elia – an improved version of the Italian Elia type of 1901). These were later considered almost useless in actual combat conditions.

Experimentation

A new design of moored mine was under development by the Vickers company and a type of oscillating mine (one that could maintain a pre-selected depth) was being developed by Lieutenant Sandford.

Technique and plans

Very limited. Admiral Sir Percy Scott, in 1914, scathingly commented that, '. . . we had no up-to-date minelayers, nor an efficient mine; no properly fitted minesweepers; no arrangements for guarding our ships against mines. . .'[3]

Minelayers

Seven obsolete cruisers of the *Apollo* class had been converted into a minelaying role during the years 1905–10. These ships formed the only minelaying squadron in the fleet in 1914. These old cruisers, built between 1892 and 1894, were 3500-ton ships with a maximum speed of 20 knots. They were armed with six 6-pdr guns and could carry 150 mines apiece.

Little wonder then, that Professor Arthur Marder was to comment later that: 'The offensive power and real place of mines in naval strategy were not appreciated at the Admiralty before the war.'[4]

---

[3] Scott, Admiral Sir Percy, *Fifty Years in the Royal Navy*, London, 1919.
[4] Marder, Professor Arthur J, *From Dreadnought to Scapa Flow: Volume 1. The Road to War 1904–14*, O.U.P., 1961.

Foreign attitudes

How did the British situation with regard to sea-mine capability compare with some foreign navies? In truth, it would appear that most of these nations regarded mines and minelaying of rather greater importance than the Admiralty, a natural re-action, perhaps, from weaker naval powers. A few foreign navies were even more disinterested than Great Britain. Others, although more interested in the mine's potential, lacked the technical expertise to change their situation. In the former group could be placed the United States, the third naval power by 1914, who concentrated mine warfare almost exclusively on harbour defence. In the latter camp, Turkey, for example, lacked the scientific knowledge or capacity, but eagerly sought stocks of mines from abroad for her needs, also principally defensive.

More enterprising was Italy, aspiring to be a major naval power in the Mediterranean. Italy had developed a wide range of types and was continually experimenting with the different aspects of mine warfare, including aerial minelaying. Indeed, as we have already seen, a large proportion of British mine stocks was based upon an early Italian design, the Elia. As with the torpedo, Italy was in the forefront on all types of under-water weaponry. Japan, despite her dire experience at the hands of the mine off Port Arthur a few years earlier, was another leading naval power that paid only limited attention to mines, although she did have types stocked for both offensive and defensive minefields. Much the same attitude was to be found in France, whose navy, in any case, was undergoing a period of stagnation or even decline. The French Navy did, however, utilise the innovation of the hydrostatic pressure-activated firing mechanism in their Sauter-Harle mine in a similar manner to the Italian Bollo type. Nevertheless, total stocks of such weapons were very limited.

As might be expected, it was the Russian Navy that laid a particular emphasis on mine warfare. This was, after all, Russia's traditional speciality and she had large stocks of all type of sea mines in 1914. The shallow waters of the Baltic were ideal for such a policy, and her harbours and ports were heavily protected in this respect.

The most important consideration for Great Britain, in this as in all other aspects of naval warfare in 1914, was the attitude of Germany. As might also be expected, that nation had ample skill, techniques and mechanical capacity available, and had thrown her considerable talent and resources at mine development. In 1914, Germany probably led the world in technique, know-how and stocks. The buoyant contact type of mine, fitted with the Herz horn firing gear, was far superior to any British mine. It proved far more reliable and was available in huge numbers from the outset of the war. Furthermore, Germany was fully committed to the offensive use of these weapons and had few scruples as to how and where they could be used, as long as they were effective. This fact was fully illustrated by the activities of the minelayer *Koenigin Luise* from the very first day of the war, and which resulted in the loss of the British light cruiser HMS *Amphion*.

So much for national attitudes to mine warfare and the material on hand to carry it out, but what of the methods employed to actually seed the mines? Compared with the seven ancient converted cruisers, which represented the Royal Navy's main strength in this area, Germany was far more prepared and attuned to minelaying and utilised warships of many types, including some of her most modern vessels. Germany had, in fact, built two specialised craft for minelaying work, the *Nautilus* and the *Albatross*. Plans were also carried out to convert two more such ships from merchant vessels, the *Koenigin Luise* and the *Meteor*. Both of these latter vessels, were, in the event, very quickly sunk by the Royal Navy, although not before they had caused considerable damage.

Germany's use of high-speed, lightly protected warships to lay mines was also widespread. During the war years, two light cruisers, the *Regensburg* and the *Graudenz*, were converted to minelayers. These two ships were 5000-ton ships with a top speed of 27 knots, were armed with seven 5.9-inch guns and could carry 120 mines. Every subsequent class of German light cruiser had a minelaying capability built into its original design. Thus the ten ships of the Frankfurt, Elbing, Koenigsberg (2) and Dresden (2) classes, all had a carrying/laying capacity of 120 mines. Even more formidable were the two custom-built cruiser-minelayers, *Bremse* and *Brummer*, built in 1916. Of 4000-tons displacement and armed with four 5.9-inch and smaller guns, they had the great speed of 34 knots and could carry a cargo of 360 mines apiece.

Using light cruisers to laying mines was not restricted to the German Navy. The Italian light cruisers *Marsala*, *Nino Bixio* and *Quarto* were similarly equipped. In addition, Italy had built the specialised minelayers *Goito, Minerva, Partenope* and *Tripoli*. These latter vessels, however, were small and slow, carrying a deck load of just sixty mines, and had a top speed of only 19 knots. Many Russian light cruisers, were similarly fitted out. In all three of these nations' navies, provision was made for the stowage and laying of mines on both battleships and lesser vessels. Russia was conducting minelaying trials with submarines, an important new development and one that Germany, again, was far advanced in. By 1915, the first small U-boats specially built for minelaying, the *UC I* class of fifteen submarines, were entering service, and these could carry twelve mines. These ships were followed by submarine classes, each larger and more wide-ranging than the previous one.

It was soon discovered that the best qualities for surface minelayers, especially when connected with an offensive policy against the enemy fleets and harbours, were very high speed, a low silhouette for nocturnal and clandestine activities, and a shallow draught. These specifications, it was obvious, were already met by one type of warship above all others, the destroyer.

Destroyer minelayers

Taprell Dorling, 'Taffrail', in his definitive history, stated: 'I do not think that in 1914 anyone seriously contemplated minelaying from destroyers.'[5]

Here Taffrail is, for once, in error. For example, from 1912 onward, Germany was building into all her new destroyer classes the capacity for laying mines. The twelve ships of the *S-*

[5] Dorling, Captain Taprell, DSO, RN, *Endless Story* Hodder & Stoughton London, 1931.

13 class were 690-tonners, armed with two 4.1-inch guns, one 3.5-inch gun and four torpedo tubes and had a speed of 36 knots. Such an armament and speed compared very well with equivalent, and larger, British destroyers being built at the same time, but in addition, the German ships had a capacity to carry and lay eighteen mines. This trend was continued in Germany with the subsequent V-25 class (six ships), S-31 class (ten ships), G-37 class (six ships) and V-43 ships, all of which were completed between 1913 and 1915, and all of which had the minelaying capacity of twenty-four mines. The later war-built S-53 class (fourteen ships) and V-67 class (eighteen ships) had a similar capability. One ship, the G-96, was converted while on the stocks to increase her mine stowage to forty, and this larger figure was followed by most subsequent German destroyer classes. Russia and Italy also widely employed some of their destroyers in the minelaying role at this time.

Nor, in a very limited manner, had the Royal Navy ignored the minelaying potential of the destroyer before the war, despite Taffrail's assertion to the contrary. This awareness manifested itself in the newest destroyers to join the pre-war fleet during 1914. These were the twenty ships of the Laforey class, of 1112 tons displacement and mounting three 4-inch guns and four torpedo tubes. They had a top speed of 29 knots. These British destroyers had built into their design a very modest minelaying potential, in that they were provided with a mining hatch and derrick for hoisting out and laying the standard Vickers Elia, Mk IV mine, each of which weighed half a ton with their sinkers. Provision was made in the destroyers', steering compartments for the Laforey class ships to carry four of these mines, the hatch being located abaft the rearmost 4-inch gun on the starboard side of the after deck.

Stationary minelaying operations were envisaged for these ships, with each individual mine being lifted out and placed precisely; this of course negated the destroyer's prime attribute, her speed. It is doubtful if any of the Laforey class destroyers ever did carry their mine load as designed. On joining the fleet on the eve of the outbreak of the war, they were immediately sent to join the 3rd Destroyer Flotilla as part of the famous Harwich Force, where they saw considerable action in the first years of the war in their true destroyer role. However, these ships had little or no cause, or opportunity, to utilise their minelaying function, other than in practices. This was one idea, which was stillborn, although it is an interesting insight into the early British approach to the concept. Significantly, it was not repeated. Destroyer minelaying was to take on a very different meaning to this idea, and it was not long before the woeful lack of suitable vessels in the Royal Navy was apparent.

Early British minelaying operations

This initial inertia was given a jolt by the activities of the German minelayers off our east coast in August 1914. Soon, voices were being raised at the Admiralty, arguing that Britain should follow suit. Opposition was equally firm, the argument again being that wholesale mining operations would mean restrictions on the Royal Navy in seeking out and destroying the enemy. Eventually, it was agreed to lay defensive mine-fields to cover the Dover Straits and, at the beginning of October 1914, the minelaying cruisers, joined later by two French vessels, started sowing their mines off Ostend and Zeebrugge and to the north-east of Goodwin Sands.

With the menace of the U-boat also finally being appreci-ated, after a series of tragic losses of old cruisers to such attacks, a series of small defensive minefields were also laid off selected east coast ports. But, when attention was directed towards a more offensive policy, that of laying mines to block the German ports and bases in the North Sea, and especially in the Heligoland Bight, considerable opposition was expressed.

Admiral Sir Herbert Richmond was one of the advocates of such an aggressive policy and the Cabinet itself was also considering the matter as opportune. Those against such a policy, however, were many and powerful, both inside the Admiralty and the fleet itself. Both the Chief of the War Staff and the First Lord, Winston Churchill, were totally opposed to such an option. After some wrangling, the matter was discussed by the Cabinet on 12/13 October; General Kitchener wished to mine the estuaries of the rivers Scheldt and Rhine as well as the Heligoland Bight, to seal the Germans in tightly. Churchill remained steadfast in his opposition to any such ideas. As was his custom, Churchill followed his conviction through and widely circulated a paper expressing his viewpoint. Any thoughts of such 'ambush' mining on the lines put forward by Kitchener were rejected by Churchill as unsound, and he refused to give ground. This rejection angered many pro-mining officers at the time, who felt they had not been allowed a fair hearing.

General Kitchener expressed dismay at such a negative policy. Support for him came from Admiral Jackie Fisher, who had blown alternately hot and cold on the issue before the war, but now came out firmly in favour of the mine. The Commander-in-Chief of the Grand Fleet, Admiral Sir John Jellicoe, was asked for his opinion on the matter. He too, was initially against the wholesale mining of the Heligoland Bight, but, by early 1915, had changed his viewpoint. Jellicoe's view was coloured by the need to obtain the earliest possible warning of any sortie by the German High Seas Fleet, and the sweeping of British mines prior to any such operation, would provide him with this information.

Accordingly, a limited amount of offensive minelaying was finally sanctioned and, in January 1915, the old cruisers penetrated the Heligoland Bight at the best speed of 15 knots to lay the first such field off the Amrun Bank. This was followed by two more sorties in May of the same year. After these sorties had been completed, however, all such operations ceased abruptly and the Apollo class ships were paid off and became depot ships as they were too slow. All credit should be given to these ancient vessels for what they achieved in making these lays. In view of their lack of speed, their mission could be seen as suicidal, for they were very vulnerable to even small German warships or submarine patrols. That they got in, laid mines and got out again unscathed might be considered more luck than judgement and there was obviously no point in pushing such good fortune any further. What was required was faster craft.

The Admiralty first turned to mercantile conversions. Among many such ships taken over were two very handy vessels, 5400-ton fast passenger ships with a light draught, designed for a speed of 21 knots, which were being built for the Vancouver–Seattle run on the Canada/United States western seaboard. These ships were the *Princess Irene* and *Princess Margaret*, both of which were adapted to carry a load of 500 mines. Unfortunately, the former soon became a war loss, being destroyed on 17 May 1915 while at Sheerness preparing her mines for laying. She blew up with all hands in a shocking explosion, caused, it was suspected, by the over-sensitive cocking mechanism with which British mines were fitted at this time. Happily, this device was replaced with a much more satisfactory type almost immediately.

Shortage of suitable fast minelayers did not overmuch affect the issue, for the Admiralty again clamped down on offensive fields as a reassertion of their original policy. Churchill had got his way as usual. It must be remembered that most minelaying operations at this period of the war were under direct Admiralty control, with very few exceptions, and the ineffectiveness of the British mines in the fields already laid down, had dampened that body's brief burst of enthusiasm very quickly. The British mines were unstable when laying, as the *Princess Irene* disaster had demonstrated only too graphically. Also, they were poorly moored, hundreds broke adrift and became more of a menace to Allied shipping than the enemy, and worse, they were invariably ineffective in use, causing little or no loss to the Germans, despite several of their ships striking them.

By mid-1915 therefore, British offensive minelaying had, for all practical purposes and intent, come to an almost complete halt. The total abandonment of the policy was a sad reflection of the pre-war inertia in this field. Matters were not to alter for another twelve months, when radical changes in the method of delivery were put forward.

2

A REAPPRAISAL

Although British minelaying stagnated during 1915, the mine's effect on sea warfare was increasingly felt and criticism grew at the failure of the Royal Navy to respond in kind. The sinking of the *Audacious* had demonstrated that not even the most powerful of modern warships was immune, and the Dardanelles fiasco foundered on a few German mines laid by the Turks, which had quickly sunk three old British battleships and damaged others. In addition, German mines in the North Sea and English Channel destroyed four destroyers and two submarines during the same period.

The British response appeared muted for several reasons. The Government was reluctant to risk good relations with neutral nations like Holland and Norway whose own mercantile shipping would be put at risk; there was the proven inefficiency of the British mines themselves; there was the need to build up adequate stocks before starting a large campaign; there was the necessity of developing and producing new types of mines to replace the older types; and there was the time required to convert ships into efficient minelayers.

In the latter category came the passenger vessels *Paris, Biarritz, Orvieto, Angora* and the Channel Islands steamer *Gazelle*, all of which could carry the standard Service mine, while the *St Margaret* was first converted to lay the Elia. However, none of these ships had any great turn of speed and themselves presented large targets.

Of the new, experimental mines then under development and the old types needing greater production capacity and modification, the standard Service mine received the largest orders, despite the fact that the German horned mine had been examined and found highly superior. The German type called for a high degree of skilled labour in its manufacture, which was possibly one reason why it was not adopted at this time, when coupled with the critical shortage of shells for the Army and other demands on our few skilled armament manufacturers.

Mines of the oscillating type were also ordered, but in smaller numbers, from the firm Beardmore, which produced the Leon pattern. A specifically anti-U-boat mine weapon was required and Admiral Sir Arthur Wilson proposed the development of an electro-contact *net* mine, 7500 of which were ordered. Following the German example again, two British submarines were converted into minelayers, the *E-24* and the *E-41*. Each was capable of carrying and laying twenty of the Herz horn-type mine. By the end of 1915, Lieutenant Sandford's work had improved the oscillating type and these new mines were placed in production, the DO type being designed for laying by surface vessels.

Despite all this, little practical minelaying was carried out. Meanwhile, Admiral Sir John Jellicoe had been increasing his requests for the mining of the Heligoland Bight as a more effective way of bottling up the German submarines. His campaign culminated in a note to the Admiralty dated 14 August 1915, in which he again reiterated the need for such a mining policy, '. . . I am more than ever convinced that it is absolutely essential to the satisfactory conduct of the war'.

This plea had a limited effect, for, during the latter half of 1915, additional mines were laid in the Heligoland Bight but this resulted in only a thin line of defence, and was far from the complete blocking operation that Jellicoe had in mind. Again, this was due to the hazards and risks involved in using slow and vulnerable ships to do the work as much as anything else. The inefficient mooring methods utilised by British mines meant that, although a line might be marked on a chart, and was reinforced from time to time, the continual breaking away and drifting of these mines, combined with their continued doubtful efficiency, made the real barrier a slender one in fact. In contrast, the German mines were increasingly restricting the movements of the Grand Fleet, which added to Jellicoe's irritation. The loss of the old battleship *King Edward VII*, mined off Cape Wrath in January 1916, only reinforced it.

By the beginning of 1916, some progress had been made in Britain, both in the provision of further delivery vessels and in stocks of mines on hand, although both were still woefully inadequate. The equipment to make the actual placing of mines more effective and accurate, also improved. Four further submarines were taken in hand for conversion to minelaying, *E-34*, *E-45*, *E-46* and *E-51*. On 7 March, the first combat minelaying from a British submarine was successfully conducted in the Heligoland Bight by *E-24*. Two further passenger ships, the *Pedita* and the *Wahine* were also converted, but both were, again, small and slow ships.

Some surface minelaying was extended with such vessels that same spring, with good results, for a combined net and mine barrage was laid across the approaches to the Belgian coast between the Scheldt and Ostend in April 1916 as an anti-submarine measure. This field utilised mines of the electro-contact type. Further fields were also put down off the east coast of England and the southern North Sea. However, for the more dangerous task of sowing mines deep inside enemy home waters, a faster vessel was still the obvious requirement. The C-in-C, Grand Fleet, continually made representations about this point to the Admiralty.

Two inventions of this period did much to improve the minelaying procedure itself. The first such was the fitting of sinking plugs. These devices could be fitted as required and provided an active life limitation for any minefield laid as a temporary expedient, rather than a permanent block. This enabled tactical minelaying, with the resultant flexibility and unpredictability this involved. Friendly forces could thus use the mined area again after a specific time lapse, to lay further minefields if necessary, or to conduct other offensive operations without too much restriction – the restriction that Churchill had so despised. The other aid was the fitting of a simple device for measuring the extent of each lay as it was made, thus ensuring greater accuracy in the plotting of existing fields. This point became increasingly pertinent as the number and complexity of the minefields grew over the years. It consisted, in the simplest of terms, of a long length of strong wire, which was accurately measured as it was played out astern of the minelaying ship during the laying operation.

All that was required now, was a more reliable and powerful mine and a fast means of delivery. Although the former was not to appear for another year, in the form of the Mk HII, which was an exact copy 'nut for nut, bolt for bolt' of the original German horned mine, the provision of the latter became a reality at last in 1916, when the first of the British destroyer minelayers joined the Grand Fleet. This was HMS *Abdiel.*

Genesis of the destroyer minelayer in the Royal Navy

As early as August 1915, Sir H Jackson (who had succeeded Lord Fisher as First Sea Lord) had asked if it would be possible for one of the new flotilla leaders then under construction, to be adapted as a fast minelayer. The flotilla leaders were considered most suitable for this role as they were, in effect, enlarged destroyers retaining the high speed of the flotilla vessel but with greater dimensions in order to accommodate the extra staff and complement of Captain (D). They were a relatively new type of warship, their introduction into the Royal Navy being brought about by the increasing speeds of the new destroyers of the 'L' and 'M' classes. The light cruisers and scouts that had hitherto sufficed for the job could no longer maintain such speeds and a class of such specialised ships was therefore laid down early in the war.

The first four flotilla leaders were followed by a further three of the same type, all to be built in the shipyard of Cammell Laird. Of these first seven ships, it was the *Kempenfelt*, nearing completion at the same company's yard, which was initially selected for the conversion to minelaying, having been launched in May 1915. The *Kempenfelt* was due to run her trials in August and the Director of Naval Construction submitted a detailed report of the further work entailed in order to convert her to her new role.

It was estimated that ships of this type would be able to accommodate between eighty and ninety of the Service mines, together with their sinkers, on rails on the upper deck. The question of the delicate balance of the ship's stability with such a heavy deck load in addition to her normal armament had to be considered. Such a mine cargo would obviously increase the ship's draught aft, and also reduce her maximum speed from a designed 34.5 knots to about 30 knots. The vessel's radius of action would also be affected, being reduced from a designed 4290 nautical miles at a speed of 15 knots, to much less. Because high speed was the entire *raison d'être* for the exercise, this was calculated on a speed of 25 knots and a radius of action estimated to be reduced to 800 nautical miles. This was still sufficient, of course, for high-speed dashes into the Heligoland Bight, her intended field of action.

Although it was stated that the mines could be accommodated on the special rails placed to port and starboard along the *Kempenfelt*'s after deck without unduly disturbing existing fittings and fixtures, some strengthening was obviously required. This, it was stated, could be achieved by fitting two stiffeners along the ship's upper deck directly below the mine rails themselves. Considering that each mine weighed 1500 lb, this was a remarkable testimony to the inherent strength of the original design.

In order to ensure stability when a full load of mines was embarked, the destroyer would have to disembark a certain amount of top-hamper. In the case of the *Kempenfelt*, this entailed the removal of her midships 4-inch gun from between her second and third funnels, both sets of twin 21-inch torpedo tubes and associated torpedo davits, as well as the after 4-inch gun. This left her with just two 4-inch guns forward with which to defend herself. Additional weight compensation was found by emptying the after 4-inch magazine. Structural alterations entailed only the conversion of the existing torpedo warhead room to stow associated mining gear and equipment and the replacement of the hatch to the steering compartment aft.

The mine rails themselves were easily fitted to the ship. The whole set consisted of twin rails with stanchions inboard, bolted port and starboard of the upper deck aft from abreast the after funnel. These rails each terminated in the mine 'chutes built out over the stern and with loading davits fitted forward and a power winch located astern inboard of the mine 'chute sponsons. Either 'H' mines or those of the Elia type could be accommodated, with the standard mine resting on its sinker, giving a total weight of about half a ton. Attached to the bottom of each sinker were small rollers, which enabled the whole assembly to be moved relatively smoothly along its rail path. The winch hauled the mines aft in succession, whereupon they were released at set intervals according to the pattern of laying required. The need to extend these rails as far forward as possible led to the resiting of the ship's boats even further forward, a dead giveaway for those skilled at warship recognition.

Secrecy was, naturally, the key-note and during an inspection of the *Kempenfelt* while she was still fitting out, Admiral Ommaney decided that the mine load should be hidden from prying 'neutral' eyes at sea, so that the ship's clandestine missions and the ports from which she operated, could remain unidentified. The simplest and most convenient way to do this was a simply constructed canvas screen stretched outboard of the mine rails, with the ship's normal guns, torpedo tubes and similar apparatus painted on in a series of silhouettes. Close-to, this might appear a primitive form of camouflage, but it was very effective at sea at any sort of distance. An added value for later destroyers, which were required to convert back to the normal roles with a minimum of delay, was that such screens could be quickly assembled or dismantled.

Consideration given to extending the scheme

Thought was also given to similar conversions, with a more limited mine load, of smaller, standard destroyers. After some consultation and calculation, the conclusion reached was that most of the existing ships would be too unstable for this work, although the exception to this was thought to be the Thornycroft-built 'Special' design of the standard 'M' class destroyer. Two of these ships were under construction, the *Mastiff* and the *Meteor*, but they were not actually taken under conversion at this time.

Conversion of the Abdiel

Meanwhile, the *Kempenfelt* had been undergoing her prelimi-
nary trials. During this series of speed runs, defects kept
appearing, which delayed her completion and acceptance into
service. It was therefore decided to convert one of her later
sisters to take her place. The *Gabriel* was the flotilla leader
selected and the necessary alterations were put in hand
by Cammell Laird for her completion as a minelayer by
December 1915. However, when Admiral Ommaney in-
spected the ships under construction, he found that *Abdiel* was
due to complete for her trials a month earlier, and so she
was selected for the conversion instead. Third time proved
lucky, and the modifications went ahead on the *Abdiel*
according to plan. After running her trials, the *Abdiel* was
officially handed over to the Royal Navy on 24 March 1916,
and was immediately sent to join Admiral Jellicoe's great
command at its Scapa Flow base.

First destroyer minelaying conducted

The C-in-C was no doubt pleased to welcome this useful addition to his very limited minelaying potential and *Abdiel* was
soon gainfully employed. Since the pause that had followed
the early operations, 1915 had seen a limited extension of
British minefields across the Heligoland Bight. Although the
poor quality of the mines was not to be resolved for more than
twelve months, *Abdiel* was sent out to conduct nightly lays to
reinforce these minefields from time-to-time during the spring
of 1916, mainly in the vicinity of Horns Reef.

   With no escort whatsoever, *Abdiel* proved herself to be ideal
for this work, although it proved a case of 'learning on your
feet' for her commanding officer, Commander Berwick Curtis.
Fortunately, a more able or competent destroyer officer would
have been hard to find, and he quickly became highly expert
at this brand-new and nefarious form of sea warfare. Curtis
had that unique blend of imperturbability and quiet efficiency
that seemed second nature to destroyer skippers of that period.
Taffrail paid a glowing tribute to him:

He was a charming man to serve with, unassuming, unselfish and a firm believer in letting people do their job without fuss and bother. He detested petty supervision as he hated paper work, inefficiency, and BF's, and backed up his subordinates through thick and thin. To him, shocking weather or alarming incidents were merely 'pretty fruity'.

Things went wrong sometimes, as things must when one is laying mines in a sort of complicated herring-bone pattern without lights, and often in vile weather and low visibility. 'Budge' Curtis was not merely responsible for his own ship, but for seven or eight working in company. But never once did we seem him the least perturbed or flustered. His language was sometimes a little florid about things that did not matter, though no worse than our own . . .[6]

It was ever the C-in-C's intention to mine the whole of the Heligoland Bight, but, with such limitations as listed above, this proved impossible. However, from the *Abdiel*'s early sorties into that region was born a special role for her in Jellicoe's preparations to lure the German High Seas Fleet into battle. These plans finally bore fruit on 31 May 1916, with the Battle of Jutland. In seeking to entice the reluctant enemy forth, Jellicoe was under no illusion that they might venture very far afield. However, he hoped that a special submarine trap of three boats south of Horn's Reef to cover the northern exit from the Heligoland Bight, with two more submarines in place off the Dogger Bank, might prove useful. As a further extension of the C-in-C's grand design, plans were also made for *Abdiel* to block the return of the German battleships to their home ports, by sowing mines in the enemy-swept channel south of the Reef, to the north-west of the island of Sylt.

The naval battle took place without the decisive conclusion so ardently sought by the Royal Navy. But, at nightfall on 31 May, the Grand Fleet was between the desperate German ships

[6] *Ibid.*

and their bases. They only had to remain so to resume the battle the next day with full confidence in complete victory. At 21.32, Jellicoe sent a signal to Curtis to carry out his mission, '. . . in accordance with instructions previously issued . . .' The *Abdiel* at once proceeded at her best speed, which, in her laden condition was about 32 knots, to the vicinity of the Vyl Lightship, south of the submarine patrol line. At 01.24 on 1 June 1916, the *Abdiel* reached her laying position in pitch-blackness, and commenced her appointed task. It took the destroyer exactly forty minutes to complete her deadly work. Then, at 02.04, she slipped back through the opposing fleets undetected and reached safety undisturbed.

Usually, the work of the destroyer minelayers was frustrating, in that they could never be certain whether their work was rewarded or not. The *Abdiel*'s lay on the morning of 1 June was an exception to this rule. Vindication of the efficiency and accuracy of her work was quickly forthcoming. Curtis could hardly have expected so positive a result for his night's efforts. At 05.20 that same morning, the German fleet had felt its way thankfully through the British destroyer flotillas astern of Jellicoe's main fleet with few casualties, and had reached the assumed safety of its own swept channels. The modern battleship *Ostfriesland* was then rocked by a large explosion and began taking in water. The German ship had struck one of the mines laid by the *Abdiel*, not one that she had laid earlier than morning, but one she had sown on an earlier sortie into these waters, on 4 May. Badly damaged, the German battleship was nursed into her home port of Wilhelmshaven to undertake repair. She did not rejoin the High Seas Fleet until 26 July.

Conversion of the Legion

Despite this spectacular success, the idea of converting yet more destroyers to a minelayer role took some time to implement. Again, this reluctance was probably due to the continued unreliability of the standard British mine, which rendered any expansion at this time of problematic worthwhile value. Nonetheless, some progress was made in fitting out a few more destroyers as they became available due to the stresses and strains of war. For example, the *Legion* was herself severely damaged by a mine while serving with the Dover Patrol in November 1916. Her hull aft was broken in two places, the shafts distorted and the steering gear was completely smashed. The *Legion* was taken in for extensive repairs, and the decision was taken to convert her into a minelaying destroyer. When the *Legion* emerged some six months later, she had mine rails and equipment fitted, a capacity for forty 'H' or 'BL' mines and a much-reduced stability, her deep GM (metacentric height) being just 0.95 feet. This followed the decision, taken in January 1917, to fit out a whole squadron of light cruisers and a whole flotilla of destroyers as fast minelayers.

1917 – rapid expansion

The slightly older destroyer *Ferret* of the *Acheron* class was also converted. Badly damaged by mining, she too was converted while being repaired, having winches, rails, bogies and spon- sons added before she resumed active life as a minelayer. In compensation for the added weight, the *Ferret* landed her after 4-inch gun and one of her torpedo tubes. The *Ferret* could thus carry forty of the 1850-lb 'H' mines. So successful was this conversion that two of her sister ships, the *Ariel* and the *Sandfly,* were similarly taken in hand, as was the more modern *Meteor* of the 'M' class, which, it will be recalled, had already been earmarked for such a conversion earlier.

Improvements to British mines

The January 1917 decision coincided with, – or was more likely brought about, and undoubtedly influenced by – the acceptance into service of a new British design of mine and sinker, the Mk HII mine on a Mk VIII sinker. This was coupled with the authorisation of a great increase in the quantities of mines to be produced. There was an increase of 2500 per cent, to a total of 100,000 new mines!

Other innovations took place at this time to match this vast expansion. Acoustic attachments to the standard moored mine were introduced, as was a magnetic firing system and the production of heavy sinkers, hydrostatic safety switches and plummet sinkers for the deep laying of minefields. All this was brought about by a complete reversal of the Admiralty's traditional backward attitude to mine warfare. Naturally, this expansion required an expanded fast minelaying force to apply them in the most effective way.

Therefore, the light cruisers *Aurora*, *Bellona*, *Blonde*, *Boadicea*, *Blanche*, *Galatea*, *Inconstant*, *Phaeton* and *Royalist* were taken in hand for conversion to fast minelayers, as was the new battle-cruiser *Courageous*, although, in the event, this latter conversion never took place. Among the destroyers, it was the newer ships of the 'R' and 'V' classes then building, that were now selected to reinforce the older destroyer minelayers. Thus, in January 1917, the proposal for the conversion of the *Tarpon* and *Telemachus* of the former class and the *Vanoc*, *Vanquisher*, *Vehement*, *Venetia*, *Venturous* and *Vivacious* of the latter class were taken in hand.

It was, perhaps, no coincidence that it was the arrival of Jellicoe at the Admiralty that saw the initiation of these changes in minelaying policy, for he had long advocated more positive action in this regard. The chief opponent, Winston Churchill, having been replaced after the Dardanelles fiasco, was now out of the way and unable to interfere.

Thus the January proposals for the *Tarpon* and *Telemachus* included the fitting of sponsons over their sterns, in the same manner as with the *Ariel*, the after gun and all torpedo tubes being landed to compensate for the addition of the minesweeping apparatus. The two destroyers could, however, in view of the growing submarine campaign conducted by the Germans, retain, '. . . one depth charge if necessary.' The *Telemachus* was also to be equipped with Types IV and 15 wireless telegraphy (W/T) equipment, which entailed the fitting of a mainmast to carry the aerials for them 45 feet above sea level.

In that same month, the First Sea Lord enquired whether at

least four of the new 'V' class destroyers could be similarly converted without their final completion dates being affected. It was found that these larger destroyers were capable of carrying increased loads of sixty mines of the 'H' type, which, on their Mk VIII sinkers, weighed 1840 lb. As usual, part of their normal armament had to be sacrificed in compensation for their minelaying role, and in the case of the 'V's this meant the removal of the after 4-inch gun and ammunition, the after set of torpedo tubes and their minesweeping gear. Again, as with the precedent set by the *Ariel*, *Ferret* and *Legion*, the minelaying gear was screened from general gaze by the erection of a painted screen. The first four ships thus taken in hand were the *Vanoc*, *Vanquisher*, *Vehement* and *Venturous*, followed shortly afterwards by the *Venetia* and *Vivacious*.

These bigger destroyers proved eminently suitable in their new role, and later minelaying adaptations were extended to others of the same class, and also the 'W' class destroyers that followed them. The ships selected for conversion in 1918 were the *Velox*, *Versatile*, *Verulam*, *Vesper*, *Vimy*, *Vittoria*, *Vortigern*, *Walker*, *Walrus*, *Warwick*, *Watchman* and *Whirlwind*.

Abdiel *further modified*

Even with the conversion of these larger destroyers, there was still a need for flotilla leaders to be fitted out in this role, more so when whole flotilla strength lays became established early in 1918. The *Abdiel* had, by that period, some eighteen months' hard war service behind her in this role. It was decided, in January 1917, with the new impetus in this form of warfare about to be initiated, to update her for this more demanding duty. The *Abdiel* was therefore taken back into dockyard hands and fitted with a rebuilt bridge structure, which incorporated, among other improvements, two 10-inch searchlights in the bridge wings. Interestingly, the *Abdiel* retained her original short, stubby funnels, although all her non-minelaying sisters had their fore funnel raised by several feet to obviate the smoke obstruction to their bridges. This smoke hazard was not felt to be an issue for night minelaying, as high-speed steaming was only required to get in and out of the danger area, not while actually laying the mines, and the lower silhouette remained a greater advantage to her. Thus, *Abdiel* remained, among her class, the only one to keep her distinctive silhouette to the end of her long career.

It was also proposed at this time to upgrade the *Abdiel*'s total mine-carrying capacity by replacing the existing rails with new ones, which would have increased her working load to a total of eighty of the B Elia mines. At the same time, mounting one Mk IV 4-inch gun and two pairs of torpedo tubes in addition to her existing modified armament of two 4-inch guns and one 2-pdr pom-pom was proposed. This would have increased the *Abdiel*'s weight by about 16–17 tons. However, as the number of ordinary mines in service was now considerable, it was decided to postpone this modification until they had all been used up. *Adbiel*'s further modifications therefore did not take place until early in 1918.

Final First World War conversions

It is convenient here to conclude the story of the destroyers fitted for minelaying up to the end of the war in November 1918, before going on to describe their actual wartime operations. The 'R' class destroyer *Skate* was added to the list while under construction, and, because of this, she was to prove one of the most long-lived destroyers in the Royal Navy.[7] The flotilla leader *Gabriel*, a sister ship to the *Abdiel*, was converted as a minelayer leader in mid-1918, with a capacity of some 60 tons of mines fully laden, plus four depth charges. In addition, one of the larger, newer classes of flotilla leaders, the *Seymour*, was also converted to a minelayer leader with a similar carrying capacity. In all the ships described, conversion back to normal destroyer functions could take place within a period of 24 hours. It should also be remembered that not all the 'V' and 'W' class ships that were built with minelaying potential, were actually *used* as a minelayer in combat during the First World War.

[7] The *Skate* was the only 'R' class destroyer to survive right through the Second World War, although not exclusively as a minelayer. She was not scrapped until 1947 – a life span of almost thirty years.

Table 1
British flotilla leaders and destroyers converted for minelaying 1916–18

Name of ship	Designed tonnage	Mine capacity	Year of completion	Maximum speed
Abdiel	1687	80	1916	34
Gabriel	1655	80	1916	34
Seymour	1673	80	1916	34
Walker	1457	60	1918	32
Walrus	1457	60	1918	32
Warwick	1457	60	1918	32
Watchman	1457	60	1918	32
Whirlwind	1457	60	1918	32
Valentine	1118	60	1917	32
Valorous	1118	60	1917	32
Vanoc	1457	60	1917	32
Vanquisher	1457	60	1917	32
Vehement	1457	60	1917	32
Velox	1457	60	1917	32
Venturous	1457	60	1917	32
Venetia	1457	60	1917	32
Versatile	1457	60	1918	32
Verulam	1457	60	1917	32
Vesper	1457	60	1918	32
Vimy	1457	60	1918	32
Vittoria	1457	60	1918	32
Vivacious	1457	60	1917	32
Vortigern	1457	60	1918	32
Skate	1036	40	1917	36
Tarpon	1036	40	1917	36
Telemachus	1036	40	1917	36
Meteor	980	40	1914	36
Legion	991	40	1914	31
Ariel	763	40	1911	30
Ferret	750	40	1911	30
Sandfly	750	40	1911	30

3

THE MOMENTUM GATHERS

The combination of more reliable and more diverse types of British mines, adequate stocks of the same, suitable vessels from which to lay them and the growing submarine menace all led, by the summer of 1917, to an increase in mine warfare as part of Royal Navy policy. There were two main areas in which the first destroyer minelayers carried out the bulk of the operations. Following the pioneering work of the *Abdiel* in 1916, she, joined by the new destroyers *Tarpon* and *Telemachus*, was employed during 1917 in extending the minefields in the Heligoland Bight. Initially, while the stocks of new mines were built up, these fields were quite small and easily coped with by the Germans, but gradually the pace quickened towards the end of 1917.

Some friction took place with the neutral nations of Denmark and Holland, as these minefields infringed on their territorial waters. Eventually, these countries stationed four new lightships in the area to identify the western edge of the declared British mine area, to help guide their own merchant ships safely away from them. Not surprisingly, the British destroyer minelayers quickly utilised these lightships as their own 'points of departure' during their clandestine nocturnal runs into the enemy's swept channels, and continuous references are made to them in their reports of proceedings.

As Professor Arthur Marder was later to record:

By July [1917], however, as Jellicoe kept strengthening the minefields in the Bight as rapidly as the delivery of mines permitted, they were beginning to constitute a real danger to the U-boats. From mid-August minelaying in the Bight, as well as in the Dover Straits, by surface and submarine minelayers, became one of the chief A/S measures. The principles adopted were to mine just outside neutral territorial waters in positions where it was believed that U-boats left and entered these waters, and to lay mines across the suspected tracks of enemy submarines.[8]

The first of the new HII mines were laid in the Heligoland Bight on one such mission that autumn, on the night of 24 September 1917. As yet there were but few destroyers ready and so the work in this facet of their busy lives was interspaced with more normal destroyer activity. Taffrail described how the destroyers went about their work at this period:

> . . . for the first seven months of the commission we never quite knew whether we were a destroyer or a minelayer. On more than one occasion, when at sea off the Firth of Forth, we received orders to return into harbour forthwith, to complete with oil-fuel, proceed into the basin at Rosyth dockyard, remove our after gun and torpedo-tubes, and to convert ourselves into a minelayer. It generally took five or six hours, after which we proceeded up the river to Grangemouth to embark our forty mines.
>
> When we really got into the swing of it we could take these on board with cranes in something under an hour. What took the time was their testing, and waiting for the tide at Grangemouth, the entrance to which could only be negotiated for two hours on either side of high water. We were generally ready for service, however, within twenty hours of receiving the signal to convert. Then came another trip down the river and the receipt of a secret envelope containing operation and sailing orders. Finally, after a signal 'Prime mines', away we went on our mission.[9]

---

[8] Marder, Arthur J, *From Dreadnought to Scapa Flow, Vol. 4*, p 226.
[9] Taffrail, *Endless Story, op. cit.*, p 274.

Further south, these same destroyers, along with the older *Ariel*, *Ferret*, *Legion* and *Meteor*, as they became operational, moved to their operational base of Dover, where they also performed their deadly work out of Dunkirk. They took part in further extensions to the minefields laid off Ostend and Zeebrugge in order to stop up the holes of the U-boats' southern lairs.

The first of these missions, in which the two Rosyth-based destroyers participated, took place on the night of 13/14 July 1917. Not only was this their first full minelaying sortie, but almost their last! By this time *Abdiel*'s experiments had got the state of the art to a nicety, but initially, there was much argument about the best method the destroyers could use to space the mines equally at higher laying speeds than normal. In October 1915, for example, it had been estimated that, at a speed of 30 knots a minelaying destroyer would be required to drop fifty mines for each mile covered if she was to form a worthwhile line. This would mean putting a mine into the water every 3.4 seconds, or about five seconds for each alternate mine. Taking the overall diameter of a mine as about 38 inches, the speed of the minelaying train to achieve such a standard would have had to have been 38 feet per minute! It was also calculated that, for a safety margin, each winch would have to be capable of hauling 0.75 tons at 45 feet per minute.

The technique varied for lays with the full flotilla. A single destroyer could go out and achieve this type of field without too much difficulty, but for a whole unit of eight ships to lay in succession along a determined track with absolute accuracy, a great deal of very detailed planning was required. The indispensable Taffrail described how this was done in practice with just a four-destroyer force:

> The rear destroyer laid the first half of her mines, swung to port to lay the other half, and disappeared. No. 3 followed suit, turning to starboard to lay her last twenty mines. Then No. 2, which swung to port. The mines, by the time we had finished laying them, were intended to be placed something like this:

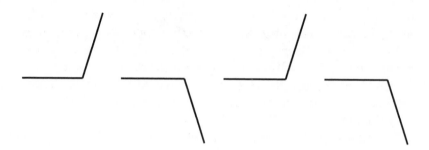

twenty mines in each leg or **V** so to speak, or 160 in all. The idea of the curious patterns was to make it more difficult for them to be located and swept up.

The optimum speed of the laying, as conducted by a whole flotilla, was 12 knots, the distance between each mine using this speed, being 150 feet. The mines laid, of the old Elia type on their heavy sinkers, weighed almost half a ton apiece. Halfway through the first leg the mines aboard the *Telemachus* jammed at the curve of the rail and had to be manhandled overboard. Moreover, while this was being done, two German destroyers passed by at a range of 500 yards! It was perhaps extremely fortunate that the enemy apparently mistook the *Telemachus* and her consorts for friendly ships, or failed to see them at all; in any case, no challenge was made and the British ships completed this lay unmolested. However, they were not to be spared casualties.

While on their way, *Tarpon* herself was mined. The detonation took place right aft, blowing the ship's propellers off and badly buckling and straining her hull. She was taken in tow with some difficulty and finally reached Dunkirk, where she was patched up sufficiently for her to sail to her home port, but her final repairs were found to need extensive work. Almost the whole stern section of the ship had to be totally rebuilt as new, and it was not until early 1918 that *Tarpon* rejoined her sister ships once more.

Further minelaying operations in the area of Cape Gris Nez to the Varne lightship were initiated on 21 November 1917.

The Dover-based destroyers *Ariel, Ferret, Legion* and *Meteor* all participated in this scheme during the last months of 1917 and on into 1918. The *Abdiel, Telemachus* and, when repaired, *Tarpon*, along with the light cruiser adaptations and converted mercantile conversions, continued to be thus employed, but only rarely in the Heligoland Bight.

Meanwhile, Lieutenant Sandford's principles with regard the oscillating mine, using a hydrostatic valve and compressed ammonia gas, had resulted in the 'DO' type of mine being produced in small numbers for laying from surface ships. These 'O' mines (the 'SO' was designed to be laid from submarines) sank beneath the surface to a pre-set depth and drifted with the tides. As part of the new aggressive action in the Heligoland Bight, it was decided that one experimental field of this type should be laid and the destroyer *Ferret* (commanded by Lieutenant A H L Terry) was selected to carry out the mission. The Rear-Admiral (T), at Harwich, was duly informed of the decision on 26 December.[10]

The *Ferret* was despatched to Portsmouth forthwith and, under the supervision of the Superintendent of HMS *Vernon*, the Royal Navy Mining School, she embarked forty of the 'DO' mines. These were set to sink twenty-four hours after being laid and were to be placed 450 feet apart, the forty mines thus covering a total distance of 3 miles. Once embarked and checked, this cargo was to be taken by the *Ferret* back to Harwich to await instruction from the Admiralty, via Commodore (T), as to which night the operation was to be conducted.

The general details of this lay were that it was to take place in the immediate vicinity of existing British minefields W11 and A21, which were already in position, and A23, which was planned to be laid in the near future. The *Ferret's* mines were to be planted in a direction 180° (South true) from that position, which would be decided upon according to the time and state of the tide when the operation was ordered. Terry was to fix his position by the Terschelling Bank Light Vessel, or by one of the light buoys before commencing the lay.

---

[10] Admiralty Telegram (AT) 842, 1240/28/1/18 and Admiralty Message (AM) M.00273 26/12/17 refer. (ADM 137/840)

It was not until several weeks later that the order was received for the lay to take place that night, 28 January 1918. The mines were now to be laid 200 feet apart and other orders were changed in view of the elapsed time and changed conditions. *Ferret* was instructed to make the Terschelling Bank Light Vessel in time to lay the first mine in position 53°51'30"N, 4°20'30"E by 21.00 that night and to lay her mines in a line 360° from that position. In the interim, British minefields A23 and A25 had been laid, and Terry was given strict instructions not to make his lay unless he could obtain a good departure from his marker boat. Secret Chart 'Z1' was provided to give him his departure route north of A25 with comparative safety, but *no* covering force was assigned to the little *Ferret*.

Despite the hazardous nature of his task, Terry duly carried out his instructions to the letter. Even so, this experiment was not to be repeated. This was due, according to Cowie, to the, '. . . limited application and difficulty of manufacture' of this type of mine, and all further production of the 'O' mine ceased.

A much longer operation was by then well into the planning stage. The Kattegat entrance to the Baltic Sea was one area that required large minefields to block it, in conjunction with the long-term plans for the Northern Barrage, and it was decided to achieve this by laying a series of deep minefields here.[11] The next task was a whole series of shallow minefields to be laid near the western boundary of the British proclaimed area, and this involved quite large-scale forces. The whole series of minelaying sorties, code names Operations A26, A27, A28 and A29, were planned in early February 1918. Admiral Sir David Beatty, C-in-C Grand Fleet, SNO[12] Rosyth and Vice-Admiral Commanding, East Coast, were all three duly informed by the Admiralty of the overall plan on 13 February, after the completion of the deep field.

---

[11] Cowie states that the following ships laid the deep field in these operations; the minelayer *Princess Margaret,* minelaying cruisers *Aurora, Penelope* and *Boadicea* and the minelaying destroyer *Abdiel.* All these had support provided by the Grand Fleet of one light cruiser and six destroyers as close escort and one battle squadron, one battle-cruiser squadron and one light cruiser squadron plus destroyers as distant cover.
[12] SNO=Senior Naval Officer

A26 and A28 were to be conducted simultaneously, the other pair by a second force as soon as possible after the first two. Screening and supporting forces for both operations were to be arranged by the C-in-C, Grand Fleet, who was to inform the Admiralty when the ships were ready to comply with A26 and A28. Admiral Commanding, East Coast, was to do likewise for A27 and A29. The Admiralty would instruct both commanders when the lays were to take place. The minelayers were to use their own discretion to select the routes to be followed, but on approaching the laying area, their positions were to be checked by the South Dogger Bank Light Vessel. No British mines had been laid within thirty miles of the intended position of these new fields; save for some dummy mines, and these were located well clear of the route. Strict W/T silence was to be maintained, '. . . except in the case of great emergency.'

Should it prove necessary to abandon any of the operations, both minelayers and screening ships were to return to the Humber, and should the weather deteriorate sufficiently as to prevent an accurate lay being carried out, then the CO of the force could abort. HII mines on Mk VIII sinkers were to be used, but deep switches and special plummet reels for deep laying were not necessary for these shallow fields.

Table 2
Forces involved in laying shallow minefields,
operations A26, A27, A28 and A29 – February 1918

Force A – Embarking mines at Grangemouth for A26 and A28			Force C – Embarking mines at Immingham for A27 and A29		
Ship Mines	Type	Mines	Ship	Type	
Aurora	Light cruiser	74	Princess Margaret	Minelayer	400
Penelope	Light cruiser	74	Vanquisher	Destroyer	46
Blanche	Scout	66	Venturous	Destroyer	46
Boadicea	Scout	66	Telemachus	Destroyer	40
Bellona	Scout	66	Ariel	Destroyer	40
Abdiel	Flotilla leader	70	Ferret	Destroyer	40
			Legion	Destroyer	40
Total capacity		**416**	**Total capacity**		**652**

Each ship was to lay two lines of mines, one ship laying lines A and B, another lines C and D, and so on. The mines were to be laid in groups of four, the distance between each individual mine being 100 feet, and each group of four being 300 feet, which gave forty mines to the mile. The number of mines in each line were as follows:-

In lines A, C, E, G, I and K – each line 36 mines
In lines M, O, Q, S, U and W – each line 24 mines
In line Y – 220 mines.

The minelayers were to lay any remaining mines in lines B, D, F, H, J, L, N, P, R, T, V, X, Y and Z respectively. The depth setting for each mine was to be set so that their tops would be eight feet below the surface at low water. In the original scheme, the scout, *Bellona* was to have been a part of Force A, but she was not available on the initial run. Navigation lights were forbidden and only dimmed blue lamps astern on each ship were permitted. As each ship commenced her lay, she was to make four short flashes to the next ship ahead. After laying thirty-six mines, they were to alter course twelve points to port and give two flashes to the next ship ahead and sound two short blasts on the siren. The cruising order for Force 'A' was *Aurora, Boadicea, Blanche, Penelope* and *Abdiel*. Captain Berwick Curtis, DSO, in *Abdiel* was to take the accurate time when she put her helm over for the last turn into position. He was then to commence laying thirty minutes after this, each preceding ship advancing six minutes before commencing her own lay.

The first pair of operations took place on the night of 18/19 February 1918, Force 'A' departing from the Forth at 05.10 and rendezvousing with Force 'C' at 17.05. The minelayers were provided with an escort of eight destroyers: *Valentine, Vimiera, Vega, Vectis, Violent, Ulster, Rival* and *Tower*, under the command of Commander C A Freemantle, until 21.00, when they were detached. *Ulster* had been sent back to base at 08.20 with serious engine defects.

Due to a considerable north-westerly set, the combined force passed four miles north of the Dogger Bank Zuid Light Vessel at 23.20, before altering course to the north and checking their position with No. 2 buoy. The *Abdiel* then commenced her lay at 02.20, while the *Aurora* laid the final mine at 03.02. The minelayers rejoined their escort at 07.00 on 19 February and the whole force returned to the Forth without incident.

However, it is doubtful whether the Germans were completely deceived by all this careful preparation. Even in the fourth year of the war, and with unrestricted submarine sinkings taking place, the North Sea was not the totally deserted area of sea that it was to become in the second conflict. As the CO, Force 'A' stated in his subsequent report:

> From about fifteen miles west of the Dogger Bank Zuid Light Vessel, until about the same distance west of the Dogger Bank Noord Light Vessel, a constant succession of sailing trawlers was sighted. Many of these were well inside the Buoy line, and it was not possible, under the clear weather and moonlight conditions prevailing, to avoid passing some of them within a distance which, I fear, the ships must have been visible. Many were sighted far to the eastward of the track followed, and of the minefield as laid.
>
> Two large steamers were sighted, one of which was visible during the laying, but was about five miles to the westward, and it is not likely that she could have seen the squadron.

The vessels that comprised Force 'C' for the laying of A27 also reported these unwelcome visitors in the course of their mission. It was noted that: 'Several sailing trawlers, presumably Dutch, were observed in the vicinity of the Minefield.'

Force 'C', the converted cross-channel steamer *Princess Margaret* and the minelaying destroyers *Legion, Ariel, Ferret, Venturous, Vanquisher*, with the more experienced *Telemachus* bringing up the rear, had sailed from the Humber around 09.00 on 18 February. After the rendezvous, Force 'C' was placed some eight miles astern of Forces 'A' and 'B'. This group obtained their fix on the South Dogger Bank Light Vessel at 23.50 and, at 01.58 on the 19th, reached position 51°12'0"N, 4°51'15"E, and commenced their lay. Due to the inexperience of some of the destroyers, which had only just joined the force after conversion, they exceeded their time limits on lines M, O, Q, S, U and W; line Y commenced and finished about one-and-a-half miles NNE of the position ordered. In addition, a mine jammed on the rails aboard the *Venturous*. As a result, she only laid nineteen mines on line Q, the rest being put down on line R. The destroyer's minefield covered a rectangle based on a line from the commencing position to 55°17'30'N, 4°56'0"E, extending one mile to the north-west, while the *Princess Margaret* laid her two lines to the north of it. Fortunately, there were no further incidents to mar the night's work and, after joining forces again, all seven ships arrived back at the Humber at 14.00 on 19 February.

The next pair of operations, A28 and A29, followed much the same pattern, and took place on the night of 24/25 February 1918. *Aurora, Penelope, Abdiel, Blanche, Bellona* and *Boadicea* sailed from the Forth at 02.30 that Sunday, escorted by the destroyers *Valentine* (Captain Freemantle), *Vimiera, Vega, Vectis, Vanoc, Vendetta* and *Tower*. This force proceeded to rendezvous with *Princess Margaret, Legion, Ariel, Ferret, Venturous, Vanquisher* and *Telemachus*, who had left the Humber at 09.00 on the same day, with the light cruiser *Conquest* as escort.

Just over four hours later, while approaching the rendezvous point, disaster almost overtook them, for a German U-boat sighted the force and made an attack. The British squadron was in position 54°16'N, 1°3'E, when the *Conquest* reported sighting a torpedo with a red head passing between the columns from astern at 13.10. This missile passed between *Conquest* and *Princess Margaret*, the former being stationed 2½ cables one point from right astern of the explosive-packed minelayer. It proved a lucky escape. Force 'C' met Forces 'A' and 'B' as planned at 16.10 and the *Conquest* turned back, unescorted. The remaining escorting destroyers were retained by Force 'A' until the Dogger Bank Zuid Light Vessel was sighted at 20.35, bearing NE, distance four miles, whereupon they in turn were detached.

The *Abdiel* commenced her lay at 23.35 with Force 'A' and again the *Aurora* completed the field at 00.19 on the 29th.

During the operation, the unreliability of the old *Elia* mine was once again forcibly demonstrated. Two mines from *Bellona* and one from *Blanche* detonated after being laid. Force 'C' commenced laying at 20.42 and also reported difficulties with the mines: 'Owing to the bright moonlight it was possible to observe the behaviour of the mines to a certain extent, and some appeared to remain on the surface.' Again, one steamer and some fishing vessels were sighted after passing the Light Vessel, working well inside the dangerous 'forbidden' zone. None of these foolhardy neutrals was actually in view during the laying period, however. All the British ships returned safely the next morning. Force 'A' picked up their escorting destroyers at 07.00 and proceeded to the Forth, while most of Force 'C' returned to the Humber. However, the *Princess Margaret* was escorted north by *Telemachus* and *Vanquisher*, parting company with them off May Island at 05.12 on 25 February.

The reason for this redeployment was that the *Princess Margaret* was required to operate with the light cruisers and scouts in the laying of the deep field, although this was subsequently abandoned until April owing to bad weather conditions. She anchored in Burntisland Road at 07.00. The two destroyers, meanwhile, had sped back southward. For them, a whole new era of destroyer minelaying operations was about to begin.

4

THE FORMATION OF THE 20TH FLOTILLA

The *Abdiel* also steamed south to Immingham at the end of February. The 20th Destroyer Flotilla was established here, with the special mission of laying mines inside the German swept channels in the Heligoland Bight. The earlier, shallow minefields, and the planned deep fields, were all in response to the C-in-C, Grand Fleet's proposal that the approaches to all the German naval harbours in the North Sea should be intensively mined. Admiral Beatty concluded that such a policy was the correct one for 1918. The conversion of extra destroyers for such an intensive campaign resulted in a further twelve 'V' and 'W' class ships being converted, as we have seen. In the event, they were not eventually called upon to function in their minelaying role during the war, for Beatty's plan was only half-heartedly adopted. The opposition to it was almost as strong as earlier, when Jellicoe's similar scheme had also been rejected.

The partial carrying out of this plan resulted in the setting up of a highly trained and high-speed force of destroyer minelayers. Their main function was to fill in the lanes that the overworked German minesweepers had to clear day-in, day-out in our steadily growing mined areas in the Heligoland Bight. Although actual results may not have been spectacular in terms of major warships or submarines sunk, the amount of effort expended by the Germans in just keeping limited routes open was enormous. Moreover, these selected boltholes were much easier to watch and patrol than the completely funnel-shaped entrance to the Heligoland Bight. As our minefield grew, so the enemy was forced to sweep further and further afield in order to maintain his entrances and exists. The Germans thus laid themselves more and more open to hit-and-run raids by more conventional forces. Nor was the element of surprise easy for the Germans to achieve. The original composition of the 20th Destroyer Flotilla was as indicated in Table 3.

Table 3
Original composition of the 20th (Minelaying) Flotilla, February 1918

Ship	Type	Commanding Officer
Abdiel	Flotilla leader	Captain Berwick Curtis, DSO, RN
Vanoc	Destroyer	Commander E O Tudor, RN
Vanquisher	Destroyer	Lieutenant-Commander K A Beattie, RN
Venturous	Destroyer	Lieutenant-Commander G P Bowles, RN
Vehement	Destroyer	Lieutenant-Commander V Hammersley-Heenan, RN
Telemachus	Destroyer	Commander Taprell Dorling, DSO, RN
Tarpon	Destroyer	Lieutenant-Commander F E Wright, RN
Legion	Destroyer	Commander F A Clutterbuck, RN
Sandfly	Destroyer	Lieutenant-Commander E H Dauglish, RIM
Ariel	Destroyer	Lieutenant F A Rothera
Ferret	Destroyer	Lieutenant A H L Terry

In order to make the work of the German minesweepers even more difficult and hazardous than it already was, anti-sweeping cutters were introduced as part of the mines moorings. More deadly in its effect was the implementation of the delayed-release sinkers. Fitted with soluble plugs whose rate of melting could be varied with infinite variety and cunning, these mines were put down in one lay. They then rose to their varied depths in batches, according to their settings, within days or hours, the depth taking being set on the hydrostatic principle. However, they were initially unreliable in operation and, to ensure the safety of the minelayers, fields were laid with 'Dummy' mines, which were equally frustrating for the enemy. These had to be swept as they were indistinguishable from the genuine article, but could be laid with more confidence by the destroyers, until improvements were made.

Thus the first operation conducted by the newly formed 20th

Flotilla did, in fact, involve the laying of 'dummy' mines in the enemy-swept channels. On 9 March, at midday, the *Abdiel* led the *Telemachus, Vanquisher, Venturous, Ariel* and *Ferret* to sea from Immingham on the first of these runs. It was a dark night, and no trawlers or other enemy shipping were encountered. The flotilla reached its minelaying position at 55°43'N, 4.58°E at 00.35 on 10 March. Commencing with the stern ship, the *Ferret*, the laying began, a total of 284 mines being put down up to a position 55°52'30"N, 5°27'00"E. No detonators or primers were used and no sinking plugs either. The mines were pre-set for 5 feet below the Low Water (LW) level and spaced at sixteen to the mile. The whole operation proceeded without a hitch.

This was field A30. Field A31 was a 'real' minefield, the same six destroyers being employed. They sailed from Immingham at 09.00 on 14 March and headed east via 'H' Channel through our own defensive minefield barrier along the east coast, to the South Dogger Bank Light Vessel to position 55°18'45"N, 6°23'30"E. From this spot they laid 284 mines in twelve lines, A, C, E, G and J lines contained twenty mines each; L line thirty-two mines; B, D and K twenty mines each; F and H lines twenty-six mines each; and M line forty mines. These were put down in groups of four, each mine being 100 feet apart with 300 feet between each group. The distance between each line was a quarter of a mile. The mines were set for a depth of 6 feet below LW and sinking plugs were not employed.

On this occasion, the flotilla had a narrow escape from detection by German patrols. While on their outward track and still laden with primed mines, they were buffeting through a moderate sea and taking onboard considerable spray. When, at 21.45, two groups of unknown ships were sighted at a range of two miles. The British destroyers were making 20 knots, the enemy an estimated 10 knots. The Germans proved far from alert. Indeed, they advertised their presence as the two groups passed each other in the murk, steering ESE by displaying 'peculiar' lights and flashing signals to each other in Morse, with little attempt at concealment. The Germans obviously felt completely secure, but they missed the chance of a lifetime, for the British ships were in no position to offer serious combat, laden as they were. In the words of Captain Curtis:

Owing to the darkness and spray it was impossible to make out distinctly what they were, but the opinion of the Flotilla is that they were either destroyers or large trawlers. As these vessels apparently did not see us and made no W/T messages, I left them alone, considering that it was my first duty to lay the mines without being observed, and that I could not hope to make an accurate run to the minefield from my departure point if I had deviated from the course to investigate. The state of the weather and the fact that my ships were loaded with primed mines, also assisted my decision. Unfortunately, these craft were not sighted on the return journey after laying the mines.[13]

Taffrail remembers this incident and the hazards such unexpected encounters always brought:

Occasionally we sighted the enemy, as witness the night when we passed a large bunch of German minesweepers escorted by destroyers, steaming back to their base. Oblivious to all danger, they were talking to each other with their signalling lamps, while we passed so close to leeward that we could smell the reek of coal from their funnels.

We could have made cat's meat of that little party had we been allowed to fight. However, orders were peremptory. We must not fight with mines on board unless attacked. Had the night been clear and calm, instead of overcast, very dark, wet and gusty; had the Germans been keeping better look-out; someone might have fired a gun at that line of dark shapes which slid past them at no more than 500 yards, and we should have replied. But no such thing happened, and we sped on into the darkness ahead to our dirty work thirty miles beyond.[14]

[13] Report of Captain (D) 20th Flotilla, 15 March 1918. (ADM 2856/W.1361)
[14] Taffrail, *Endless Story, op. cit.*, pp 383–4.

As well as German patrols, there was the very real danger of running foul of either British or German mines. This could be caused by an error in navigation through waters becoming more and more liberally bestrewed with these monstrosities or else there could be mines that had broken adrift, a not uncommon event in the stormy North Sea. These concerns always ensured that these nocturnal visits were heart-in-the-mouth affairs. Our own minefields in this area, thirty-two at this time, and to grow to more than seventy by the war's end, were carefully plotted and marked on the charts, but nobody could risk passing too close, say within a mile of them, in case of errors. The German minefields were, naturally, a totally unknown factor, although frequent sightings of drifting mines gave some clues as to how and where they were distributed about the Heligoland Bight.

The destroyer's main advantage in this type of clandestine warfare, apart from her speed, was her shallow draught compared with major warships and converted merchant vessels. By using high tide for most of their runs, they could be reasonably certain of avoiding the worst effects of accidentally straying into a mined area themselves, but the dangers were very real indeed. The Germans were incredibly slow in catching on to what the British destroyers were up to (a position totally reversed during the opening months of the Second World War incidentally). However, after a while, they began serious attempts to ambush the 20th Flotilla with specially prepared minefields set shallow in areas that looked like potential targets for British activity. It was a combination of guesswork, luck and pure chance that granted the 20th Flotilla immunity for a long while. But, eventually, their nemesis was to catch up with them, as was perhaps inevitable. Still, at the outset, luck was with the 20th Flotilla.

The next sortie, to lay minefield A32, was an example of the unknown horrors that lay bobbing about beneath their slim keels as they dashed in and out of this deadly stretch of water. Again, the same six destroyers were employed. They sailed from Immingham and arrived, via the South Dogger Bank Light Vessel and the Dutch Free Channel, an internationally neutral area through the fields, to a position 55°23'45"N, 6°14'E. Here, they laid 284 mines set for a depth of 6 feet below Low Water Level, but with no sinking plugs. Lines A, C, E, G and J contained twenty mines each; L forty mines; B, H and K twenty mines; D and F twenty-six mines; and M thirty-two mines. It proved another dirty night – black and with heavy driving rain. As a result, some navigation problems were encountered, which meant that the field ran out two miles further north than specified.

The 20th Flotilla had already been warned by the Admiralty that enemy mines had been discovered some six miles south of the North Dogger Bank Light Vessel. This accounts for why Captain Curtis used the Dutch Free Channel for both inward and outward passages, rather than the gap between A26 and the dummy field laid earlier. This gap was only four miles across, too narrow for safety on a night like the 18/19 March. Curtis also believed that even dummy mines, although safe, were laid shallow and likely to damage the ships' propellers at speed. Even so, enemy mines were seen 'watching' on several occasions to remind them of what they were up against. Two of these were actually floating in the Dutch 'Free' Channel, 'pear shape and painted yellow', while a new type was also sighted, 'pear shaped and painted green'. But at least on this trip no enemy surface ships were encountered.

Again, Taffrail recorded the incident:

The German minefields were an unknown quantity. We knew that many had been laid, some for the express purpose of putting a stop to our excursions. Many times we saw enemy 'floaters'. On several occasions yellow painted monstrosities, bristling with horns, came to the surface in the wake of one of us after its mooring wire had been cut by a fast-moving propeller. We simply had to take our chance, trusting to the Almighty. I must confess, however, that when I saw the chart of the German mine-fields, which was delivered up after the Armistice, I had an attack of cold shivering. Much of the water that we had considered innocuous, and had gaily careered over at twenty-five knots, teemed with explosive abominations.[15]

[15] *Ibid.*

By this time, the more potent British replies to these weapons were becoming available to the 20th Flotilla in sufficient quantities to justify their use. HII mines on Mk VIII sinkers fitted with thirty-day sinking plugs and with an 'O' exploder fitted to every fifth mine, promised much heartache for the Hun when embarked for the laying of minefield A33. Only five destroyers took part in this operation, which took place on the night of 22/23 March. The *Ariel* was not available and was left behind; otherwise the composition of the force was as previously listed.

The flotilla proceeded via 'H' Channel and the Terschelling Light Vessel to lay these horrors from a position 53°47'15"N, 4°56'00"E, from 23.00 onward. Each mine was spaced 100 feet apart in groups of four, with 300 feet between each group, and three-quarters of a mile between each line. The night was clear and bright, with a flat calm sea, so a very precise lay proved possible. Fortunately, neither enemy nor neutral ships were met, and enemy mines were not observed, This field, typical of those put down at this period of the war, was laid out as in the figure on page 45.

The 'O' exploder, fitted to some of these mines, was a simple obstructer device, designed to make life unpleasant for the German minesweepers. It was intended to cut the minesweeping wire itself by means of a sharp cutting device, forced against it by the automatic detonation of a small charge of gunpowder activated by the sweep. This device was only in the experimental stage, hence it was fitted to only one mine in every five. However, stocks were even more limited than the new mines themselves and for the next operation, the laying of A34 field, the small quantity on hand at Immingham was exhausted. Thus, although five-mine spacing was used on this occasion, two lines had to be content with merely two apiece. Otherwise, it was the same mixture as before, with *Abdiel*, *Legion*, *Telemachus*, *Vanquisher*, *Ariel* and *Ferret* laying a total of 264 mines on the morning of 27 March.

This field was unique in two ways. First, the lay was conducted in daylight, although not planned that way, and second it brought the 20th Flotilla into contact with German surface forces in a far more positive way than had hitherto been the case. It had been the intention of Captain Curtis to

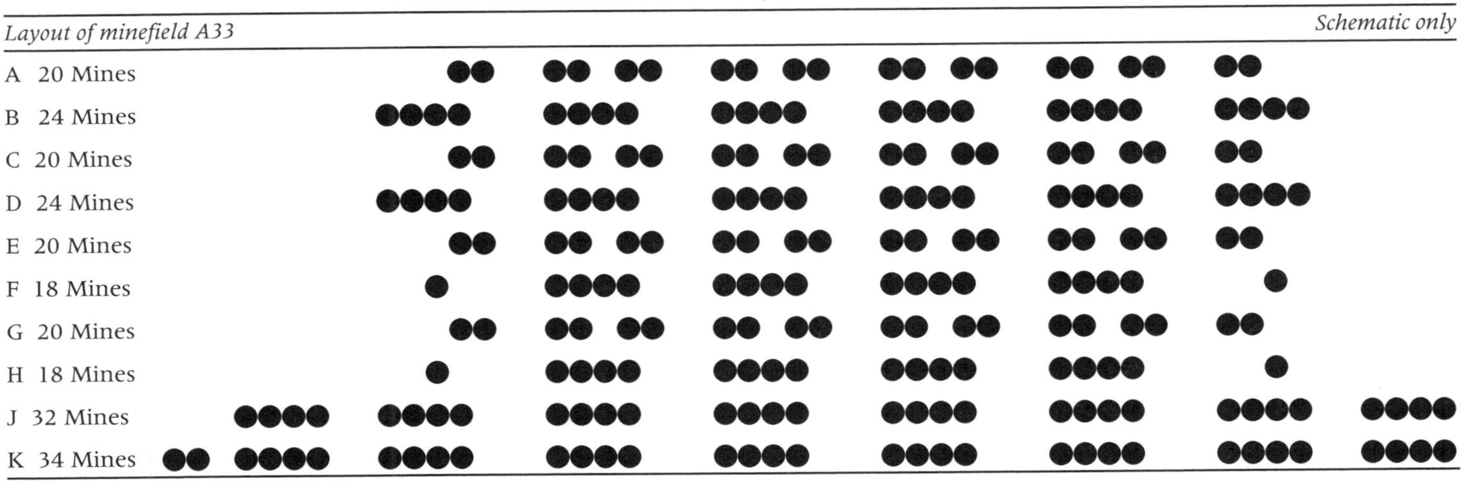

Layout of minefield A33

Schematic only

A 20 Mines

B 24 Mines

C 20 Mines

D 24 Mines

E 20 Mines

F 18 Mines

G 20 Mines

H 18 Mines

J 32 Mines

K 34 Mines

arrive at the laying position at 03.00, but the flotilla ran into thick fog *en route* to the South Dogger Bank Light Vessel. The destroyers therefore had to feel their way slowly and patiently until they discovered the lightship, before they could make a good, accurate departure. Thus, it was not until 01.30 that they actually found this vessel. As the mist remained blanket-like and still, it was felt that it would serve in lieu of the more usual darkness to shield their activities and the risk of daylight laying was accepted. The flotilla pressed on.

All was well, and the destroyers were within four-and-a-half miles of their lay commencement area. Suddenly, out of the fog, the bows of three enemy trawlers steaming slowly south-ward in line abreast about three-quarters of a mile apart were seen. It was all over in an instant. The blunt bows loomed up while the silent minelayers rushed across in line ahead in front of them and vanished into the gloom again like misty wraiths, at 20 knots. The German patrol boats responded by switching on two horizontal red lights and flashing a challenge 'DU', but Captain Curtis ignored them and continued to make his lay as planned. The distance between the two forces had been 300 yards and the decks of the enemy ships had been completely deserted. They were soon left far astern. Amazingly, the German vessels made no sighting reports during the whole time that the British destroyers were busy about their minelaying business some five miles further on. The enemy patrol trawlers seemed content to anchor and wait for the fog to lift.

This it gradually did, until, by the time the last mine had plopped into the water, the two groups were in plain sight of each other in the watery sunlight. It being too good an oppor-tunity to waste, Captain Curtis decided to try to capture these tardy sentinels, and so detailed two of his destroyers to each German trawler. Only now did the enemy crews show some signs of animation, but by then, it was far too late. The German ships sent out W/T reports from 05.15. It was later learned that two German light cruisers and a flotilla of destroyers were in the area searching for the 20th Flotilla. Had they had been warned on the first sighting, they may have found them. Indeed, the German survivors stated that the two cruisers were close by to the east, and they had not expected to see the British ships return from that direction until after their first view of them.

Taffrail took *Telemachus* toward the centre enemy ship and later described what ensued:

> We were just about to go alongside ours, when I saw a man rush aft along her deck and release something which fell into the water with a heavy splash. I realised what it was – a depth charge – and promptly went full speed astern. It was as well. The depth charge went off with a shattering explosion, and practically blew the stern off the outpost boat. Another few seconds, and it would have pulverised our bows as well. We rescued the crew from their boat, and made them prisoners.[16]

The other German vessels showed no such aggressive intentions, as Captain Curtis later reported:

> I ran *Abdiel* alongside the western one and the *Legion* did the same to the eastern one, but the sea was so heavy that the boarding parties could not get on board. I therefore told the captain to get his anchor up and steer N.78 W, which he did with great alacrity, the *Vanquisher* spurring him on. I then returned to assist *Legion* while the remaining four were picking up the crew of the blown-up trawler and cruising round to keep off submarines. All this time Telefunken W/T got very busy and strong and was reported as getting louder, so I considered the wisest course was to blow up the remaining two trawlers and get away as soon as possible, observing that the weather was getting worse every minute and the speed of my flotilla is only twenty-five knots, on account of *Ariel* and *Ferret* and in such weather, probably much less. I therefore took off the crew and blew up the trawler with a demolition charge and sent *Legion* on ahead with the rest of the flotilla

---

[16] Taffrail, *Endless Story, op. cit.,* p 384.

except *Vanquisher*, whom I ordered to take off the crew of his trawler and we then sank her with a few rounds of 4-inch.[17]

Captain Curtis regretfully mused that he wished he could have brought both surviving enemy ships back as prizes as they were 'beautifully fitted up', each with a 4-inch gun, searchlight and many bombs and depth charges. Only the leader's boat was fitted with W/T, but in view of the close proximity of the enemy cruisers, it was felt to be too great a risk to take. From what the Germans later told their captors, strong German forces were at sea hunting for them. Indeed, they had initially mistaken the 20th Flotilla for one of their own destroyer squadrons quartering the area. Captain Curtis noted that, 'The Germans made no resistance at all and appeared quite pleased at being captured . . .' In total, three officers and sixty-nine men were taken captive from the three outpost boats, which were the converted German trawlers *Mars*, *Scharbentz* and *Polarstern*, the latter being the leader of the patrol group.

Despite an unpleasant voyage home through a rising gale at 22 knots, this little incident had been an unexpected and heartening event in an otherwise grim and anonymous war for the crews of the British destroyers. It was almost a light relief from the constant tension that accompanied such missions. It was probably the only time that they ever met the enemy face-to-face. Taffrail recorded his own feelings:

> We landed our guests under an armed guard on the jetty at Immingham, and, whatever other people might have thought, I certainly felt sorry for them. They were quite pleasant fellows, seamen like ourselves, and I noticed when they were put ashore that all their uniform buttons and cap-ribbons had disappeared. They had exchanged them for cigarettes and chocolates. Your British bluejacket is insatiable as a curio-hunter. That

---

[17] Report of the CO 20th Flotilla, dated 29 March 1918. W. 1361 refers. After much hard war service the top speeds of all destroyers were usually three to five knots less than that credited to them in reference books, or when first built. *Ariel* and *Ferret* were the oldest boats of the flotilla.

morning's work brought the six destroyers taking part the sum of £360 in prize bounty, or £5 for each man captured.[18]

As March gave way to April, however, there were to be few such diversions for the men of the 20th Flotilla. The pace was increasing and the coming of the lighter nights in the North Sea saw no slackening in the tempo of their operations.

[18] Taffrail, *Endless Story, op. cit.*, pp 384–5.

5

ALARMS, EXCURSIONS
AND ACCIDENTS

The encounter with the German patrol boats was very much
an exception to the rule for the 20th Flotilla. Their work was
considered top secret so, as well as hardly ever knowing
whether the results of their labours were worthwhile or not,
they could not talk of their exploits, even obliquely. They were
denied the satisfaction their more fortunate colleagues felt
after a surface action in the Dover Straits, or an encounter with
German destroyers in the convoy operations off Norway and
suchlike. If their work was therefore anonymous, nonetheless
it was not without serious risk. It should also be emphasised
that it did not lack purpose or fail to achieve major results. The
fact that the results of their work was, perforce, kept hidden
from themselves and the public as a whole at the time, and
have been largely overlooked by historians ever since, should
not detract from either their achievements or purpose. Nor
were mere scalps of ships sunk the sole criterion for judging
their work, as Cowie points out:

> To revert to the main purpose and effect of the mine-
> fields, it will be seen that without sinking any ships at all
> they would have forced the enemy to a course of action
> which he would not otherwise have adopted. In fact,
> however, some twenty-eight German destroyers and
> torpedo boats were sunk, together with nearly seventy
> minesweepers and armed trawlers. These minefields also
> accounted for four U-boats at least. This comparatively
> small number was not so much due to the alleged in-
> effectiveness of the mines as to the fact that their

presence forced the enemy to route his U-boats through the Kattegat or to pass them through the inland water-ways via Bruges to Zeebrugge and Ostende.[19]

The next two operations were fairly routine. On 1 April the Admiralty signalled that the flotilla was to lay minefield A35 with live mines on the night of 2/3 April between positions 53°51'30"N, 4°47'15"E and 53°55'15"N, 4°47'15"E in plan 6, modified to allow *Abdiel* to lay thirty-two mines in line J. The mines were to be set for 6 feet below LW and 38-day sinking plugs were to be used, as were 'O' exploders if they were available at Immingham in time. (In the event, they were not.)

Accordingly, *Abdiel, Legion, Vanquisher, Ariel* and *Ferret* sailed at 11.00 on 2 April. They proceeded via the Terschelling Light Vessel to the laying point, which they reached at 23.00. From there, they laid a total of 238 mines, the ships turning to port after completion in accordance with instructions. Nothing was seen of the enemy, apart from a lone steamer and two fishing craft in the vicinity of the Light Vessel itself.

Abdiel, Legion, Telemachus, Vanquisher, Ariel and *Ferret* laid a similar field of 278 mines in the same waters on the night of 5/6 April. It proved to be a dark and misty night, and the ships once more carried out their nefarious work unobserved. This was minefield A36 and A37 was soon to follow, using exactly the same methods. This field was put down *by Abdiel, Telemachus* and *Vanquisher*, the 'fast' division, as it was closer to the enemy coast, and high speed was considered necessary. The three destroyers sailed from Immingham at 23.00 on 10 April, but thick fog prevented them from proceeding any further than Grimsby Roads, where they were forced to anchor until midnight while waiting for the weather to lift a little. The mist remained very thick on their outward passage, however, right across to the Danish coast. The flotilla was, nonetheless, able to get a good departure fix from the Lynvig Light during a brief lifting of the murk, although Blaavland Point Light could not be seen. The Dutch schooner *Jantine Fenegine* was the only vessel encountered during this operation. The destroyers laid a

---

[19] Cowie, *Mines, Minelayers and Minelaying, op. cit.,* p 82.

total of 158 mines in six lines, in the designated position, before returning safely home.

Another dummy field followed, laid on the night of 11/12 April by the 'Slow' division, *Legion* (Commander Francis Clutterbuck) and *Ariel*. The pair left Immingham at 20.30 and proceeded via the Terschelling Light Vessel to a position 53°36'45"N, 4°33'E. They then laid eighty mines set for a depth of 20 feet rendered safe by the removal of the detonator's and primers. Special dummy detonator holders were inserted to fool the enemy, and the mines were spaced 300 feet apart.

Occasionally, the Admiralty got wind that the Germans were planning special reception committees for the 20th Flotilla. When this happened, heavy support was laid on by the light cruisers, destroyers and large flying boats of the Harwich Force. One such occasion was the laying of minefield A38. This large minefield was to be laid with its mines fitted with a variety of 7-, 14-, 21- and 28-day release plugs. It was arranged for the Harwich Force to be out in support and patrolling to the position of 54°55'N, 5°35'E by daylight. They would take some of the Large America flying boats with them, towed on lighters behind the destroyers, and then launch them at dawn to conduct aerial reconnaissance. Because of the acute danger of operating in such waters, the Harwich Force was to be preceded by destroyers fitted with high-speed mine sweeps and all the ships were to stream their own paravanes. Even with all these precautions, the sortie was risky.

As E F Knight wrote:

The great minefield which was declared by our Government in the summer of 1917, the preparations of which was a gigantic undertaking, extended from the Frisian Islands to about latitude 56 degrees north. The Dutch, for their own purposes, removed their lightships from their coasts to the western side of this minefield, thus forming a line of lights running north and south, roughly along the 4th degree of east longitude. This our sailors facetiously named Piccadilly Circus. It was the business of the submarines to lay mines on the eastern part of this minefield, that is, near to the coast. Our surface minelayers laid their mines further seaward; while still further west our large minelaying ships laid their mines just inside Piccadilly Circus.[20]

And so, the work went on as early spring gave way to spring and summer. On the night of 21/22 April, *Abdiel, Legion, Telemachus, Ariel, Sandfly, Tarpon* (finally rejoining her compatriots after the damage received on her first operation had been made good) and *Vanquisher* laid minefield A40 with 318 mines 6 feet below LW in fourteen rows, with 38-day sinking plugs fitted. A41 was laid by *Abdiel, Telemachus, Ariel, Sandfly* and *Tarpon* on 24/25 April. The ships departed from the Dogger Bank South Light Vessel to a position 55°7'30"N, 6°20'30"E and commenced their lay at 02.00 on the 25th. This field consisted of twelve lines of mines without sinking plugs. In contrast to earlier lays, the night was a bright, clear moonlit one, affording the flotilla no protection whatsoever. However, the only untoward incident was the sighting of a bright, fixed, white light to the east of the minefield. Captain Curtis was of the opinion that this was at the masthead of a vessel at anchor, but went on, 'If it was an enemy outpost vessel, I do not think she saw the flotilla as she was too far off and she did not challenge or extinguish her light.'[21]

The third 'Dummy' minefield occupied the attentions of *Abdiel, Legion, Telemachus, Venturous, Ariel* and *Tarpon* on the night of 27/28 April. Dummy detonator holders, drawn specially from the mining depot, were substituted for the real primers and detonators. Some 278 of these harmless mines were deposited from a position 54°16'00"N, 4°42'15"E, the ships turning to starboard on completion of the lay.

The beginning of May saw the east coast lashed by a succession of storms for a period, which postponed the next sorties. *Sandfly* and *Ferret* joined the other six destroyers to carry out the laying of A43, and the 20th Flotilla sailed at 10.20 on the last day of April. However, it was forced to turn back owing to strong east winds and heavy seas. Captain Curtis had initially

[20] Knight, E F, *Harwich Naval Forces*, Hodder & Stoughton, 1919, pp 134–5.
[21] Report of SO 20th Flotilla, dated 25 April 1918, W. 1361 refers.

persisted in his attempts but as the evening drew on, the seas grew rougher instead of moderating and they had to abort the sortie. The flotilla sailed for a second attempt from the Humber on 2 May and, at 02.00 on 3 May, took departure from their old friend the South Dogger Bank Light Vessel, laying sixteen lines of live mines, a total of 358 in all. The ships turned to port on completion of their runs.

The sea on this occasion was smooth and the weather was fine, and they once again witnessed the mysterious bright white light below the horizon to the east for a few minutes at 02.00. A similar glow was observed at 02.30 to the south-east and burned for five minutes. At the *Abdiel*'s masthead, a signalman with night glasses reported that he could see a small ship in that direction but it was a pitch-black night and nothing could be observed from the destroyer's deck. The light was a long way off and the moon was rising nearly behind it, while there were thick black clouds to the west that is, *behind* the flotilla. This being the case, Captain Curtis observed that he did not think they were seen, even if these strange lights were some sort of German patrol. 'I found it very difficult to see the TBDs, who were formed in line ahead after laying and only one mile off,' he was later to recall.[22]

On their way home the British destroyers passed in sight of a large section of the Dutch fishing fleet, whom they encountered standing up the Free Channel under full sail. It was impossible to avoid them, as no fewer than six drifting mines were sunk, one of them a yellow, submarine mine laid by the Germans. This completed Operation A43.

Operation A38, which had been planned earlier but postponed, took place on the night of 5/6 May, with the same eight destroyers participating. Again, a combination of strong easterly winds and heavy seas caused the flotilla to turn back after they had got as far as the South Dogger Bank Light Vessel. They had to try a second time, sailing at noon on 7 May. This time they were more successful and deposited a total of 358 HII mines on Mk XII sinkers as far south as 54°4'N, 5°39'45"E. The

[22] Report of SO 20th Flotilla, dated 3 May 1918, W. 1361/1 refers. TBDs – Torpedo Boat Destroyers, the old-fashioned name for destroyers, which was still widely in use in 1918.

winds were still strong, however, and the sea was steep, which made perfect station-keeping difficult. Various delayed settings, ranging from nil to twenty-eight days, were laid in sixteen lines.

The dark waters off the Dutch and north German coasts, with their hidden dangers of minefields, sandbanks, treacherous currents and enemy patrols, were full of latent perils, but the flotilla continued to enjoy a remarkable immunity. To those who had read Erskine Childers' famous pre-war novel *The Riddle of the Sands*, these waters were truly the enemy's very back doorstep and were indeed mysterious. In addition, there were the unknown machinations of the enemy, during the four years of warfare, which increased the element of tension in their work. The strange lights and the knowledge that the Germans might have all sorts of hidden traps and unknown devices waiting for them, added to the normal strains of operating light, unarmoured craft, laden down with a lethal cargo, deep inside enemy territory. That the Germans were plotting something to stop their work was expected, and, as with the strange lights spotted earlier, the next sortie gave other hints that something nasty was brewing on the other side of the North Sea.

Operation A45 took place on the night of 10/11 May. The flotilla, less *Ariel*, laid a total of 318 mines in the same general area as before. However, this night's lay was interrupted from time to time by distant explosions and the sightings of lights over the horizon. Captain Curtis reported the night's weird happenings:

At 22.41 – position 54°22'N, 4°13'E – heard and felt a heavy muffled explosion bearing about S.E.

At 22.48 – position 54°20'N, 4°15'E – heard another explosion bearing about E.S.E.

At 23.05 – sighted white light N 83 E – ship's position 54°15'N, 4°20'E.

At 23.10 – heard third explosion bearing about N 60 E – ship's position 54°13'30"N, 4°21'30"E. White light bearing about the same (N 60 E) and drawing aft. Ship's course and speed – S 17 E – 20 knots.

From these facts I am of opinion that the light was about six miles off and judging from the way in which the explosions shook the ship, they could not have been much further. Therefore, I suggest that this may have been a ship laying mines there and the explosions possible prematures. I did not close and investigate and I am certain the flotilla was not observed as the night was dark with low visibility.[23]

But when the first trouble did befall the 20th Flotilla, it was not from any evil plans of the Germans, but through the machinations of an older and equally treacherous enemy, the fogs and mists of the North Sea. Hitherto, the flotilla had, on encountering such conditions, either turned back to await more favourable weather, or, if the mist had not been too bad, had pressed on in order to gain a reliable bearing before laying their minefields. It was often tense, nervous work, groping about in thick weather in enemy waters, as Taffrail again reminds us:

The North and South Dogger Bank Lightships were the points from where we laid off our positions for the runs of anything between eight and one hundred miles in to the laying positions in the 'Bight. After losing sight of them, we had to work on 'dead reckoning', for there were no other lights to guide us. And steering a serpentine course between old minefields, often in wild weather, or in North Sea fogs so thick that the next ahead was invisible, must have been a nerve-wracking business for the *Abdiel*'s navigator. But I never knew him to fail, even if the spray was breaking heavily over the bridge and the chart in its open chart-table must have been reduced to the consistency of blotting-paper.

We worked in close order, and, of course without navigation lights. Moreover, as flashing signals in enemy waters were impossible, all our operations had to be done by time. Some hours before arriving at the laying-

---

[23] Report of SO 20th Flotilla, dated 11 May 1918, 463/W. 1361/3 refers.

ground, therefore, a zero time, indicated by a long flash on a shaded lamp, was made by the *Abdiel*, and stop-watches were started in every ship. The speed was reduced to the laying speed of 10, 12 or 15 knots later, just before we arrived at the spot, and five minutes after-wards the leader would swing round to the laying course. The rear ship started to lay the first half of her mines immediately she steadied on the new course, and then swung out of line to lay the rest. The last ship but one started her lay the moment her next astern was seen to alter out, and so on to the head of the line, with the result the field was laid in a series of obtuse-angled Vs.

At the end of the operation all the laying destroyers were supposed, theoretically, to arrive in a single line some distance to the flank of the minefield. On the clearer nights this was possible without much difficulty. On the really dark nights, however, when hulls could not be seen at more than 200 yards, or in fog or hazy weather, the manoeuvre became positively exciting. However, as the evolution was worked out to fractions of a minute, any delay caused by a ship putting her helm over a few seconds late, or by a mine on its sinkers refusing to travel along the rails, became cumulative, and affected every other ship in the flotilla.[24]

It was at midnight on 13 May, not an auspicious date, that *Abdiel* led *Telemachus, Tarpon, Venturous, Ariel, Sandfly* and *Ferret* to sea once more to carry out operation A46. They proceeded through position 'T' (56°00'N, 3°32'E) and position 'U' (56°30'N, 5°34'E) and position 'V' (56°33'N, 7°57'E) to posi-tion 55°56'30"N, 6°16'15"E, arriving there at 01.25 on 15 May, intending to lay their field as planned. The weather was fine and the sea calm, but from time to time the flotilla ran into very thick patches of fog. It was in one of these that, just before the lay was to commence, four of the flotilla lost touch. The *Abdiel* at once turned sixteen points to try and find them and make a fresh start. After steaming five miles on this fresh

[24] Taffrail, *Endless Story, op. cit.*, pp 380–81.

course, Captain Curtis was satisfied that they had rejoined him and, at 01.49, he turned the flotilla for the minefield once more. They were soon eighteen miles from the lay commencement point when they ran into the fog bank, but Captain Curtis did not consider this invalidated his decision to go ahead with the lay as planned. As he later was to write:

> . . . all necessary Signals had been made and the rest of the operation would be done by time – fog or no fog – I considered I was justified in carrying on, provided the flotilla kept touch, which, up to the present, they have always managed to do in misty weather.[25]

However, on this occasion they failed to do so. Worse, there were two collisions of which, Curtis, leading the line, was not immediately aware. Taffrail described how it was seen from the bridge of the *Telemachus*, one of the ships involved.

> We had altered course through 180°, and were jogging along at ten knots astern of the *Abdiel*, when, to my horror, I suddenly saw a destroyer on the starboard bow steaming at right angles for the narrow gap ahead of us. We must have sighted each other simultaneously, and to rattle the engine-room telegraphs over to full speed astern and yelp thrice with the siren was the work of a moment. The helm also went over in a frantic effort to swing clear.
>
> But fifty yards is fifty yards. One cannot pull up 1000-tons like a taxi-cab. Collision was inevitable from the moment we saw each other.
>
> Looking anxiously over the bridge rails, I found myself gazing into the eyes of a white-faced little group of men on the *Sandfly*'s forecastle as her bows slid past ours.
>
> 'Gaw' blimey!' howled a voice, 'Where the blinkin' 'ell are you coming to?
>
> In point of fact, the boot was rather on the other foot, for we were in station and the *Sandfly* was not. But there

[25] *Ibid.*

was no time for further badinage. With a sickening bump and the grinding crash of twisting steel, our sharp bows struck the *Sandfly* fair in her foremost boiler-room. It carved a V-shaped gash through which the water poured like a mill-race.

It was a sickening moment, for the collision, through no fault of ours, had occurred within thirty miles of the enemy coast and a full 250 from home. The *Sandfly* was badly damaged, and would have to be towed, while we were in the very thick of probable enemy patrols. Daylight was due in an hour and a half, and our wireless operators could hear a Zeppelin chatting to a friend in Germany, and a ship within five miles chiming in. We prayed all we knew that the fog would continue.

This was not the end of the sorry tale. The *Ariel*, next astern of *Sandfly*, had also found herself in the same unenviable position with the *Tarpon*, next astern of *Telemachus*. Luckily, these two ships had slightly more time in which to avoid the worst of the resultant collision, and, although they had touched, the momentum was lost before the actual moment of impact. Neither of these two destroyers was badly damaged. Meanwhile, Captain Curtis had carried on, oblivious to the carnage in his wake. Not until he arrived at the laying point did he discover he was completely on his own. Captain Curtis again turned his ship N 72° E as before. After five miles, he found the rest of his flotilla gathered protectively around the *Sandfly* and *Telemachus*.

After ascertaining that *Telemachus* was not crippled, Captain Curtis left her and the *Ferret* to assist the *Sandfly*, while he tried for a third time to proceed with the operation. But, once again, he failed. This time it was because, in the fog, another destroyer, *Venturous*, lost contact. Rather than try for a fourth search in the darkness, which might result in yet another accident, Captain Curtis carried on with *Abdiel*, *Tarpon* and *Ariel* only. These three vessels laid a total of 152 mines in eight lines. On conclusion of this lay, Curtis sent *Ariel* on alone at 22 knots to position 56°00'N, 1°50'E, to make a W/T report, as he did not consider it advisable to do so from the vicinity of the minefield itself. The rest of the flotilla returned to Immingham, with the *Ferret* towing *Sandfly*, and *Telemachus* keeping them company at a best speed of 8 knots.

Taffail wrote:

> . . . it took us thirty-six interminable hours to get the damaged *Sandfly* home, take her up the Humber, and tuck her into a dry-dock at Immingham, safe but not quite sound. As for the *Telemachus*, she was entirely undamaged, with hardly a scratch in the grey paint round her bows. But our steel submarine ram below the waterline had made a nasty mess of the *Sandfly*.

6

SUMMER IN THE HELIGOLAND BIGHT

Although the patterns of mines laid by the 20th Flotilla varied, all were combinations of the basic format for individual minelaying. Speed was varied according to the type of pattern to be put down and to a set formula, but it must be remembered that the mines were hauled aft by winch and then manhandled over the stern of the ship. Apart from the stoppages, which could cause much delay even though rare, considering the conditions in which many of the lays were conducted, it was a tough physical job for the men. The variation in gaps between mines could obviously also vary considerably. This, of course, cut both ways. Perfect spacing might appear desirable on the charts worked out for specific areas, but a certain randomness was always worked in, hence the destroyers sometimes finished their dog-legs to port and sometimes to starboard, in order to confuse the enemy minesweepers. Therefore, a certain degree of irregularity in spacing probably, if unintentionally, caused a similar effect.

Accuracy in the placing of the fields was, as we have seen, paramount. It was essential to place the fields precisely, not only to have maximum impact on the enemy, but also in order that an accurate plot of friendly fields could be kept, in order that our own ships could safely circumnavigate them with a degree of confidence. The first essential was an accurate 'fix' for navigation purposes, and here the neutral Dutch Light Vessels, as we have seen, played a very convenient role as marker for the 20th Flotilla. Fixed buoys and other lights were also so utilised in the shallow waters of the enemy coast, but these, of course, could be moved at will by the enemy with nasty results, and so could not be relied upon. They could also break adrift in heavy weather and storms. One important device was invented, or adapted, by the British minelaying destroyers at this period, which greatly facilitated accurate plotting. It was the Taunt-wire measuring apparatus. Cowie describes it as follows:

> This gear, originally designed for use in ships laying submarine telegraph cables, consisted in simple terms of a long length of piano wire paid out astern of the minelayer, the amount of wire run off being measured with a high degree of accuracy and recorded on a form of cyclometer.[26]

For the protection of our own ships, which had to penetrate the enemy minefields, the adoption of paravanes was the most acceptable solution for larger ships of light cruiser and upward dimensions. Briefly, it consisted of two 'otter boards' as used by steam trawlers. These extended a galvanised steel wire towrope to either bow. In the design perfected by Lieutenant D Burney, these paravanes were given registered numbers. Even numbers were adjusted to run port side of the ship only, those with odd numbers to starboard. The steel ropes were similarly paired, the right hand wire being used exclusively on the port side, the left to starboard.

On larger ships fitting these paravanes was easy in that they were towed from the ship's forefoot, right forward under the bow, and rode easily well out on each side of the bow. The mooring wires of the mines fouled by these galvanised wires were pulled in by the momentum of the ship toward the paravanes, and away from the vessel hull. The wires were made with a sawing edge, which cut through the mine mooring wire. Cutters were also fitted near the paravanes to do the same job. Once severed from its mooring, the mine floated free and could either be ignored or sunk by rifle fire. In the destroyers, such large fittings were not considered practicable because their draught was deepest astern, and

---

[26] Cowie, *Mines, Minelayers and Minelaying, op. cit.,* p 55.

many had a rounded forefoot. In these ships the paravane equipment had to be specially adapted, as the mine gear of the 20th Flotilla destroyers obviated the more usual expedient of towing from astern via gear fixed to the quarterdeck. By 1918, the *Abdiel* was fitted with this special gear, which was why she usually led the line. When her sister ship *Gabriel* joined the flotilla in August, she, too, was fitted with this equipment. The other destroyers, in general, just had to take their chances.

The unfortunate events of 15 May in no way slowed down the tempo for the flotilla, although while the *Sandfly* was under repair, they had to operate for a time at reduced strength. Several new conversions were pending however, and were due to join the flotilla's numbers soon. Until then, the veterans soldiered on.

Other measures to maintain secrecy are mentioned by Taffrail:

> The work at the time was considered very 'hush-hush' and secret, and, in order that it should not be known what we were doing, the large white numbers painted on our bows were frequently altered to mystify anyone who might sight us at sea. For the same reason it was desirable to conceal the rows of mines on our deck, which was done with canvas camouflage screens spread over the after part of the ship and painted with a gun, torpedo-tubes, and deck-fittings against a background of sky. One artist even ran riot and painted in a few sea-gulls and some men on deck! But the camouflage screens certainly served their purpose. At a few hundred yards, unless one suspected, it was impossible to tell that we were not ordinary destroyers. [27]

The mention of the alteration of pendant numbers is interesting. In fact, *all* British destroyers underwent considerable changes in their pendant numbers throughout the war, especially during 1918, when these identifying numbers were

[27] Taffrail, *Endless Story, op. cit.,* p 380.

changed almost monthly. Minelaying destroyers might have changed their pendants more frequently than most, but this is not thought likely. Some of the changes affected by the ships of the 20th Flotilla are listed in Table 4, although this is not the entire range of numbers carried.

Table 4
Pendant number changes in the 20th Flotilla during 1918

Ship	1-1-18	1-4-18	14-6-18	13-9-18	By 1919
Abdiel	F49	F49	F49	F49	F60
Gabriel	F00	F00	F00	F91	F67
Vanoc	F27	F27	F27	F84	F61
Vanquisher	F08	F08	F08	F85	F62
Venturous	F21	F21	H96	F87	F63
Vehement	F12	F12	F12	–	–
Telemachus	F23	F23	H98	F81	F66
Tarpon	F22	F22	H97	F79	F65
Meteor	H78	H78	H78	D84	G45
Legion	H54	H54	H54	H54	G95
Sandfly	H99	H99	H99	F95	H63
Ariel	H07	H07	H07	–	–
Ferret	H32	H32	H32	F93	H93

However, one cannot help but gain the impression that the only people likely to be inconvenienced by such measures as changing pendant numbers and the painted screens were one's own countrymen rather than the enemy. Perhaps one of the biggest assets enjoyed by the flotilla was the fact that they sailed right into the enemy's lap, the last place the German patrols expected to find British destroyers! Still, there can be no denying the fact that their activities were causing the Germans no little loss and a great deal of inconvenience. On several occasions the Germans attempted to bring the flotilla to book.

Among the many German forces of war likely to be encountered by the British destroyers, the flotilla could number light cruisers, destroyers, patrol boats, submarines and the great Zeppelin airships, which constantly hovered over the area and tried to direct surface forces to intercept them. Chance meetings with most of this list took place as spring nights gave way to the lighter ones of summer and the flotilla continued to flirt with death.

To carry out Operation A48, Captain Curtis sailed with the *Abdiel, Legion, Telemachus, Venturous, Tarpon* and *Ferret* at noon on 18 May. Leaving the Humber, this force set course to a position some seven miles south, true, from the Terschelling Light, which they reached at 20.05. From there they headed to their laying position of 53°51'15"N, 4°31'45"E, which they reached at 00.03 the following morning.

It was a routine operation, with 278 Type HII mines on MkVIII sinkers laid in twelve lines (the ships turning to port), and they were all fitted with 38-day sinking plugs. They sighted two steam and one sailing trawler earlier on and sank two drifting mines on the return, but apart from these small events, the night was without incident.

A similar mission was carried out by the *Abdiel, Legion, Vanoc, Venturous, Tarpon* and *Ferret* on the night of 25/26 May. The flotilla took their departure from the Bovbierg Light at 22.45 and laid 284 mines in twelve lines without sinking plugs attached and set for six and ten foot depths. The night was clear, with a large area visible under the bright moonlight, but no neutral or enemy ships were sighted except the usual Dutch fishing craft. However, on their way back to Immingham, at 09.15 on 26 May, the *Abdiel* sighted a U-boat on the surface at a range of about five miles SSW. In the words of Captain Curtis:

> We altered course towards her and increased speed, whereon she dived at once. She showed her periscope again about three quarters of a mile to the northward of the Flotilla, having dived under us; we turned at once and when near the spot where she was last seen, dropped six depth charges and two more in the other likely looking spots. I continued the search until 10.30 but finding nothing in the form of a wake or oil track, gave it up and continued on our course to the Humber.[28]

[28] Report of SO 20th Flotilla, dated 26 May 1918. W.1361/7 refers.

It must be remembered that although fitted for minelaying, the flotilla still carried depth charges, but that detection of submarines underwater was largely a matter of guesswork. Had these ships been fitted with Second World War ASDIC detection echo-sounding gear,[29] that submarine might not have survived.

The next minefield to be put down, A51, involved a combined operation with ships from both the Grand Fleet and the Harwich Force. Clearly, the Admiralty had got wind of something big being planned across the North Sea. As Taffrail put it:

> Sometimes, after one or other of our operations, we received a congratulatory telegram from the Admiralty on our return to harbour. This acted like a tonic upon officers and men, and it was pleasant to know that our efforts were appreciated. Nevertheless, we never quite knew why we were patted on the back for some excursions, and not for others.[30]

Practically the whole of the flotilla was employed in this operation, *Abdiel, Legion, Tarpon, Ferret, Vanoc, Venturous, Vanquisher* and *Vehement*, and they all sailed from Immingham at 13.00 on 31 May. They proceeded via the South Dogger Bank Light Vessel to their laying position of 55°17'0"N, 6°0'30"E, which they reached at 01.15 on 1 June. From here, they laid 376 mines in sixteen lines, the destroyers dog-legging to port. No sinking plugs were used and the weather remained clear and fine with a moderate sea.

On conclusion of this part of the operation, the flotilla proceeded to a position off 'Piccadilly Circus', ten miles south of the Light Vessel. Here, they met the 1st Light Cruiser Squadron and four other destroyers. They cruised in company with these ships and later the Harwich Force also joined up with them. However, whatever enemy movement this deployment had been made to anticipate, never materialised. The *Legion* and *Ferret* were detached at 06.00 and the whole flotilla

[29] SONAR in American parlance.
[30] Taffrail, *Endless Story, op. cit.,* p 383.

parted company from the 1st Light Cruiser Squadron at 15.00, still off the South Dogger Bank Light Vessel having sighted nothing more menacing than the usual ships of the Dutch sailing fishing fleet.

The same force, less *Venturous*, was again at sea on the night of 4/5 June, having left the Humber at 13.00 for roughly the same area again. That the enemy were apparently astir also this night was apparent when, at 23.00 on 4 June, the night being clear and the sea slight, the flotilla sighted a Zeppelin, very high up, which appeared out of a heavy bank of clouds to the west. The radio operators reported that she made no W/T reports and Captain Curtis considered that it was too dark for her to have seen the wakes of the British ships. Had she done so, the night might have ended differently as German destroyers were also out in force.

About three-quarters of an hour after this sighting, when the flotilla was in position 54°32'N, 4°39'E, and still steering south-east and at a speed of 20 knots, *Abdiel* spotted four enemy destroyers. They were in line ahead to the south-east, with a further pair to the north of them. Captain Curtis, again with his deck load of mines, did not think it the right moment to offer battle.

> I altered course 16 points at once. They made no sign of having seen us and as we had a very bad background, I do not think they sighted us. After steaming N53 W for five miles I altered course again for the minefield and came across their wake, which bore away S 80° E, I could also see smoke in that direction and an occasional gleam of light. I calculated their position at 23.50 to have been 54°30'N, 4°48'E, course S 80° E, and speed about fifteen knots. I did not follow them after laying the mines as they had too great a start and their course led over some of our own minefields. Had I finished laying mines when I met them first I think I could have inflicted a good deal of damage on them considering the superior numerical force I had with me.[31]

[31] CO 20th Flotilla Report, dated 5 June 1918. 754/W.1361.10 refers.

Perhaps the hardest part of a minelaying destroyer skipper's job was the passing up of such golden opportunities as this, which they would normally have welcomed with open arms. However, their orders were very precise. The flotilla laid 330 mines that night and, on return to the Humber, vented some of their pent-up frustration by carrying out a 4-inch full-calibre shoot at a towed target in the War Channel. However, it was no substitute for the chance of a real crack at the Germans. Hopes of a surface encounter, high in the earlier operation but not realised, and almost forced upon them on this occasion, but avoided, again receded into the background.

The relentless routine continued nonetheless as the summer drew on. On the night of 21/22 June, the *Abdiel, Legion, Ariel, Sandfly* (happily back in service once more), *Ferret, Telemachus, Vanoc, Venturous* and *Vehement* prepared to sail to lay minefield A57. Unfortunately, while departing Immingham dock, the latter destroyer fouled her propeller with a wire and had to be left behind. The remainder sped off at 14.00. *En route*, they passed the British submarine *E-29* at 22.37 and exchanged signals with her. She warned them that she had sighted enemy submarines several times earlier that day. In the event, however, no U-boat showed itself to the flotilla that night and they laid 364 mines from position 54°27'N, 4°33'30"E.

On completion of this operation *Abdiel* was due for a boiler clean, having been almost permanently at sea since February. However, before this was done, and before Captain Curtis could enjoy a brief respite from the tensions of their operations, minefield A58 was to be laid. The whole flotilla took part in this operation, less the *Tarpon*, which was refitting. With nine destroyers in company, *Abdiel* laid a record 456 mines. They located the Terschelling Light Vessel at 23.10 and commenced laying at 01.00 on 27 June. Their lay and return was once more without incident. This fairly large field was put down with the mines fitted with 38-day sinking plugs. The track and position of the field was as indicated on Map 1.

With *Abdiel* finally withdrawn for refit, Captain Francis Clutterbuck of the *Legion* became the senior officer of the flotilla. It was Clutterbuck, therefore, who led the next

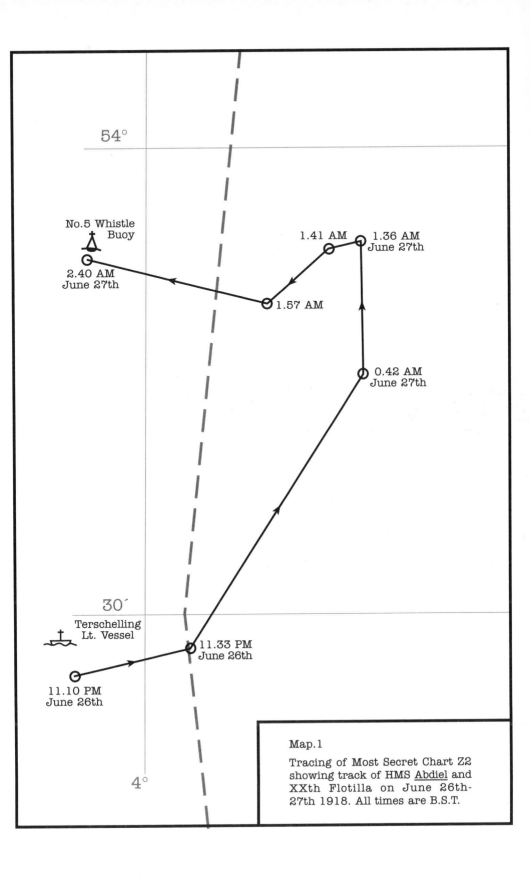

No.5 Whistle
Buoy

2.40 AM
June 27th

1.41 AM   1.36 AM
            June 27th

1.57 AM

0.42 AM
June 27th

54°

30'

Terschelling
Lt. Vessel

11.33 PM
June 26th

11.10 PM
June 26th

4°

Map.1

Tracing of Most Secret Chart Z2
showing track of HMS Abdiel and
XXth Flotilla on June 26th-
27th 1918. All times are B.S.T.

missions into the Heligoland Bight. The first of these operations took place on the night of 29/30 June. *Legion, Telemachus, Vanoc, Sandfly, Ariel* and *Ferret* passed the Spurn lighthouse at 14.00 on 29 June. They proceeded via E. Buoy to a position some seven miles south true of the Terschelling Light Vessel and thence to a point 53°39'45"N, 4°16'15"E, where they commenced minelaying at 00.43 on 30 June. Other ships were also astir, the *Vanoc* exchanging challenges with a British force bearing north-east at fifteen miles range at 21.45. Challenges were also exchanged with the submarine *H26*, south of the lightship, but no hostile vessels or airships were sighted on this night.

A similar pattern followed for minefield A60, which was laid on the night of 2/3 July. *Legion, Telemachus, Vanoc, Venturous, Sandfly, Ariel* and *Ferret* were the destroyers employed, although the *Sandfly* had to abort the mission after two-and-a-half hours steaming due to engine defects. The third operation led by Clutterbuck took place on the night of 5/6 July, when minefield A61 was laid by *Legion* with *Telemachus, Ariel, Ferret, Vanoc, Vehement, Venturous* and *Vanquisher*. The only problem encountered was that the line of destroyers became slightly strung out during the lay, which resulted in the northern end of the minefield being elongated.

Although the *Abdiel* remained in dockyard hands, Captain Curtis returned from leave and led the flotilla for a while from *Venturous*. The ship led the *Legion, Ariel, Sandfly, Ferret, Vanoc, Vanquisher, Vehement* and *Telemachus* on a run into relatively fresh waters on the night of 8/9 July, to lay minefield A62. The flotilla passed some four miles to the north of the North Dogger Bank Light Vessel and commenced their lay in position 52°2'10"N, 5°55'0"E at 00.30. They put down 384 mines in eighteen lines. The night was a fine one and, save for the lights of a solitary Dutch sailing craft five miles away, nothing was sighted. The track and position of this lay are shown on Map 2.

Much the same procedure was followed by *Venturous, Vanoc, Vehement, Vanquisher* and *Telemachus* (the 'fast' division) on the night of 13/14 July when 224 mines were laid to form minefield A63, and again when the whole flotilla, less *Abdiel*, laid A64 consisting of 424 mines on the night of 17/18 July. For the

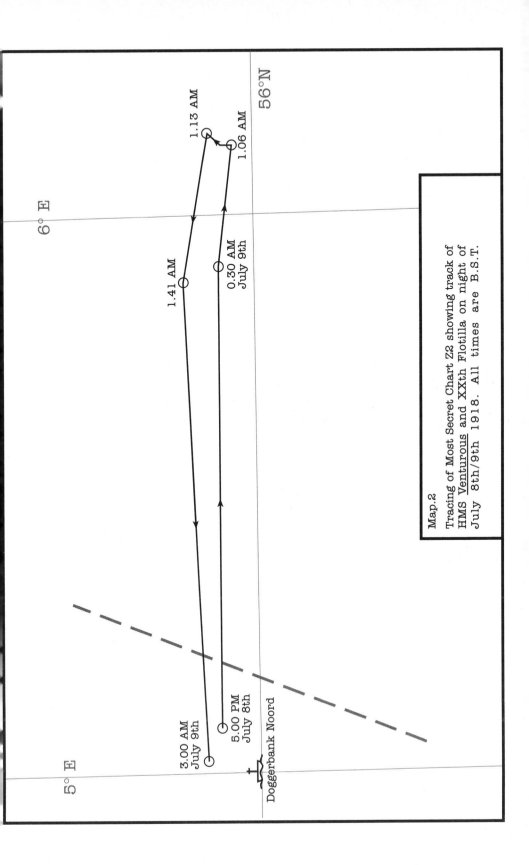

Map.2

Tracing of Most Secret Chart Z2 showing track of
HMS <u>Venturous</u> and XXth Flotilla on night of
July 8th/9th 1918. All times are B.S.T.

5° E

56° N

6° E

1.13 AM

1.06 AM

1.41 AM

0.30 AM
July 9th

3.00 AM
July 9th

5.00 PM
July 8th

Doggerbank Noord

latter operation, the 7th Light Cruiser Squadron was in support, but nothing untoward took place.

Toward the end of July, the *Abdiel* finally rejoined the flotilla and Captain Curtis was able to move back aboard his leader ship once more. The routine was now well established and it seemed as if nothing would disturb it. Far from the end of their sorties seeming to be in sight, it appeared that they were fated to carry on undisturbed by the enemy until the war's end. However, this was *not* to prove the case.

7

DISASTER!

Initially, all seemed to be well, and laying continued as before. However, it is now known that the Germans, incensed by the growing toll taken of their minesweepers and destroyers in what should have been 'safe' waters, were making determined efforts to bring the 20th Flotilla to book. Where intensified patrols with cruiser support had failed, new minefields, cunningly placed, might succeed. The flotilla had already had several hints from their previous sorties that something like this was afoot, but they were ordered to continue work. So they did, night after night. But, eventually, the Admiralty ordered them into dire danger once too often.

The next minefield to be planned, A65, was another large one. The full strength of the flotilla was therefore deployed. A total of 496 mines were laid, all without sinking plugs, from a position 55°58'N, 7°27'15"E, in twenty-two lines. The operation followed Plan VI, with all ships turning to starboard. It was a clear night and an accurate departure was taken from the Lynvig Light. But on their way out to the laying area, at 16.30 on 24 July, the *Vehement* sighted two periscopes of a U-boat, which was hull-up at a range of 1000 yards. At once, the nearest destroyers swung out of line to attack, but the submarine crash-dived, and, although five depth charges were dropped during a quick hunt, there was not time for a prolonged attack. However, there is little doubt that a further entry was made on the dossier detailing the movements of the flotilla back in Wilhelmshaven as a result of this sighting.

The whole flotilla was out once more on the night of 28/29 July (less *Legion* and *Telemachus*), for the laying of minefield A66. The ships left the Humber at 13.00 and took the usual course via the South Dogger Bank Light Vessel and the Dutch

Free Channel along the edge of 'Piccadilly Circus' to a position 54°26'35"N, 5°11'50"E. From here they deposited 416 mines in eighteen lines, all fitted with 38-day sinking plugs. There was a strong northerly wind blowing, but although this whipped up a moderate swell, the night was fine and there were no untoward incidents.

Further orders awaited them on their return to base, via Admiralty Message No. 888, dated 31 July. These orders were to conduct yet another of these by now routine lays, and the flotilla was soon busily employed embarking a new cargo of mines through the whole of 1 August. Nine ships were to be used to lay minefield A67 and, at 08.45, the *Abdiel* again put to sea with *Telemachus, Tarpon, Sandfly, Ferret, Vanoc, Vanquisher, Vehement* and *Ariel*. They passed through positions 55°38'N, 3°15'E at 18.13, 55°56'N, 5°0'E at 2205 and 35°N, 5°17'E at 22.30, to reach their deployment area of 55°34'30"N, 5°17'E at 23.35. From this position, the flotilla deployed in single line ahead in the order *Abdiel, Telemachus, Vanoc, Vehement, Vanquisher, Tarpon, Sandfly, Ferret* and *Ariel*.

All was proceeding entirely to plan when, at 23.47, disaster struck. Taffrail recorded his impressions of what occurred:

> We were steaming in single line at high speed, preparing to lay our mines within half an hour, when, at 11.45 p.m. [*sic*] there came the thudding crash of a heavy explosion from somewhere down the line. We, in the *Telemachus*, were following the *Abdiel*, and, looking aft, we saw a brilliant gout of ruby and orange flame mingled with smoke and water standing out of the sea to a height of quite 200 feet. It was an unnerving sight. No British mines were in the vicinity. We were on top of a German minefield. [32]

It was in position 55°33'N, 5°24'E that the *Vehement*, the fourth ship in the line, struck a mine right forward. The result was

---

[32] Taffrail, *Endless Story, op. cit.,* p 385. As well as being wrong on the exact time, the author also stated that *Vehement* was the fifth ship in line. In fact, she was the fourth, as the Official Report makes clear.

devastating, as eyewitnesses later recalled. The captain of the *Vehement*, Lieutenant-Commander Vernon Hammersley-Heenan, had a miraculous escape from death when the entire forefront of his ship up to the bridge blew up. He was thrown from the bridge into the sea by the force of this explosion, landing some 400 yards astern of the wreck, completely knocked out. Fortunately, he quickly came to on hitting the water and blew up his inflatable waistcoat. In the darkness, he found another survivor who was drowning; he succeeded in reaching this man and keeping him afloat and alive until they were both picked up some time later by the *Vanquisher*. For this very gallant act, he subsequently was awarded the life-saving medal of the Royal Humane Society.

The senior surviving officer aboard the stricken destroyer was Sub-Lieutenant David R Wilson, and he at once assumed command. He later recorded the subsequent events thus:

> I was on the upper deck abreast the after superstructure at the moment of striking and heard two distinct explosions followed by the roar of escaping steam. The shock was not great and I perceived that the ship remained on an even keel. Fire was observed before the foremost funnel and it was not until some considerable time had elapsed that the extent of damage done was ascertained. All that part of the ship forward of No. 1 Stokehold had been blown away but although the fire prevented close examination, the remaining bulkheads appeared to be holding.[33]

The loss of life was fearsome, for the ship's company were naturally at action stations at the time, which meant they were pretty evenly divided between the fore and aft parts of the ship. With the whole forward part of the vessel before the fore-funnel devastated, there were few survivors from that section.

The Gunner (T), William Sutherland, recalled how:

> Immediately after the explosion I was working on the mines altering the plummet settings, in accordance with

---

[33] Report dated 2 August, ADM1/8534/226 refers.

the orders of the Captain. I immediately walked forward and saw Lieutenant Wilson. He passed the remark, 'What has happened?' I said, 'Apparently we have been mined.' I walked to the fore part of the ship, saw that the ship was gone as far as the foremost funnel, by a torch I had in my pocket. I came aft again and ordered the mines to be unprimed and the depth charges to be unprimed.

I looked down below to see if the lights were burning and saw that they were correct. I afterwards ascertained that Leading Seaman Pawley and the Chief ERA had restored the lighting. I got in consultation with Mr Wilson, the Commanding Officer, and the Engineering Officer, as to whether the mines should be thrown overboard. The Commanding Officer decided that it would be best to keep them on board to keep the stern of the ship down. I then removed the wounded men in a Whaler alongside and the ship was taken in tow by H.M.S. *Abdiel*.[34]

The Chief Artificer Engineer himself, Harry Huxley, described his own experiences as follows:

I was at the Engine Room hatchway, on the upper deck, when the explosion occurred and I had a first-hand impression of what happened. I immediately went below to the engine room, saw that the steam was low, due to an explosion of one of the boilers, and immediately gave orders for the bulkhead valves isolating No. 3 boiler to be shut off. This was done immediately. I then gave orders for the oil fuel emergency valve to be shut and the safety valve of Nos. 1 and 2 boilers to be lifted. The 'peace' tanks contained about five tons of oil and I gave orders for this to be run off to the sea by the drain valve fitted for that purpose, and the tanks washed out with seawater. The hands from No. 1 boiler room got on

[34] Statement contained in Court Martial Inquiry, 2 September 1918, ADM1/8534, refers.

deck safely. I attributed this to the excessive air pressure, which was, then in No. 1 boiler room.

I went forward and saw that the ship had the forepart blown away. During this time, the engines were still steaming ahead. I returned to the engine room and gave orders to stop the engines and go slowly astern to take the way off the ship. I next gave orders for the after steering and telegraph positions to be prepared. On this being completed, I reported to the Commanding Officer that the ship was ready to steam astern with one boiler.

A fire broke out immediately before and in No.1 boiler room. I made several attempts to enter No. 1 boiler room but could not do so owing to the fire.

Meanwhile, Sub-Lieutenant Wilson had got hoses rigged along the upper deck to the fire, and water was thrown on that part of the upper deck immediately affected and into the foremost stokehold to lower the temperature. Any loose projectiles that were rolling about were thrown overboard, while Gunner (T) Sutherland attended to the unpriming of the mines and depth charges, as related, and also removed the pistols from the torpedoes. The Carley floats were cleared away, both the ship's boats being wrecked and unseaworthy, and a gun's crew was told off to keep a lookout at No. 3 gun.

Meanwhile, Captain Curtis assumed, quite correctly, that they had run onto a hostile minefield. He decided to abort the operation and remove his remaining ships from this death trap as quickly as possible, returning by the route that they had entered it. *Abdiel* herself, the only ship fitted for carrying para-vanes, had none available on this operation. He therefore ordered the flotilla to stop and then proceeded to close the *Vehement* in order to try and get her away from the mines and save her if possible.

Aboard *Telemachus*, the wreck quickly came into view.

She was still afloat, her bows deep in the water and her stern well in the air. But the bows, from abaft the bridge to the stem, had almost completely disappeared. All that remained was a tangle of twisted steel plating, in which the oil fuel and cordite blazed in a sickly yellow glare, and clouds of black smoke went drifting slowly to leeward. It was a clear night. That flaming beacon must have been visible for many miles.

While *Abdiel* prepared to take the wreck in tow, the nearest destroyers lowered their boats to search for survivors and take off the wounded men. Sub-Lieutenant Wilson recorded:

Abdiel then closed and passed her heaving line across. Hawsers were hauled in and wires made fast. Casualties were lowered into *Vanquisher's* whaler, which cast off. *Abdiel* then went ahead and by using our starboard engine, it was found possible to keep fairly well astern of her. A second fire, due to shell explosions, caused some trouble but was gradually got under control by Chief Artificer Engineer Huxley and his staff. Preparations were completed for abandoning ship and confidential books brought up and sunk. By this time, *Abdiel* had us well in hand and was making about seven knots. There seemed no danger whatever of going down as bulkheads were holding well.

As Lieutenant-Commander Hammersley-Heenan was later to report:

All confidential books and documents were thrown overboard, those ordered to be kept in the steel chest were there with the exception of the General Signal book but as it is weighted should have sunk. The vocabulary in force and wireless books in force were in the W/T office and should be in the chest supplied for that purpose and locked according to my standing orders. It was impossible to ascertain anything about them, as all W/T ratings were lost. All Grand Fleet Secret Orders were in the steel chest. The remaining confidential books were placed in a weighted bag and thrown overboard. Secret Charts were locked in weighted cylinders supplied for the purpose. All books were thrown overboard in about 20 fathoms of water and some miles away from where the ship was finally sunk.

While the tow was being established, without warning yet further tragedy struck the flotilla ten minutes after midnight. The last ship of the line, the *Ariel*, was turning under starboard helm at 18 knots to comply with the withdrawal signal, when she, too, struck a mine forward. Once again, the explosion of the mine detonated the ship's forward magazines. In a grisly repeat of the *Vehement* disaster, the whole of the fore part of the ship was totally blown away from about six feet before the whaler's davits. Again, casualties were heavy, her captain, Lieutenant F A Rothera, being among those instantly killed, as were most of her other senior officers.

Her Gunner (T), Mr E G Hillier, found himself the senior survivor.

> I was thrown in the air by the force of the explosion and on recovery found myself the only executive officer left. I at once took the necessary steps to close all hatches on the upper deck and the motor boat [was] turned out, the whaler having previously turned out [*sic*]to the force of the explosion. The Surgeon Probationer attended to the wounded, and in the meantime I instituted a thorough search of the ship to ascertain if there were any more wounded, but found none.[35]

The Chief ERA Alfred James Bullen was on deck forward of the engine room on the starboard side when *Ariel* was struck. He described the aftermath:

> There was a cloud of steam and when I got clear (I was pinned down on deck) I went forward to No. 2 Boiler Room and found Stoker Petty Officer Mott lying across the hatchway badly injured. I succeeded in removing him to the deck and assisted the Doctor to give him an

[35] Report dated 3 August 1918, ADM1, 8534, refers.

injection of morphia. I then attempted to enter No. 2
Boiler room again, but found after descending about
three rungs of the ladder that the gratings were blown
away. I then entered the engine room and found no
steam whatever. The Doctor asked me for my torch on
my return to deck. I proceeded aft to get another one
from the Captain's cabin. I did not find one there but got
one from the First Lieutenant's cabin. On arriving on
deck, I met the TI who told me the Gunner had abandoned ship, and he was just leaving. The TI jumped
overboard. I then looked along the deck with my torch
and sung out, but could not see anyone.

In fact, the little *Ariel* was sinking fast; within twenty minutes
of the initial detonation, it was clear that she could not last
much longer. In the words of Gunner (T) Hillier:

At about 00.30, finding the ship was settling down fast,
I reluctantly gave the order 'Abandon Ship', observing
that, in my opinion, there was no possible chance of
saving her. The ship was abandoned in a thoroughly
orderly manner in the motorboat, whaler, dinghy and
Carley float. Before leaving the ship, I carefully
searched everywhere and finding no one else on board
I then dived and swam to the whaler, eventually being
picked up by HMS *Vanoc*. The ship sank altogether
about 01.00.

Alfred Bullen also dived off and swam to the Carley float about
thirty yards distant.

I then heard someone singing out to be saved and picked
up Stoker Petty Officer Mitchell, who was badly
wounded. I then heard someone else singing out and
picked up two more survivors, one of whose name was
Durrant. I tried to proceed to pick up others but was not
able to as there were two oars one side of the Float and
one the other because of the wounded; she kept sliding
round. Whilst the *Vanoc*'s dinghy was preparing to take

us in tow, HMS *Ariel* sank with a loud explosion. I was taken with the remainder on the float to HMS *Tarpon*, being the last to leave the float.

There were many heroes in the darkness of that awful night, among them Leading Seaman Arthur Rushbridge who gave up his lifebelt to Robert Mitchell who was seriously wounded. When the *Ariel* slipped beneath the waves at 01.00, she took with her the four senior offices and forty-five of her ship's company. She was the flotilla's first loss.

All attempts were now concentrated on getting the remains of the *Vehement* clear of the minefield and then home safely. At first, all seemed to be going well. The stoutly constructed little ship had stood up well and her bulkheads were apparently holding firm. Taffrail recalled:

> The grey dawn was breaking in the east when the remains of the *Vehement*, still blazing furiously, and with an occasional shell or cartridge exploding in the heat of the fire, were finally in tow. Even so, the position was still one of horrible uncertainty, for we could not know which way to steer. The minefield might be laid in any direction. North, south, east or west – all might be equally dangerous. We steered north, trusting to Providence. And Providence was kind. It was not until afterwards that I discovered the German minefield stretched twenty miles north and south.

However, all their efforts proved to be in vain. Sub-Lieutenant Wilson described his ship's last moments:

> At about 3.30 am, the ship suddenly began to settle by the head. I signalled this back to *Abdiel*, passed the word for hands to muster at abandon ship stations and slipped the towing hawser. The upper deck abreast the foremost funnel was awash but on conferring with Chief Artificer Engineer Huxley I learnt that we were sinking no further and still capable of being towed slower.

Bill Sutherland remembered that:

> We steamed astern 100 revolutions with the starboard
> engine, and the helm was kept hard a starboard. The
> ship appeared to tow very badly, well up on the port
> quarter of *Abdiel*. We were towing thus for some
> considerable time until daylight was breaking. I was
> then on the after part of the ship when she suddenly
> lurched forward as if she was going down. The
> Commanding Officer gave orders to slip the tow and
> this was done. We were closed by *Telemachus*. The fore
> part of the ship was settling in line with the water.
> Captain of *Telemachus* stated that he did not consider
> towing was further feasible. I thought his statement
> correct as the ship was then at a considerable angle
> with the surface of the water. Permission was asked to
> scuttle her and this was granted. The Engineering
> Officer undertook with his ratings to open the weed
> traps. The Commanding Officer stated some scuttles
> should be opened. I proceeded to the flat with the
> Commanding Officer and opened the scuttles. When
> we came on deck, there was a Whaler alongside with
> several ratings in it and I went into this whaler accom-
> panied by the Commanding Officer. After the explosion
> occurred first, a considerable fire started in the fore part
> of the ship. This was got under – or partly under – after
> some time. Another slight explosion occurred in the
> fore part of the ship; I believe due to a lyddite shell
> exploding as several of these were found on the upper
> deck as if thrown from the shell room or forecastle
> by the explosion. The second fire burned very fiercely
> and the upper deck became very hot over the foremost
> boiler room, so that life buoys and matting had to be
> collected to stand on the deck. The fire, although stren-
> uous endeavours were made to extinguish it, was not
> altogether extinguished until the ship dipped in the
> fore part at about 3.30 am. I consider the extra lurch of
> the ship was due to the foremost boiler room becoming
> full of water.

Chief Artificer Engineer Huxley later stated:

> I stood right forward when the ship went down by the
> head and saw the water seething round the fore part.
> The orders then came to abandon ship. I asked per-
> mission from the Commanding Officer to scuttle her. I
> gave orders to Chief ERA Pollard to proceed to the
> Engine Room and remove the weed trap covers. I went
> into No. 2 boiler room and gave orders to the Stoker
> Petty Officer to abandon ship, to stop his oil fuel pump,
> and ordered him up, and his men, on deck. I followed
> him up and went to the engine room and saw Chief ERA
> Pollard and Leading Stoker Talbot removing the weed
> traps. I then ordered them on deck telling them to take
> the engine room register with them. When I got on deck
> there was a whaler coming alongside from the
> *Telemachus* which Leading Stoker Talbot and I went on
> board.

Sub-Lieutenant Wilson wrote:

> *Telemachus* then put her bows alongside in readiness to
> take off any of our men who were on board, and
> Commander Taprell Dorling expressed his opinion that
> he did not think the condition of the ship rendered
> towing feasible. He accordingly signalled to *Abdiel* and
> asked permission to scuttle us. Permission was granted. I
> gave the order to abandon ship. The remaining hands
> quietly took their places in the whalers and Carley floats
> alongside and stood by. Two stokers went below and
> opened up the valves and Gunner (T) Sutherland
> and myself went aft and opened scuttles in the cabin flat.
> We then got into the boats and shoved off leaving the
> ship about 3.50 am. The question of shoring up the bulk-
> heads forward was thoroughly gone into but owing to
> the fierceness of the fire was found impracticable.

With *Vanoc* and *Tarpon* closing astern after rescuing the crew of
the *Ariel*, it was left to the *Vanquisher* and *Telemachus* to finish

off the gallant *Vehement*. This was done with gunfire and two depth charges set to explode shallow close to the wreck. The destroyer finally vanished below the surface at 04.11. With her went Lieutenant George Hatch, her first lieutenant and forty-seven men.

The flotilla then continued to follow its inward route to safety and arrived back at the Humber on 3 August. Captain Curtis later reported that:

> I deeply regret that this unforeseen accident should have occurred and I am convinced that everything possible was done to save life. I am certain of my position as the weather was clear with no cloud and the sea flat calm and I had obtained a good departure position from the North Dogger Bank Light Vessel, the presence of enemy mines being totally unsuspected. I saw one mine on the surface and it appeared to be black and pear shaped. From rough observations the line of mines appeared to run in direction ENE. *Telemachus* suspects having rubbed another mine which did not go off.

This close to death did Taffrail come that night. But, as he was later to write:

> We turned our bows to the westward and steamed away. We had left our base nine strong and returned seven. In the brief space of twenty-two minutes over one hundred of our flotilla-mates had gone to their death. But we carried on, because we had to. Less than a week afterwards we were laying mines within seven miles of Zeebrugge.

Tragic as these losses were, the work of the 20th Flotilla continued unabated. Perhaps, in view of the dangerous nature of their work, it is more remarkable that these were the only losses they suffered in the last year of the First World War. Their success had obviously prompted retaliation by the enemy, but it had come late. As Captain Cowie was to record:

It was not until the middle of 1918 that the enemy appears to have endeavoured to lay mines himself as a trap for the British minelayers.

This blow was a setback, but it failed to halt the 20th Flotilla.

8

SOWING THE
DRAGON'S TEETH

The rapid development of all types of British sea mines and their associated equipment reached fruition in 1917–8. Among the many 'firsts' chalked up by our scientists and naval research teams was a magnetic firing system for incorporation with ground mines. Standard moored mines were also fitted with an acoustic device, another first for the Royal Navy. In response to the desperate situation with regard the U-boat war, it was planned to replace the ineffective cross-channel Mine Barrage between the Goodwin Sands and Dunkirk with a combination field of both these new types. The moored magnetic mines were laid in shallow waters and the moored acoustic mines in deeper regions. The strong tides of the Channel had been responsible for scores of conventional moored mines breaking adrift, especially close-in. However, the new magnetic mine, being a ground mine, would be immune to this type of attrition and remain a viable barrage at all times.

These magnetic mines were known as M-sinkers. It resembled a large concrete pyramid and the magnet, working on the dip needle principle, was housed in the apex of it. These mines lay on the bottom of the sea and could clearly be seen as they could only be used in the shallowest of waters, but that did not matter when deployed against submarines. Conventional minesweepers could not sweep these weapons. Special wooden-hulled minesweepers had to be used to detonate them by towing magnetic sweeps astern,which the Germans did not possess at the time, as they were a totally new concept. The heavy charge of amatol explosive was protected for forty minutes after laying by safety-plugs of sal ammoniac. They

1. *Abdiel*: an early photograph taken on 24 March 1916, as first completed. Note low funnels and after guns not shipped and also special minelaying sponsons and fittings at her stern. The usual canvas screen is in position to hide the details of her special equipment and note the absence of any camouflage or pendant numbers on her light grey hull. *(Ministry of Defence, Navy).*

2. *Legion*: one of the first destroyers to be converted to the minelaying role, and one of the founder members of the 20th Flotilla, is seen here sporting her two-tone colour scheme leaving the Humber. The painted canvas screens aft have been embellished with reproductions of the silhouettes of her after 4-inch gun, torpedo tubes and superstructure. Although obvious close up, at any sort of range and in the half-light of a North Sea winter, such a deception was quite effective.

(Imperial War Museum, London).

3. *Abdiel*: here seen alongside a minelaying cruiser in a Scottish port with a full load of mines on their rails ready for an operation in the North Sea early in 1918. The view along her mine rails to the chutes is interesting and illustrates just how the mines ran down to the sponsons astern and out, and how the canvas screens were kept in place. Notice the wood covering over her torpedo mounting place and the cortecine deck walkways. *(Imperial War Museum, London).*

4. *Telemachus*: shown here in August 1917, as first completed in her minelaying role. She has not shipped her full load of mines and still retains one set of torpedo tubes.
(National Maritime Museum, London).

5. *Telemachus*: a detailed model of her as a minelayer, constructed by Mr J. Forrest Thomson of Glasgow. *(J. Forrest Thomson)*.

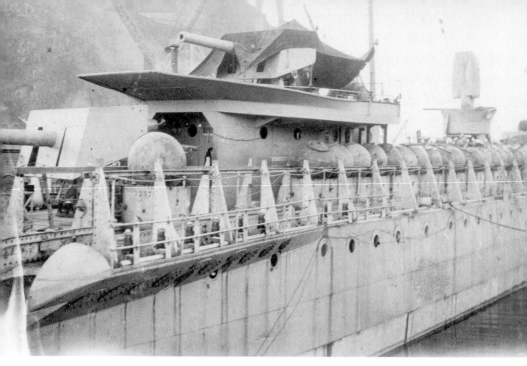

6. *Vehement*: the ill-fated destroyer-minelayer as completed in her minelaying role, showing to good advantage the rails with mines and sinkers in position aboard during her fitting out. The stanchions are in position to rig the canvas screens but both after guns are still mounted at this time. *(National Maritime Museum, London).*

7. *Vanoc*: shown here fitting out at John Brown's yard in 1917, with the after bank of tubes and both stern guns in place, but with mine rails and sponsons fitted and a range of dummy mines aft. *(John Brown, Shipbuilders).*

8. *Vanquisher*: she shows her Pendant Number F64 forward and is much weathered from numerous North Sea sorties. The canvas screens are in place, as is 'x' gun, but the sponsons aft give her away. *(Imperial War Museum, London)*.

9. *Gabriel*: a 1918 photograph showing all the wartime modifications with raised funnels, protection against splinters around the bridge and improved wireless telegraphy equipment. Although her canvas screens are in raised position, she is unladen and resting high in the water at her mooring buoy. *(Ministry of Defence, Navy)*.

11. *Seymour*: another of the large flotilla leaders to be converted to the minelaying mission towards the end of the Great War. Her conversion took place too late for her to participate in actual minelaying operations, while her early post-war scrapping similarly precluded any operations in the Second World War. She is shown here post-war, although she was converted in August 1918.

(National Maritime Museum, London).

12. *Velox*: typical inter-war appearance of the standard 'V' and 'W' class destroyer conversions which were only used in the minelaying role rarely once hostilities had ceased. They were never thus employed during the Second World War although, initially, some were still capable of conversion. Long-range convoy escorts and anti-aircraft 'WAIRS' proved to be more in demand after Dunkirk, however.

(National Maritime Museum, London).

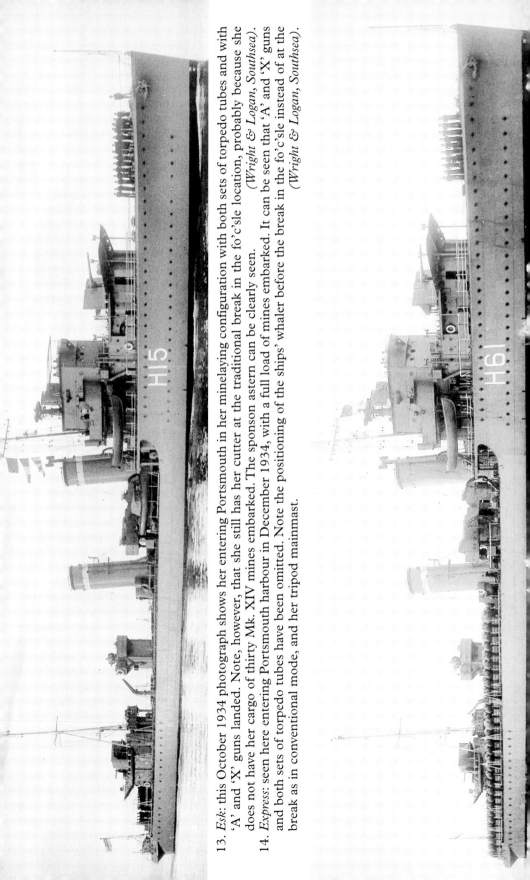

13. *Esk*: this October 1934 photograph shows her entering Portsmouth in her minelaying configuration with both sets of torpedo tubes and with 'A' and 'X' guns landed. Note, however, that she still has her cutter at the traditional break in the fo'c'sle location, probably because she does not have her cargo of thirty Mk. XIV mines embarked. The sponson astern can be clearly seen.   *(Wright & Logan, Southsea).*

14. *Express*: seen here entering Portsmouth harbour in December 1934, with a full load of mines embarked. It can be seen that 'A' and 'X' guns and both sets of torpedo tubes have been omitted. Note the positioning of the ships' whaler before the break in the fo'c'sle instead of at the break as in conventional mode, and her tripod mainmast.   *(Wright & Logan, Southsea).*

15. *Stronghold*: seen leaving Portsmouth on 25 August 1936. One of the small 'S' class that survived mass scrappings in the 1930s. She was converted to minelaying after alarms were raised by the Anglo-Italian war scare during the Abyssinian crisis. In this view she still retains both sets of torpedo tubes but her after 4-inch gun has been put ashore. She was to be one of the most active destroyer minelayers, working in the Far East. *(Wright & Logan, Southsea).*

16. *Scout*: another of the little 'S' class survivors given minelaying potential as witness the sponsons astern. Here seen in her conventional guise at the Spithead Review of the fleet in July 1935. *(Wright & Logan, Southsea).*

17. *Sturdy*: a further example of the 'S' class survivor destroyers given minelaying potential as witness the sponsons astern. Depicted in her conventional guise on the eve of Second World War, in August 1939 she was not to lay any mines, being wrecked off the west coast of Scotland in a gale in the winter of 1940.

(Wright & Logan, Southsea).

17a. The destroyer minelayer HMS *Thanet* in heavy weather. She is in full destroyer mode with after gun shipped and mine rails and equipment landed ashore. She laid minefields in the Far East prior to the Japanese invasion but was later lost in action there.

(Author's collection).

18. An 'I' class destroyer-minelayer returning to Dover with troops of the BEF embarked during the evacuation from Dunkirk, May 1940. In this photograph the tripod mainmast can be clearly made out aft, while, in the foreground, the massive adjustable paravane boom pivoted to the reinforcing angled derrick at the fore end of the bridge can be seen in great detail. Also visible is the davit at the waist, just abaft the multiple 0.5 inch machine-guns mounting. *(Imperial War Museum, London).*

19. 'I' class destroyer-minelayer. A view showing her approaching her berth alongside a 'V' class destroyer (*right*) at Dover harbour in May 1940, during the evacuation from Dunkirk. The massive pivoting tow-wire arm can been seen on her starboard bow just abaft her anchor. This was used to keep the paravane cutting wire down to the bows when streamed. The angled projections on either side of the bridge on which the paravane boom pivoted can also be made out. Note 'A' gun landed because these ships had been switched from active combat minelaying duties to troop evacuation overnight and no time could be spared to re-embark her full destroyer armament.

(Imperial War Museum, London).

20. Disaster in the 'Bight. The crippled *Express* as viewed from the destroyer Kelvin at first light on the morning after her mining. *(Imperial War Museum, London)*.

22. Disaster in the 'Bight. *Express*: the anti-aircraft and torpedo ratings of the Kelvin watch as preparations are made to take the damaged ship in tow.

(Imperial War Museum, London).

23. Disaster in the 'Bight. *Express: MTB-30* closes the damaged destroyer to render assistance. *(Imperial War Museum, London).*

24. Disaster in the 'Bight. Another view of *MTB-30* closing the damaged *Express* while boats from the *Kelvin* close her to take off the wounded and surplus crew.

(Imperial War Museum, London).

26. Disaster in the 'Bight. *Express*: the whaler from the *Kelvin* returning after taking a line to the damaged destroyer. Her anti-aircraft guns are fully manned and on the quarter-deck aft her crew prepare for a stern tow to safety.

(Imperial War Museum, London).

25. Disaster in the 'Bight. Another view of *MTB-30* closing the damaged Express while boats from the *Kelvin* close her to take off the wounded and surplus crew.

(Imperial War Museum, London).

27. Disaster in the 'Bight. Preparing the steel towing hawser aboard the *Kelvin* with the damaged *Express* in the background. *(Imperial War Museum, London)*.

28. Disaster in the 'Bight. Some of the wounded from the *Express* being transferred to the *Kelvin* from *MTB-30*. *(Imperial War Museum, London)*.

29. Disaster in the 'Bight. *MTB-30* with wounded embarked from *Express*, comes alongside the *Kelvin* to transfer them. *(Imperial War Museum, London)*.

30. Disaster in the 'Bight. The walking wounded from *Express* are helped aft by the crew of the *Kelvin*. *(Imperial War Museum, London)*.

were painted yellow and weighed about one ton. The explosive charge was 150 lb, more than enough to sink any U-boat that passed within 150 feet of one of these fearsome weapons.

Although the Royal Navy was ready to implement this plan by late 1917, the production of these new mines had not got sufficiently into its stride for large scales lays to be undertaken until August 1918. They were originally to have been laid by especially adapted CMBs,[36] but, although the boats were ready on time, storage facilities for the mines at the Dunkirk base were delayed. This chore therefore had to be added to the many duties of the 20th Flotilla in August and September. Three such lays were made by the flotilla during this period, all of them off the main U-boat operating base of Zeebrugge.

The first operation involved the flotilla steaming south to Dover to embark the M-sinkers and then crossing the Channel to conduct the lay. Although the destroyers successfully accomplished this, the operation as a whole was considered a failure owing to a defect in the design. Most of the mines deposited at such risk, blew up soon after their safety-plugs had melted through. That August a repeat operation followed, mounted from Dover. This mission proved more satisfactory.

Early in September, the flotilla conducted a final lay off Zeebrugge, embarking the M-sinkers from Dunkirk this time, as stocks had been built up at that base. Taffrail remembered the only untoward incident of this operation:

> I remember one rather amusing incident when five of we minelaying destroyers were lying off Dunkerque ready for an operation the same night, with our mines all ready and primed. It was pitch dark, and because of an expected enemy destroyer raid, we received sudden orders to weigh and shift billet to an anchorage farther up the coast. Dunkerque Roads were rather crowded, and, while steaming ahead, the *Ferret* grazed a French trawler lying at anchor. The *Ferret*'s mine traps happened to be open, and before anybody could stop them, the

---

[36] CMB = Coastal Motor Boat, the First World War precursor to the more well known MTB (Motor Torpedo Boat) of the Second World War.

slight shock sent two mines on their sinkers trundling gaily aft and overboard.

The Frenchman, already sufficiently peevish at being rammed, flung up his hands in horror, and burst into a flood of Gallic profanity when informed in execrable French by the *Ferret*'s captain that there were two mines under his stern which would become dangerous as soon as their soluble plugs melted – otherwise, within about half an hour![37]

While the 20th Flotilla was thus employed, a lone destroyer minelayer, the *Meteor*, was also at work on this hazardous duty. She was busy laying her own cargo of M-sinkers off Ostend. A full load of forty mines was put down during August by this ship, alone and unsupported.

Yet another duty that came the flotilla's way between 8 August and early October, was the laying of a defensive minefield down the east coast of Yorkshire. The stepping up of the offensive mine barrages would, it was hoped, be so effective as to curtail to a large extent, the activities of German submarines. If this proved to be the case, then the Germans might be forced to switch their activities to the hitherto relatively immune east coast, hence the need for this additional barrier. Although fast minelayers were not a requirement for this work, lack of suitable vessels in sufficient numbers, other than the converted merchant ships *Paris* and *Wahine*, led to the 20th Flotilla being given this chore to assist them as a matter of urgency. This mission was undertaken in-between their more normal offensive runs across the North Sea and took place between August and October, by which time the destroyer had laid a total of 9000 defensive mines.

The loss of the *Ariel* and *Vehement* was partly offset during August by the arrival of the newly converted flotilla leader *Gabriel*, equipped with paravanes, as well as a capacity for sixty tons of mines and four depth charges. As additional leaders were considered essential for future plans, the even larger *Seymour* and the 'V' half-leaders, *Valentine* and *Valorous*, were also

[37] Taffrail, *Endless Story, op. cit.*, p 378.

converted into minelayers, but were never, in fact, used in this role. Another similar conversion was the 'R' class destroyer *Skate*, which had been badly damaged aft by a mine, and, like several others in the flotilla, was rebuilt later in the role of the biter rather than the bitten! The *Skate* retained her forecastle and midships 4-inch guns, director, main mast and forward tubes. However, she never actually took part in wartime operations as a minelayer, owing to the lateness of her conversion.

Although somewhat reduced in scope following the tragedy of 2/3 August, the flotilla's lays in the German-swept channels continued as before, when breaks in the other operations (as described above) permitted. Such fields continued to be put down right up to the Armistice. Chronologically, the next such field was A68, the date assigned being the nights of 29/30 August. Plan 2 was to be utilised, and the lay was to be carried out between 56°00'00"N, 5°34'45"E and 56°02'15"N and 5°43'30"E, with the ships turning to port. HII mines on Mk XII sinkers were to be employed. Four-fifths of these were to be laid with delay-release plugs set for seven, fourteen, twenty-one and twenty-eight-day periods, in equal proportions. These mines were to be set for a depth of ten feet below LWOS. The remaining one fifth were to be laid without delay-release plugs and set for a depth of six feet, without sinking plugs. The depth of water was to be taken as 26 fathoms and mooring ropes were to be adjusted accordingly.[38]

Accordingly, Captain Curtis led the 'fast' division of the flotilla, comprising *Abdiel*, *Vanquisher*, *Venturous*, *Tarpon* and *Telemachus*, from Immingham at 08.30 on 31 August, the weather conditions having postponed the lay by one day. There was still a strong WNW wind blowing and the sea was heavy, but as the distance to the field from the North Dogger Bank Light Vessel was only nineteen miles, an accurate lay was made. A total of 244 mines were deposited according to instructions. Nothing hostile was sighted; the only other vessel observed was a Dutch sailing fishing craft near the Light Vessel herself. The destroyers' return to the Humber was, however, considerably delayed as conditions deteriorated during the

[38] Admiralty Telegram 188, dated 27 August 1918, refers.

night. A full westerly gale was soon blowing and the seas became extremely rough, with the little ships 'taking it green'.

Because of their other work, a full month elapsed before the flotilla's next excursion into enemy waters. This enabled *Gabriel* fully to work up and take her place in the fast division team. On 28 September, directions for the laying of A69 included the *Gabriel* for the first time. Plan 6 was modified to allow both *Abdiel* and *Gabriel* to lay forty-eight mines in a base line, with the remainder of their loads being dropped after a port turn. The same ships as in A68 took part, plus the new leader, and the flotilla sailed from the Humber at 11.15 on 27 September. Yet again, the weather proved atrocious, with a heavy sea running right up to the time of laying. Despite this, 316 mines were put down after a good fix had been taken from the South Dogger Bank Light Vessel. Once more, there was no intervention from the Germans.

The succession of early autumn gales that lashed the North Sea throughout this period, proved no more of a deterrent than had the isolated enemy success earlier. The entire flotilla continued with its deadly business. Reading between the lines of Captain Curtis's official reports, it can be seen that this duty was a far from pleasant chore at this stage of the war. On land, great British victories had swept the Germans back towards their own frontiers and the Allies were following up these events with their own offensives, but there was no outward sign that the war was anywhere close to an early termination. Indeed, it was fully expected that the Germans would fight with even greater tenacity in defence of their own soil. Thus, plans were in hand for new offensives in 1919, and the men of the 20th Flotilla had little to look forward to other than the occasional boiler clean as respite from their task.

As an example of how a notorious North Sea 'Blow' could affect the precision and strict timetable of a minelaying operation, one has only to read Captain Curtis's report for the laying of minefield A70 on the night of 30 September. *Abdiel* had led *Gabriel, Vanquisher, Venturous, Tarpon, Sandfly* and *Ferret* to sea at 21.00 and had proceeded via the Terschelling and Haaks lightships to a position 53°2'10"N, 4°24'30"E by 07.15 on 1 October.

Arrival at minefield was delayed by bad weather and on that account I considered it more prudent to start laying from the westward and turn to starboard than to close the shore and start from that end, observing that as it was daylight the flotilla might have been seen by Dutch craft or from the shore and therefore would not have been able to lay any mines at all, whereas approaching from the westward there was a reasonable chance of getting most of the mines down unobserved. The weather was very bad with a biggish sea and heavy rain squalls and I do not think the ships were seen at all.

Having laid the mines I proceeded to the position given for Harwich Force (20 miles 240° from minefield) but not finding them there returned to the Humber via Leman and Haisboro' Lightships and war channel. At 11.35 on 1 October, when in position 53°N, 2°45'E, sighted a submarine on the surface about three miles on starboard bow. I formed in line abreast and altered course towards it, but it dived and left no trace. At 11.50, in position 53°2'N, 2°40'E, sighted three aeroplanes about six miles off port quarter steering to eastward, nationality unknown.[39]

Just how close to the hostile shore this minefield was laid in daylight can be seen from the track chart contained in Map 3. Once again, the Germans had missed a unique opportunity to catch the flotilla close to the Germans' own main bases in a compromised situation. However, they seemed to have little stomach for bad weather conditions, withdrawing to the safety of their harbours at the first sign of any sort of gale. In contrast, the British ships used the elements to their own advantage in the traditional manner of the Royal Navy. Nonetheless, if there were no active patrols in such conditions, some of the enemy picket boats were still at sea, as the next operation was to reveal.

---

[39] Report of SO 20th Flotilla, dated 1 October 1918, W.1361/31 refers.

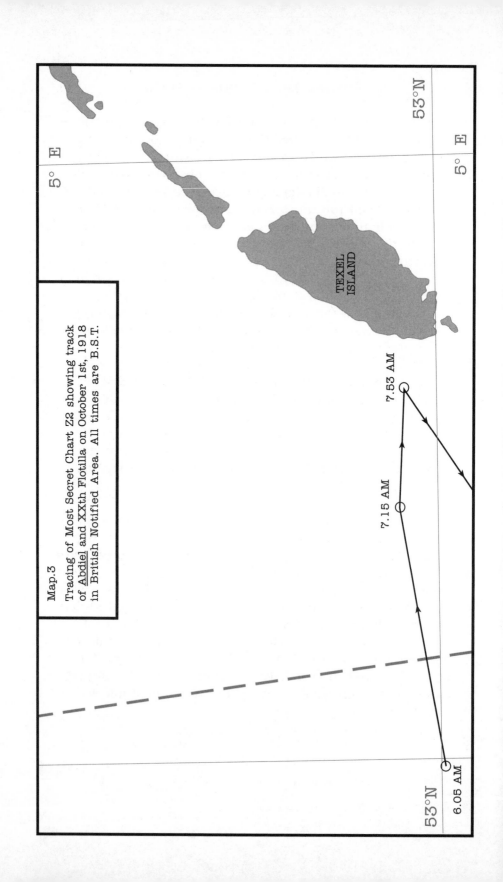

Map.3

Tracing of Most Secret Chart Z2 showing track of _Abdiel_ and XXth Flotilla on October 1st, 1918 in British Notified Area. All times are B.S.T.

TEXEL ISLAND

5° E

53°N

5° E

53°N

6.05 AM

7.15 AM

7.53 AM

Having fought the elements all night and day, the destroyers' stay at Immingham was of the briefest duration. Loading mines and refuelling filled most of the short period in harbour. Then, at 11.00 on 2 October, *Abdiel, Gabriel, Vanquisher, Venturous, Tarpon, Telemachus, Legion, Sandfly* and *Ferret* sailed to carry out operation A71. Again, Captain Curtis provided the most graphic account of what took place.

> The night was extremely dark and great difficulty was experienced by some of the destroyers in seeing when their next astern turned out of line, after laying their first groups, which accounts for the base line being extended two miles too far to the North Eastward.

The actual laying operation commenced at 22.50 and, some ten minutes later, strange lights were seen in the distance.

> Position determined by bearings on distance run assuming the craft was at anchor – the lights showed up again after about ten minutes eclipse, and as they were very bright, there seems very little doubt that they were shown from a mark vessel of some sort. On returning through position 'Z', one light was sighted at 00.05 on 3 October. I did not investigate this light, as the sea was too rough for boarding and I considered it better not to disclose the fact that the flotilla was in the vicinity.[40]

Two further runs were made in similar conditions. *Abdiel, Vanquisher, Venturous, Tarpon, Telemachus, Legion, Sandfly* and *Ferret* deposited minefield A72 on the night of 27/28 October. These ships laid 364 mines in sixteen lines between point 'X' (56°07'00"N, 3°15'E) and point 'Y' (56°06'45"N, 5°56'15"E), with no sinking plugs fitted. The night was reported as being 'intensely dark and foggy in patches'; the lay commended at 00.15 on the 28th and was conducted without incident.

The second run took place on the following night, with the same destroyers. The flotilla set sail at 15.30 and arrived at

[40] Report of SO 20th Flotilla, dated 3 October 1918, W. 1361/32 refers.

position 55°55'N, 5°0'E, at 02.50 on 30 October. On this occasion, nature was kind, the visibility was clear and the seas smooth. Despite this, nothing was seen of the enemy and 364 mines were deposited in sixteen lines from 03.45 onward, all without sinking plugs.

No doubt the pace would have continued, although by now the strain was showing on ships and men alike. But with the news of the impending Armistice, which finally took place on 11 November, all further offensive sorties by the 20th Flotilla ceased.

From small beginnings, with just one ship, the destroyer minelaying force had grown into a formidable weapon. Despite tragedy, accidents and bad weather, it had operated for almost a year on the enemy's back doorstep with remarkable success and, considering the dangers, remarkably few losses. It was, without doubt, the most experienced and able force of its kind in the world and in 1918 the position of the Royal Navy, compared with the lamentable state it had found itself in just four years earlier, was an outstanding improvement.

Home mine manufacture was gearing up into full production, the many specialist types of mines were reaching fruition and the whole production might of the United States was slowly getting into its stride. Had the war continued, 1919 would have seen the mounting of an unprecedented mine assault on German shipping, from which it could well have been rendered totally immobile. This was not to be, but the expertise of the 20th Flotilla in conducting such operations was unique and had been maintained at a high pitch of intensity and professionalism.

As for results, as with all mining operations, these were never precise. However, the First Lord of the Admiralty, Sir Eric Geddes, in a speech quoted in *The Times* on 6 January 1919, claimed that over one hundred enemy vessels – destroyers, minesweepers and outpost craft, plus two submarines – had been sunk by British mines in the Heligoland Bight in just the first six months of 1918. A total of twenty-two U-boats were sunk by mines during the whole course of the war (including victims of their own mines), a considerable

Table 5

Individual totals of mines laid by British destroyer minelayers 1916–18	
Abdiel	6293
Legion	2033
Telemachus	1898
Ferret	1875
Vanquisher	1859
Venturous	1823
Tarpon	1425
Sandfly	1242
Ariel	1237
Meteor	1082
Vanoc	965
Gabriel	850
Vehement	554
Total	**23,136**

proportion of the 178 total destroyed between 1914 and 1918. Of the 128,000 mines laid by the Royal Navy in the same period, approximately 40 per cent were in the dangerous waters of the Heligoland Bight, the Kattegat and off the Belgian coast.

Although the destroyers' individual mine loads were small compared with those of the converted merchant ships used to lay the defensive barrages, their contribution was far from insignificant, as Table 5 reveals. More pertinent is the fact that the majority of their lays were carried out inside the enemy-swept channels. They were therefore the most offensive of all minefields laid and accounted for the enemy's greatest headaches, especially from February 1918 onward. It would be reasonable, therefore, to state that the contribution of the British destroyer minelayers to the overall minelaying campaign was far in excess of their small numbers when calculating their achievements.

Nor was this remarkable contribution carried out at the expense of more vital work elsewhere. By 1918, only about fifteen destroyers were regularly so employed from a total of more than 300 destroyers in commission, an insignificant percentage as things stood at that time. Whereas no fewer than twenty destroyers were sunk by enemy mines during the war, and many times that number damaged in varying degrees, the 20th Flotilla lost only two ships in action, despite being the most exposed surface ships in combat at that time.

All in all then, the achievements of the Royal Navy destroyer minelayers were quite unique and invaluable to the overall war effort of the Royal Navy in the First World War. The question on the conclusion of the conflict was, as ever, would all the effort, expertise, courage and experimentation be utilised to keep the Royal Navy in the forefront of this type of warfare? Or would it all be thrown away, as had happened in other aspects of naval technology in the past, in the heady days of peace?

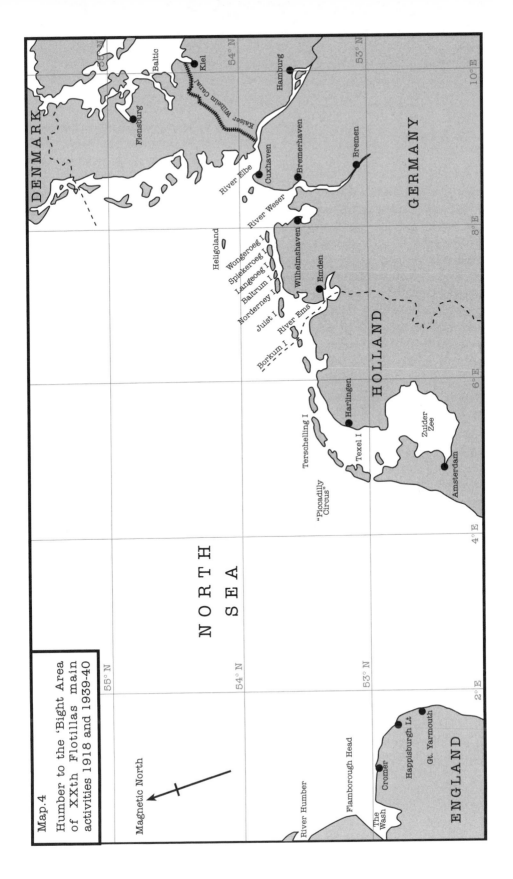

Map.4

Humber to the 'Bight Area. of XXth Flotillas main activities 1918 and 1939-40

Magnetic North

9

THE LOCUST YEARS

In the immediate aftermath of the First World War, the destruction of the Royal Navy that was to take place because of the infamous Washington Treaty could not be foreseen. The Royal Navy was at its peak of power and prestige following the wholesale and abject surrender of the German High Seas Fleet and its subsequent ignoble scuttling at Scapa Flow. Few in Britain suspected that the Royal Navy's overwhelming lead in both numbers, expertise and war experience, coupled with an age-old tradition, would ever be eroded. Yet the end of centuries of British Naval mastery had taken place within five short years of their greatest triumph! The British had not banked on the fickleness and short-sightedness of their own politicians, coupled with the burning ambition of the United States to wrest the Trident away. This combination brought about the transfer of power across the Atlantic within the briefest of periods.

The strong force of thirty or so destroyers either converted, or readily adaptable for high-speed minelaying, was initially kept intact, although Churchill's ill-advised meddling into Russian affairs in the Baltic resulted in the loss of two of the newest ships, *Verulam* and *Vittoria* in those waters in 1919. However, as neither of these destroyers had been fully utilised in the minelaying role, their loss made little difference to the strength of the flotilla as a whole.

There was little doubt that the smaller, older destroyers, would not find a permanent place in the post-war fleet of course. Many of them had been damaged before their conversion and all had spent a hard war in ceaseless usage in the front line. The smaller ships of the 'slow' division soon went into reserve and, in 1921, a wholesale scrapping of all types of warship took place, during which these four ships, *Ferret*, *Sandfly*, *Legion* and *Meteor*, went to the breaker's yard. A similar fate befell the *Gabriel*, even though she was less than five years old. Her place was taken by the slightly more modern and larger flotilla leader *Seymour*.

Of the smaller destroyers, only the 'R' class ships *Tarpon* and *Telemachus*, soon joined by their sister ship *Skate*, remained in the minelaying role, for experimental purposes. The veteran *Abdiel*, however, which had seen far harder service than any of these ships and for far longer, was retained on the active list. Indeed, her future seemed assured in the post-war fleet when, in 1926, she was taken in hand for a major refit.

It was her worn-out machinery that required replacement. Her fittings and fixtures had been modernised as recently as January 1918, and were still sound enough. In dockyard hands all her bearings were re-metalled, her boilers were re-tubed, her drums and brickwork were renewed and most of her turbine blading was replaced. It was estimated that this work would give her a further useful life span of five years. The work was completed in October 1926 and during her post-refit trials, the old ship attained the very creditable speed of 31 knots. Her funnels, uniquely, remained their original short height.

Yet despite all this work and expense, seemingly justified, the *Abdiel* was sold for scrap the following year, along with *Tarpon* and *Telemachus*, probably as yet another result of the Washington Treaty. Just two years later the *Seymour* was also put on the sales list, leaving only the experimental *Skate* of all the wartime destroyers still in active commission as a minelayer. Truly, parsimony had taken over with a vengeance.

There remained only the destroyers of the 'V' and 'W' classes, a few of which were fully converted vessels. Others remained capable of rapid conversion if required in an emergency. By the end of the decade, however, there was little practice minelaying conducted by these ships, which still remained, ten years after their launch, the most modern destroyers the Royal Navy possessed. As such, these ships were much in demand for traditional flotilla duties. Captains (D) and Admirals were therefore reluctant to part with any of them for too long at a time, for what many considered less essential, and certainly less glamorous, work. The extent to which they were converted was never of a scale equivalent to the old 20th Flotilla ships, with the one exception of the *Skate*, as Cowie pointed out:

> It will be recalled that a certain number of destroyers of the 'V' and 'W' classes, had been equipped for minelaying in the First World War, but had not actually been employed as minelayers. It should be noted that the expression 'equipped for minelaying' means that the necessary structural alterations are made and the mine rails fitted, but the full gun and torpedo armament is retained. When required for minelaying, a proportion of the armament is disembarked to compensate for the weight of the mines, and the minelaying gear is fully rigged. A more correct description would therefore be 'equipped for rapid *conversion* to minelaying' duties, and the requirement that the conversion should be capable of being carried out in forty-eight hours has always been met with ease. Reversion to full destroyer status is even more rapid, and has on occasion been completed in five hours.[41]

From time to time then, such a conversion was carried out for limited exercises. The late Captain F S De Winton told the author about one such occasion in which he was personally involved:

> I was in command of *Whirlwind*, 5th Flotilla, Home Fleet, from 1929–31. This flotilla was equipped for minelaying and my experience was as follows.
> In July 1930, *Versatile* and *Whirlwind* were detailed to test the roll of ships with mines on board. We had our torpedo tubes and 'Y' gun removed at Portsmouth to compensate for top weight, and fitted up with mines. I think we carried about sixty each. We set off to look for weather suitable to roll in west of the Scillies and south and west of Ireland. We both managed to roll about thirty degrees and the ships seemed to be rather 'stiff'

---

[41] Cowie, *Mines, Minelayers and Minelaying, op. cit.*, p 112.

with the mines embarked. On conclusion of the trials, we returned to Dartmouth and laid a minefield off Start Point. We then proceeded to Portsmouth where our mines (the ones remaining after the lay off the Start) were removed and our guns and torpedo tubes replaced. The mines were dummies; the filling was designed to give the approximate correct weight of explosive. We laid the field in daylight.[42]

All the destroyers of this period, 1930, still used the old method of laying their mines. Also, all were, naturally, still only fitted with the original narrow-gauge mines, as there was insufficient clearance on either side of the after superstructure in all these classes to allow for more modern, broader-beamed types of mine to be accommodated. In essence they laid as the 20th Flotilla had laid during the war, using the winch, wire and bogie method, known as hand laying because of the way the mines still had to be manhandled over the stern by the complicated arrangements of wire ropes.

Table 6
Fates of destroyer minelayers 1919–39

Ship	Date	Disposal
Vittoria	1-9-19	Sunk by Soviet submarine *Pantera* in Baltic
Verulam	4-9-19	Sunk by Soviet mines in Baltic
Gabriel	1921	Sold for scrapping
Ferret	1921	Sold T W Ward for breaking up
Sandlfy	1921	Sold T W Ward for breaking up
Legion	1921	Placed on disposal list
Meteor	1921	Placed on disposal list
Tarpon	1927	Sold for scrapping
Telemachus	1926	Sold for scrapping
Abdiel	1927	Sold for scrapping
Seymour	1929	Sold for scrapping
Venturous	1936	Sold for scrapping
Walrus	13-2-38	Wrecked off Scarborough
Valorous	11-38	Converted to AA escort destroyer
Valentine	6-39	Converted to AA escort destroyer
Skate	12-39	Converted to high-speed minesweeping destroyer

[42] Captain F S De Winton to the author, 27 June 1978.

The method was for a stout wire rope to be secured on the after deck, outboard of the mine rails themselves by means of a spring buffer. The wire from this was led forward, outboard of the rail still, round a bogie sheave fitted to the bogie itself, which was nothing more than a dummy sinker placed at the far end of the row of mines. The wire rope was fed through the sheave on this bogie and then, inboard of the rails, back to a powerful winch fitted near the stern opposite the spring buffer. With the winch motivated, the bogie moved slowly along, pushing the train of mines steadily along the rails. As the mines reached the end of the rail and the chute over the stern, a party of seamen manhandled each successive mine off and into the sea.

In order to achieve some system of order and time, a primitive computer apparatus had been designed. This device was the McKaffery-Klyne clock. The speed of the ship was set on this machine, as was the distance apart of each of the mines to be laid. Obviously, the higher the speed of the lay, the shorter the time interval to achieve the same gap. At 12 knots, not an excessive speed, with mines laid 120 feet apart, the interval between each mine would only be six seconds.

This rate of lay was far from easy to achieve by such physical methods, with the mines weighing so much. On a pitch-dark night, in freezing weather in hostile waters, the job called for considerable expertise and also a great deal of stamina. Obviously, with two sets of rails, the time interval could be doubled, by laying each mine alternately from the port and then the starboard chutes. Even so, it required two large groups of skilled seamen to do the job, and the slightest foul-up of the mine train on the rails could cause quite considerable time loss. The resultant spoiling of the pre-set mining plan, or the prolonging of the line, was obvious. We have noted this occurrence in previous chapters. In a test conducted by the *Skate* steaming at 23 knots, it was found that the interval gap between mines laid in this manner varied from five to thirteen seconds, the first mine taking seventeen seconds. A total of twelve mines were laid at this speed in ninety-two seconds.

By 1931, the Royal Navy had suffered yet further restrictions on its strength with the Government's signing of the London

Navy Treaty of 1930. This was compounded by Churchill's Treasury-inspired 'Escalator Clause', in which the period of no major war being envisaged for ten years was made perpetuating. As a result, the total permitted tonnage of destroyers was reduced to a mere 150,000 tons, which worked out at a maximum of thirteen full flotillas. This was to prove totally inadequate. A hesitant start at a modest replacement programme had begun three years earlier with the completion of two experimental destroyers, *Amazon* and *Ambuscade*. From this pair of ships, one flotilla leader and eight destroyers were built annually. With the Acasta, Beagle, Crusader (cut back to just four ships by a Labour Government) and Defender classes either complete or under construction, there was a call from some quarters for the next destroyer class, the eight ships of the Eclipse class (due to be laid down under the 1931 Programme) to be built with minelaying capacity, to replace the ageing 'V' and 'W' class ships.

There was a considerable divergence of opinion on this matter within the Royal Navy. For several years prior to this decision, some believed that, as no C-in-C would willingly part with new destroyers for this type of work, the Royal Navy should only retain the older boats with minelaying conversion capacity to fill this limited need. The argument put forward was that, as these older ships would not be needed in the front line anyway, they could carry out minelaying without affecting the numbers of new destroyers available for Fleet duties. On the opposing side, the argument was that an obsolescent destroyer must have been new at some point in her life. It therefore made more economical sense if they were constructed with minelaying conversion capacity, provided that their first-line duties were not in any way compromised, rather than incur the extra expense of conversion later in their lives. The pro-minelaying conversion capacity faction finally won the day and it was agreed that all eight of the new Eclipse class destroyers should be so designed and built.

However, before the plans were finally implemented, it was pointed out, after a study of all types of mines, that some of the more modern types could not be carried unless an improved method of laying was found. The Superintendent of Mine

Design was of the opinion that the old 'hand' laying method was unsatisfactory and that merely to adapt it for the broader mines would still not overcome the problem of correct spacing. He put forward a plan for a motor-driven, chain system, which utilised a rack that hooked underneath the sinkers below the rails and pulled the mines along, incorporating a variable speed gear. This 'endless chain' design was given Board of Admiralty approval in October 1931. The hull width of the new destroyers was extended to take advantage of this and their mine capacity was increased to eighty of the old HII mines, or sixty of the newly developed Mk. XIV mines. As usual, the two sets of torpedo tubes and the after gun had to be landed, but, with the new weights, 'A' gun also had to be taken off. This left just 'B' and 'X' 4.7-inch guns for defence. This risk was accepted.

Being designed from the keel up for the job meant that the fittings and fixtures for the new destroyers were very much part of the hull structure, rather than being 'tacked-on' extras as previously. This, in turn, gave a greater all-round strength to the ships. The mine rails were heavy 'D' quality channel bars and attention was given to accurate alignment of these, gauges being used by the builders when fitting. Their weight was incorporated with the ships' main structural girders. The spon-sons at the stern of the vessel were also integral and faired into the ship's side as part of the hull itself.

The chain was an enlarged bicycle-type affair in appearance, known as the 'chain conveyor'. Cowie's delightful description of it was, 'a combination of the toy train coupling and a moun-tain rack-railway'. Each mine rested on its sinker in the normal manner, the wheels of the sinker moving along the rail. Each sinker was coupled to those either side of it by means of a simple pin and socket coupling. The chain conveyor itself occupied only a short stretch of the deck aft.

It was set in a pit beneath the rails themselves and moved endlessly around two wheels, with an idler wheel at the fore end and a sprocket wheel aft, which was worked by the variable-ratio drive motor. The normal dynamo power of a destroyer was sufficient to power this when working, as no power would be required for searchlights at the time of laying, nor was there any extra load on the steering engines.

As the endless chain rotated, lugs, of which there were three, meshed into the bottom of the sinkers and pulled the whole train of mines aft at a pace dictated by the mining officer. As each mine reached the round-down at the end of the rail, the sinker carriage tilted over, automatically releasing the holding pin. The mine and sinker fell astern, with no manpower being required whatsoever. The top speed of the chain itself was 37 feet per minute. The two chains to port and starboard were interconnected, thus ensuring uniformity of the lay. The maximum speed for laying to be carried out by this method was 20 knots, the minimum was 10 knots.

The usual speed of laying utilised by the 20th Flotilla had been 12 knots. Here it should be emphasised that the expression 'High Speed Minelayers' as applied to destroyer minelayers in particular, does *not* refer to their speed while actually depositing their mines. It had been proven that speed itself at this point in the operation was of no great virtue. The difference between laying sixty mines at 20 knots instead at 10 knots would have only been ten minutes. Where the destroyers' unique advantage came in was in the getting into, and out of, enemy waters, before and after the lay. *That* was where the term was applicable.

The new system, and its operation, will be described in detail in the next chapter. However, it should be noted that, as well as being a stronger, more economic and sounder method than 'hand laying', it was also less liable to hang-ups on the train than this more cumbersome method. However, it could only be used in the specially built ships. Thus the 'V' and 'W' class destroyers, and later, the much smaller ships of the 'S' class when they came to be so converted in the late 1930s, still had to employ the old method when laying their mines, Equally, these ships were also restricted in the choice of mines they could deploy.

Although the system was approved in theory in 1931, the conservative Admiralty, through the Controller, voiced its doubts on fitting the entire flotilla with this, as yet, untried device. The Board agreed with this and only gave approval for two of the flotilla to be so fitted, the ships chosen being the *Esk* and the *Express*. The Board stamp was given to the legend and building drawings in February 1932 and the contracts for both destroyers were awarded to the Swan Hunter shipyard.

It should be noted that the new system, although requiring fewer men for the physical work, required more expertise in the actual operation for the reading of the various mechanical devices incorporated in the entire system. To supply the numbers of such skilled men to a destroyer, or flotilla of destroyers, should more be built with this same system, would become a serious drain on the Royal Navy's very finite skilled manpower pool. Such expertise was limited and the requirements might be equally so unless a permanent flotilla was again established, and there were no plans for this in 1932. Fortunately, this was mitigated, to a limited extent, by the reform of the whole mining system afloat and ashore in this period, and especially so of the latter.

A committee set up in 1930, called for, and got, the establishment of specialised mine depots. Of these depots, the principal one was set up at Frater, near Gosport, with others at Milford Haven and Wrabness, near Harwich. Special embarkation depots were put in place at Immingham and at Dover, in addition to bases around the Empire – Malta, Singapore, Hong Kong and Trincomalee. Whereas it had previously been the duty of the ships themselves to prepare the mines for laying once embarked, under the new plan a civilian organisation, under the Director of Armament Supply, was established, which took over responsibility for this and also for the examination of the mines at the embarkation depots. This relieved the ships from much of the burden of their responsibilities – those of merely setting the delayed-release mechanisms, depth-keeping settings and fusing.

This not only meant that fewer ratings had to be embarked for these duties, but it gave the destroyer crews greater periods of relaxation between sorties. As we have seen, turn-around times for the 20th Flotilla had often been within a few hours, and the men became physically exhausted. Obviously, prolonged periods working under all the many combined pressures, coupled with lack of proper rest, could result in accidents and errors. Although no fatal accidents overtook the flotilla, things were much safer under the new system.

As for the mines themselves, the new Mk XIV had been developed after the war. It was fitted with Herz horns, fourteen of them, which were activated when struck by a ship and not before. This, in turn, was found to be too sensitive and the Mk XV mine had spiked 'switch horns', which, if knocked so they moved, completed the circuit for detonation. Unfortunately, production difficulties overcame both these advanced types. Under the harsh dictates of producing large numbers when war eventually broke out again, a simplified mine, the Mk XVII, was developed from both these designs. Their dimensions were all similar and did not effect the destroyer minelayers' ability to lay them.

Work proceeded on the two destroyers. The *Esk* was designed as a divisional leader, and she was launched in March 1934, and the *Express* in May of the same year. Both ships were due to complete in the early autumn. Until they did so, obviously no trials could be conducted to assess the merits of the new equipment. As a result, destroyers of the next class, the *Fearless* class, were ordered as repeats of the conventional *Eclipse* destroyers. They were not built with any minelaying conversion facility whatsoever.

There still appeared to be some difference of opinion in the actual interpretation of the March 1932 decision. However, as things stood, no further destroyers would be ordered with any minelaying conversion capacity until the 1935 programme.[43]

All this therefore had to be debated again within a very short period. The Greyhound class destroyers of the 1933 programme were similar to the Fearless class, but later provision was made that this class would, after all, be capable of conversion to minelayers. This in no way meant that they would follow the *Esk* and *Express* in design with regard to the specialised fittings. Indeed, all eight were completed as normal destroyers in all their main essentials. When the Hero class ships of the 1934 programme came up for discussion, the DTD again raised the issue of minelaying destroyer policy as he understood it, and as it was, seemingly, being interpreted.

[43] See *Minelaying Destroyers; Legend and Design* (ADM1/9333) and *Decision to fit Flotilla Leaders with ASDIC and two-speed destroyer sweeps or as minelayers.* (ADM1/8755/57).

He noted that it was not apparent from the Assistant Chief of Naval Staff's minute, that it was ever the intention to fit these new flotillas as minelayers. The old argument about old destroyers being used for this job had apparently been perpetuated. As mines, rails and sinkers were standardised, the DTD (Director Trade Division) considered that any alteration to the standard design should be done forthwith, in order that *Esk* and *Express*-type equipment could, in fact, be so fitted at a future date. If this was not done, then considerable expense would be incurred and much structural alteration would be required should conversion become a necessity. He recommended as a start, that all new destroyers should be dual-purpose, equipped for minelaying and with the Two-Speed Destroyer Sweep (TSDS) for high-speed minesweeping, instead of one or the other.

The Head of Mining argued that the DCNS (Deputy Chief Naval Staff) statement of March 1932 was that all destroyers would have ASDIC and also TSDS *or* minelaying potential. 'This means all future destroyers and leaders were to be *designed and built* so as to be capable of conversion to minelayers . . .' He continued, 'Controller's caveat referred solely to *fitting* and not to *designing*.' This was an important definition: *Esk* and *Express* were fitted for minelaying; the Greyhound class was designed for future conversion, which would result in exactly the DTD's fear of structural alteration and expense, not to mention delay, at some future date.

Therefore until the *Esk* and *Express* had conducted their trials, '. . . no vessels fitted both for TSDS and M/L (Minelaying) will actually be ordered until orders for 1935 Programme are placed.' Thus, the interpretation of that decision had resulted in no new destroyers being designed for possible conversion to minelayers, the Fearless class being capable of TSDS only.[44]

It was then decided by the ACNS (Assistant Chief Naval Staff) and agreed by the DCNS and the Controller himself in

---

[44] In which minesweeping role ships of this class performed several times during the passage of convoys to Malta during the war; see *Pedestal, the Convoy that saved Malta*, Peter C Smith, Goodall, 2002.

February 1934, that *all* future flotilla leaders and destroyers should be built so as to be capable of conversion for minelaying. Their design should be as the Greyhound class, but amended to comply with this decision. However, the Controller made two stipulations: flotilla leaders should *not* be so included and destroyers under construction (the Greyhound class) should be so amended, providing that their construction would not be delayed, and the Hero class should not have their date of ordering delayed. This was complied with but, in fact, neither the Greyhound nor the Hero class were ever taken in hand for fitting as minelayers to take advantage of this inbuilt design modification. Despite this, many 'authoritative' reference books maintain that they were built as minelayers, which is not quite the same thing.

With this decision taken, the long-awaited trials of the new equipment went ahead in August 1934, when *Esk* finally completed. She embarked sixty mines; thirty each side and put to sea for various evaluation manoeuvres. The maximum laying speed attained on these trials was one mine per 6.5 seconds; a total of fifteen mines being laid from each train initially. When laying three mines from each rail alternately, *Esk* attained a 4-second interval, compared with the Staff requirement of one every 3.5 seconds.

The vibration was found to be bad with a full mine load embarked at speeds in excess of 28 knots. So much so that, during a one-hour trial at 35 knots, the mine register jogged back fifteen steps. This necessitated moving the mine control hut from aft to the gun platform, which proved a steadier base. A maximum speed of 37 knots was attained in *Esk*'s minelaying configuration, at full power in a moderate wind.

These trials delayed the destroyer's full commissioning, which did not take place until October 1934. In November, the *Esk* once more embarked a full outfit of mines. She made another trial run in position 'M' at Spithead, in a fresh northwest wind, at the normal laying speed of 12 knots. There was some delay in embarking the mine loads as the mines were split up between two lighters, one of which arrived late. On the lay itself, the equipment malfunctioned, the mine register failing to work at all. The same fault was occurred on the

Express. When she in turn conducted a similar run. It was found that, instead of an equal spacing of 100 feet between mines, those laid from the port side went into the water at 90-feet intervals, while those of the port side went in at 110-feet intervals. These discrepancies were believed to be caused by a permanent set in the ship's cross shaft, the main drive being positioned closer to the starboard side, which called for modification.

Once these teething troubles were ironed out, the two destroyers were put into service early in 1935. They were used as conventional destroyers with all four 4.7-inch guns, torpedo tubes and TSDS gear embarked. In this guise, they could be distinguished from their six sisters by the fact that their whalers were shipped on the forecastle deck instead of at the break in the forecastle, and their main masts were tripods to compensate for vibration. Their built-in sponsons astern were yet another giveaway for foreign naval experts in the late thirties.

10

A NEW BEGINNING

While the *Esk* and *Express* were entering service, the decision had to be made on the 1935 programme destroyers, the Intrepid class. The Greyhound and Hero classes, designed but not fitted out as minelayers, could be distinguished by tripod main masts as the two 'Es'. The Intrepid class followed this layout exactly, as completed, with the ships being more or less repeats of these two classes with 'arrangements' for minelaying, but no sponsons or rails as fitted. However, they had only been in full commission for a year when the DTD's predictions came true!

While Great Britain had been disarming to please senators in Ohio and Kansas, the dictatorships in Germany and Italy, and the war faction in Japan, had been rearming at an unprecedented pace. These countries were busy implementing a series of easy conquests. (Manchuria, Ethiopia and Austria), while the League of Nations wrung its collective hands but did nothing. The next crisis came about with Hitler's obvious designs on Czechoslovakia and during the Munich period during the autumn of 1938, it very much appeared as if war might be inevitable. Duff Cooper at the Admiralty was among the few clear-sighted men willing to make a stand. At a Cabinet meeting on 9 September, he called for a 'symbolic act' to show the dictators that we had drawn the line at last. He considered that, as they always used force themselves, such a measure might 'speak more effectively than words'. The First Lord's words were mulled over and Chatfield, the First Sea Lord, was called on by the Cabinet on 12 September, to explain just what act he might have in mind. Among the proposed measures actually taken, was the placing into full commission of four reserve fleet destroyer minelayers, and this had been duly announced in the Press.

This brought about the belated realisation of just how few such destroyers were still available and it had immediate effect. In the Mediterranean, the Intrepid class ships had formed the 3rd Destroyer Flotilla. Later that year, in October 1938, hurried plans were implemented to carry out the necessary modifications to some of these ships to bring them into line with the *Esk* and *Express*. The work was carried out at Malta dockyard, as George Mack then serving aboard the *Intrepid* herself, was later to recall:

We had another surprise, this time in Malta, as we found that five of the I class destroyers were going into the dockyard to convert to Minelayers, as we had been designed to do, and after we were completed the other four could be converted. [In fact, just four were so modified.]

Work went steadily on, as sponsons were built on each quarter, and a lot of tapped steel plates were welded from the stern, along the iron deck as far as the rear funnel, to which the mine rails could be bolted. A large electric motor was fitted in the tiller flat which turned a capstan on the quarterdeck, as well as a cross-shaft which turned chains which pulled the mine aft and dropped them over the stern. An extension was fitted to the front of 'X' gun deck to put our depth charge throwers over the top of the mines, and a couple of feet were cut off the tops of our funnels to reduce top-weight.

Eventually, in late January, our conversion was completed and we went out for trials, which meant going to a remote bay where our mine-carrier was anchored. This was a converted Holt Line merchant ship of about 8,000 tons carrying several thousand mines, and fitted with derricks capable of lifting off our guns and torpedo tubes.

Using only our own ship's company, we took off 'A' and 'Y' guns and both sets of torpedo tubes, then fetching up the mine rails from under the engine room plates, we bolted them each side of the Iron Deck. Then we loaded a full complement of 64 mines, the first six to be dropped being dummies, and after a few manoeuvres to check the ship's stability, we moved to a quiet area and laid the dummies.

All went well and after restoring ourselves back to a normal destroyer, we wearily returned to Sliema creek, with a very concentrated 24 hours behind us, and a fervent hope that we would never be called to do it again in earnest![45]

All this haste and cost could have been averted had the DTD's wise words of 1932 been heeded! Even so, only the *Icarus*, *Impulsive*, *Intrepid* and *Ivanhoe* were actually converted. Plans to alter the rest of the flotilla were abandoned with the end of the crisis. When the war really did come eight months later, it was too late to carry out the work on the other ships. These destroyers were always required for more conventional duties and so the work was never carried out on any of them. Nor was this the end of the story. In the subsequent destroyer classes laid down up to the outbreak of the war in 1939, the Tribal, Javelin, Kelly, Laforey, Milne and Napier classes, *no* provision for minelaying whatsoever was included in their design. In September 1939, therefore, only six modern destroyers were capable of this function in the entire fleet.

Moreover, among the older destroyer minelayers, more scrappings (*Venturous*) and accidents (*Walrus*), had further reduced their number. Also, the decision to convert many of these older ships to anti-aircraft escorts, though in itself a very wise move, meant that both *Valorous* and *Valentine* were lost to the minelaying force by 1939, and other ships were so earmarked. In fact the war overtook this programme and the old 'V' and 'W' class destroyers capable of being converted for minelaying, if so desired, totalled just ten, *Vanquisher*, *Velox*, *Versatile*, *Vimy*, *Vivacious*, *Vortigern*, *Walker*, *Watchman* and *Whirlwind*. Such was the demand for destroyers as anti-

[45] Mack, George, *HMS* Intrepid, edited by Peter C Smith, William Kimber, London, 1980, pp 57–9.

submarine ships in the Battle of the Atlantic that followed, that none of these were ever so converted.

However, this paucity was slightly offset by the fact that five of the old 'S' class destroyers were taken in hand for conversion to minelayers, albeit limited conversions, still using the old 'hand' laying method because of their smaller dimensions. These ships were the *Scout, Stronghold, Tenedos, Thanet* and *Thracian*. All these destroyers were sent out to the Far East and were very usefully employed, quietly and without publicity, for several years. They laid a whole series of defensive minefields off British bases in that region, off Hong Kong, Penang, Singapore, Borneo and the like. They also used up the stocks of the old-type mines held in that part of the world as insurance against the growing ambitions of Japan.[46]

The oldest destroyer remaining in the Royal Navy, the last remaining 'R' class ship, *Skate*, was taken into dockyard hands for conversion to a destroyer minesweeper trials ship in 1939. However, she later served as a conventional escort in the North Atlantic, despite her age and size! The full list of destroyer minelayers, actually converted or with the potential for conversion, which was in many cases never utilised, is shown in Table 7.

The gear for further conversion of the Greyhound, Hotspur and remaining four Intrepid class destroyers, was held at the home dockyards. Twenty sets of conveyors were stored for possible use, but none of these ships actually received any of this equipment, although some was used later in the war, as we shall see. All the mines readied for laying by the existing destroyer minelayers were ground mines. New forms of oscillating mines, originally pioneered by the *Ferret* as long ago as 1918, were under development, but, as in the First World War, they were never used.

This was the parlous state of the ships and their mine loads in 1939. Let us now examine in greater detail the equipment and methods employed then, as applicable to the *Esk* and *Express* only in September 1939, and later also to the four converted 'I' class destroyers.

---

[46] See Chapter 15.

Table 7
Destroyer minelaying potential on outbreak of Second World War – September 1939

Destroyer	Base Location	Readiness	Notes
Esk	Milford	Mines	
Express	Haven	loaded	
Intrepid		Unconverted – in	Due to convert in
Ivanhoe	Chatham	Mediterranean	October 1939
Icarus		Unconverted – in	Due to convert in
Impulsive	Portsmouth	Mediterranean	February, March 1940
Skate	Portsmouth	Converted	Due to fit out for minesweeping December 1939
Stronghold	Penang		Local Defence Flotilla
Scout			To Hong Kong to lay
Tenedos	Singapore	Converted	Defensive minefield
Thanet			
Thracian	Hong Kong		Local Defence Flotilla
Vanquisher	21st Div, 11th DF		No plans to
Walker	Clyde	Unconverted	convert
Versatile	22nd Div, 11th DF		
Vimy	Liverpool	Unconverted	No plans to convert
Whirlwind			
Velox	25th Div, 13th DF		
Vortigern	Gibraltar	Unconverted	No plans to convert
Watchman			
Vivacious	17th DF, Liverpool	Unconverted	No plans to convert

Each of these destroyers was fitted with mine rails and chain discharge gear. Prior to embarking their full outfits of sixty Mk XV or XIV mines on XV sinkers, thirty on each rail, the 'A' and 'Y' guns and ammunition, all torpedo tubes and warheads and the TSDS equipment had to be put ashore. The mine rails were cleaned, greased and the tracked cleared. The mines could be embarked on either side of the ship by means of the torpedo davits. However, before the actual laying began, the sinkers had to be coupled together to form the train on either side of the ship, the after sinker of each train being engaged with the train.

For the actual embarkation of the mines, certain members of the crew would be assigned the relevant duties. These comprised the following groups. The *lighter party* consisted of one petty officer or leading seaman and two ABs for hooking on and steadying the hoist. While the torpedo ratings were not considered vital for this work, the men employed had to have some instruction in certain parts of the drill. The *plummet guard* party consisted of two ABs, whose job it was to remove the wooden guards at the plummet end of the sinkers. The *tier party* varied in number according to the type of mines embarked. If the new Mk XIV or XV mines were used, then four seamen were required; if the old HII mines were used, only three men were necessary. All these groups came under the supervision of the mining officer, usually the executive officer of the destroyer. His duties included the inspection of each tier; checking that the length of the mooring was correctly adjusted for the field to be laid; depth adjustment; seeing that the mines were properly seated and the mooring shackle and chain were correctly stopped up; checking to see that the safety clip could be withdrawn easily; and that the soluble plug was in place.

The torpedo gunner was stationed on the mining deck in charge of the actual preparations. He was responsible for testing the communications and timing devices, the trap point and hauling winches, as well as being responsible for the fitting of the mine rails on deck. Under him were a torpedo gunner's mate and two lower ratings, to make sure the mines were secure at sea, and to cast them loose before the actual lay. Mk XIV securing pendants were used and mine stays were also fitted.

The mining officer was also the control officer for the laying operation. The control station consisted of a small hut, which was embarked and placed on the gun deck, but it was only large enough to shelter one rating. The control officer therefore had to remain exposed close by during the lay.

The controls and instruments supplied initially did not include the taunt wire gear, but this was later found to be essential, as we shall see. Before the war, it was expected that all calculations could be done by the tachometer, but this did not work out in practice. The other controls utilised are as listed below:

Order instrument
Mine dropping register
Minelaying instrument
Tachometer
A telephone from the bridge
A voicepipe from the tiller flat

Their various functions and workings were as follows: -

Order instrument

These were mechanical telegraphs, step-by-step electrical instruments or lamps covered by stencilled discs. The orders and repeats were marked as follows: -

Order	Repeat
STAND BY	AM READY
LAY MINES	AM LAYING
STOP LAYING	HAVE STOPPED
	FOUL

Mine dropping register.

The object of this device was to keep the bridge and control room informed of the number of mines already dropped at a given moment. Transmitters were fitted abaft each trap or chain discharge gear and receivers were on the bridge and in the control room or hut. In addition to the individual receivers from each rail, totalisers were also fitted which registered the total number of units laid from *both* rails.

The transmitter consisted of a switch operated by a de-pression bar, which was worked by the sinker as it passed over the sponson. Each time the switch was made an electric impulse was transmitted to the receiver. The totaliser was in series with both individual receivers.

Minelaying instrument

This was fitted in the control hut and consisted of a fixed dial marked 'Mines Laid Starboard' and 'Mines Laid Port', these graduations being 180° apart. Working over this dial was a pointer, driven from the chain on one side. When the gear was operated this pointer revolved, and the mines were released from the sprockets of the respective chains as the pointer passed the markings. This instrument therefore acted as a creep indicator, and also showed the position of the units on the chain at any particular moment.

Tachometer

This was also fitted in the control hut with the minelaying instrument, but was placed in such a position that it could be seen by the chain operator. It consisted of a dial graduated in revs per minute. Working over the dial were two pointers. One set by a hand wheel to the speed desired, acted as an index mark, while the other recorded the speed of the chain.

When laying mines, all the chain operator had to do was to regulate his control so that the two pointers were kept in line with each other. A table was provided for use with the tachometer, which gave the revolutions of the chain required to lay mines at various spacings and speeds of the ship.

It was laid down that the correct laying speeds were between 12 and 15 knots, 'when nature allows'. Mines could be relied upon to function if laid at speeds of up to 20 knots. However, above that speed, errors in depth taking and spacing were expected, owing to the disturbed state of the water in the destroyer's wake. It was also noted, from the *Esk*'s trials, that severe vibration was also likely to cause defects in the mines themselves, as well as the controls.

With regard to spacing, it was stated categorically that, 'Actual spacing of mines is never exactly as intended and the minimum is to be aimed at so that a ripple firing does not take place'. Examples given were as follows:

HII – 150 feet
XIVa and XVa – 150 feet (with a 500-lb charge)
XIVb, XVb and XVI – 120 feet (two 320-lb charges)

The time interval when hand laying the old mines from destroyers was eight seconds from the same trap.

Taunt wire measuring gear

As briefly described earlier, this gear was used to position the minefields. It accurately gave the distance that the ship had to run from a given point to the designated dropping zone, by means of measuring the amount of wire that was run off. It would work effectively at speeds of up to 20 knots.

It consisted of a drum, which carried 140 miles of fine wire. The wire was taken off the drum by means of a flier, which was controlled by a hand brake. It was then fed through guide rollers round a counter wheel, each turn of which represented 0.001 miles. From there, the wire was taken to the first lead wheel and on to a dynamometer, which took up the strain from the motion of the destroyer. From this the wire was fed to the after (second) lead wheel and then through stern rollers over the stern of the ship. When the required distance was run off, the wire was cut with a hammer and chisel.

Although this method sounds primitive, this equipment could measure very accurately up to distances of 100 miles, but a latitude correction was necessary as the wheel registered 1000 revs for every nautical mile.

When commencing a run, a fix was taken from the shore, or a buoy or lightship, and the wind, tide and length of mooring if either of the latter were being taken into account.

In order to avoid other ships when running with the taunt wire gear out, it was found better to reduce speed rather than alter course. This was because if the latter method was chosen, the wire would still give the distance between each turning point, regardless of the speed of the destroyer. Thus, it can be seen that the destroyer was on the arc of a circle whose centre was the point of departure, but if the destroyer had altered course, this centre would become the last turning point.

It was thus obvious, that should an alteration of course be found unavoidable, only the smallest movement of the ship's helm was desirable. When the destroyers were reinforcing an existing minefield or laying a line of mines parallel to another already laid, the approach was made at right angles. The reason for this was that you could never be nearer to the previously laid mines than designed, and you might be further away due to set. If there was any doubt, the new line was laid on a divergent course four or five degrees away from the old one.

McKaffery-Klyne clock

This automatically indicated when a mine was to be dropped. Settings ranged from 2½ to 18 seconds between each drop, and the clock had a starting switch. The timing drum was driven through a ratchet gearing at a constant speed, by the oscillation of a solenoid. These solenoids were made to oscillate by means of a make and break arrangement. The timing drum was perforated with thirty-three rows of holes. Each time one of the contact fingers took in one of the holes, a gong rang and a light lit at the trap, thus indicating that a mine was to be released. The relay coil was normally short circuited by the timing drum, but when the contact finger took in a hole, the relay became energised. The current then flowed through the circuit breaker to either the port or the starboard light and gong circuit. These two circuits were fitted with switches so that either the light or the gong could be cut out for Day or Silent Night laying.

A change-over switch arranged from which side laying was to commence. Before the clock was used, the drum had to be turned to the starting position to ensure that the gong rang when the switch was activated. The mines, of course, were laid on alternate sides of the destroyer. The usual spacing, as we have seen, was about 150 feet apart.

So much for the equipment. It was stressed that mines and sinkers would not stand up to too much rough usage, if this really needed emphasis! Any dent weakened the shell of the mine and thus limited the depth at which it could be laid. Lifting eyes provided on the mine always had to be used to minimise this danger. When on the sinker, the combined equipment of mine and sinker thus married together was always lifted by the lifting eyes of the sinker and *never* by those on the mine itself. The sinkers could be run for short distances on their rollers over smooth surfaces. Wooden protective covers were always fitted over the plummet end of the Mk VIII, XIV and XV sinkers and over the anchor ends of the Mk XVI sinkers.

Both mines and sinkers, prior to the Second World War, following the reorganisation, were supplied by the mine depot on demand. The destroyers embarked mines at ports in which there were mine depots. Failing that, they embarked mines at suitably equipped depot ships, from lighters under control of armament supply officers, or, if lying alongside a quay wall, from trucks.

Once the minelaying destroyers had reached the correct computed dropping zone, the preparation procedure was as follows.

About one hour before the laying position was reached, the horn covers were removed, safety pins or clips were eased, and the stays and pendants were removed. All the communication instruments were tested and the gangways between the tiers closed up. The traps themselves were never unlocked from their closed positions until all hands were closed up at the action stations. The lower deck was cleared and the ship's company was distributed throughout the vessel as far as possible, ready for an emergency during laying.

Stand-by was signalled some five minutes before the first mine was due to be dropped. It was signalled by the captain when the first mines were launched into the traps on each side, this being reported by the mining officer as 'Ready', which the control officer telegraphed to the bridge. The captain then informed the control officer of the interval and spacing to be adopted and the McKaffery-Klyne clock was set in starting position.

The timing clock was started, the first gong rung and the

Table 8
British destroyers converted for minelaying or built with minelaying conversion capability and actually so utilised 1939–45

Destroyer	Tonnage	Mine load	Completed	Speed in knots
Stronghold			1919	
Scout			1918	
Tenedos	905	40	1919	36
Thanet			1919	
Thracian			1922	
Esk	1375		1934	35
Express				
Icarus				
Impulsive				
Intrepid	1370	60	1937	36
Ivanhoe				
Obedient				
Opportune	1540		1942	
Orwell				

mine was laid with each sound of the gong, or flash of light if at night, as normally was the case in the 20th Flotilla, alternately to port and to starboard. Each unit was manhandled into the trap, the safety pin removed as it entered. When released, it was pushed out of the trap and ran down over the sponson. The winch man adjusted the hauling speed to set the dropping interval if necessary. The tiers moved steadily until the first bogie reached the furthest point of its travel. The hauling aft wire for the first bogie was declutched. The hauling aft wire was unshipped and stepped out of the way. The head of the second tier then reached the first bogie, which it pushed aft with any remaining mines of the first tier.

Should any attack develop during this critical period, the quickest method of getting rid of the mine load and sinkers was to remove the foremost ties of the trap. Then keeping the trap open, all units were heaved overboard, regardless of the spacing. If the mines were to be rendered ineffective in such conditions, the safety pins were left and it was thought that they should have been capable of withstanding the sheering stress involved. The main thing was to ditch the deadly cargo as rapidly as possible. With the chain discharging gear, much of this procedure was unnecessary. The chains laid alternately, the speed being adjusted by the tachometer reading being altered.[47]

[47] From MCDL4 and MCDL5, Lecture No. XI – *Minelayers*, 1939, and No. XII – *Minelaying Embarkation, Preparation and Laying*, Admiralty, 1939.

11

BACK TO THE
HELIGOLAND BIGHT

After being made ready during August 1939, the *Express*
(Captain J G Bickford, DSO, DSC, senior officer) and *Esk* were
immediately available on the outbreak of war on 3 September.
These two destroyers initially operated directly under the
orders of Admiral Sir Charles Forbes, C-in-C, Home Fleet. On
8 September, both ships arrived at Immingham to embark
their cargo of mines.

The British minelaying policy at the outset of the Second
World War, was twofold: offensive and defensive. The two
minelaying destroyers were to take part in an immense number
of both types of laying during the first six months of the conflict.
Initially, it was hoped to commence, in modest form (dictated by
the fact that only two such destroyers were available), a series of
offensive lays in the Heligoland Bight, picking up from where
their predecessors had ended in 1918. Plans had, in fact, been
made before the war for the laying of such fields along the most
likely enemy sea-lanes through the Heligoland Bight, which,
again, were assumed to be similar to those used in the earlier war.

As a result, a large section of the Heligoland Bight was at
once declared a dangerous mine area by the British. The
Germans responded by declaring their own mine area along
the western boundary of the British zone. This, as Captain
Cowie wryly recorded, raised a nice question in International
Law as to whether we could therefore lay mines *outside* our
own declared area but *inside* the German one! The first offensive lays awaited only suitable moon conditions.[48]

---

[48] Cowie, *Mines, Minelayers and Minelaying, op. cit.*

There was not a long wait, for the *Express* and *Esk* made their first sortie from Immingham on 9 September. By the early hours of the following morning, the pair had laid a total of 120 mines in the entrance to the suspected German main exit channels in the enemy's own mine area. This duty done, the two destroyers repeated the operation a week later and it was once again accomplished without detection.

Although both runs were achieved seemingly satisfactorily enough from the practical point of view, it was then decided to call a short halt to these offensive operations. In the words of Captain Stephen Roskill, '. . . doubts arose regarding both the accuracy of the lays and the adequacy of our intelligence on enemy movement; the programme was therefore suspended until both had been improved.'

The two destroyers therefore reverted to normal duties for a while, sailing from Immingham on 18 September to investigate a U-boat reported off Bridlington. They were subsequently detached for general duties with the Home Fleet for the next month. But, as early as the end of October, they were both readied for minelaying duties once more, *Express* sailing from Milford Haven on 30 September and *Esk* arriving there the following day to prepare in earnest.

A defensive minefield was being planned to protect the coastal convoys off the east coast of England and Scotland. The second section of this field was to be declared off the Galloper Shoal, which covered the Thames Estuary. In readiness for this, Operation RG, the two ships arrived back at Immingham on 10 November. Here, they received orders to load a full complement of mines and then to proceed to Harwich. They left the Humber on 13 November and arrived at Harwich at 17.00 the same day. On the 18th, however, the laying of Line 'X' of Operation 'RG', to which they were assigned, was postponed, and they both returned to the Humber. Plans were made to try again on 20 November. Instead, however, the first section of the defensive barrage, covering the Yorkshire coast from 55°00'N, was begun by these destroyers on 27 November.

Meanwhile, the need for additional destroyers for the resumption of the offensive fields was obvious. The Admiralty therefore ordered that *Intrepid* and *Ivanhoe* were to reconvert to this role immediately. These two ships had been operating as normal destroyers ever since their trial conversion at Malta and their return to home waters from the Mediterranean earlier in the war. George Mack again provided an eyewitness memoir of what ensued:

> 'A' and 'Y' guns were now standing on the jetty, so the forecastle and quarterdeck looked very empty, but there was the top of some bent arm just over the guardrails on the starboard bow, which turned out to be a massive arm pivoted from a bracket just above the waterline. This was obviously part of the new paravanes which we had squeezed past as we came up on the fo'c'sle, as were the two large derricks, fitted to 'B' gun deck, one each side.
>
> On 4 December 1939, we completed our conversion to minelayers in Chatham Dockyard with *Ivanhoe*, and sailed to Sheerness to get our ammunition and stores, also to try out our new paravanes. The paravane is like a miniature aeroplane or kite, which instead of flying in the air, flies out from the bow of the ship at an angle of about 45° to the centreline. It flies on the end of a serrated wire secured at the bottom of the bow, and is fitted with an automatic depth-keeping device, to 'fly' at about twenty-five feet below the surface of the sea.
>
> The big problem is getting the 'point of tow' down to the bottom of the bow. On the larger ships this is done by having two chains rove through holes at the foot of the stem, so after the paravanes are 'streamed' and running correctly, then the point of tow is hauled down to the bottom of the bow. But the bow of a destroyer is not strong enough for this, so like other small ships, they usually tow their sweeps from the stern so that they sweep a passage for other ships, but have no protection themselves, although, as they draw less water they are not quite so vulnerable. However, we were to go to places where the enemy would lay mines especially for our benefit, so the Admiralty fitted us with bow paravanes.
>
> To get the tow-wires to the bottom of the bow there

was a long arm fitted about ten feet back from the bow, on the starboard side. This arm pivoted at the waterline so its top was under the stem when we wanted to use the paravanes, but when not required, the arm was stowed in a bracket and stuck up just above the top of the guardrails. Unfortunately, this arm was right in the bow wave, so even on a calm day there was a constant fine spray of cold sea water sweeping over the bow and the forward gun, which made this permanently-manned gun even more uncomfortable.

After we completed ammunitioning, we went on 12th December to Portsmouth to join the 20th (Minelaying) Flotilla, where we loaded a dozen dummy mines, and went out to a remote part of the Solent, first to test the minelaying gear, by laying the mines, and then to stream our paravanes.

This proved to be more difficult than expected and it was past lunchtime by the time they were streamed. As I sat down to my steak, eggs and chips, or whatever we had for lunch, the ship swung round to test the paravanes by sweeping up the dummy mines. Shortly after we had sat down, the whole bow started to vibrate and a loud drumming sound was heard, which obviously came from the mine mooring wire running along our paravanes wire. It stopped just as suddenly when the mine was cut free. We all knew we would recognise this sound when we heard it again![49]

In fact, it was on 12 December that the Admiralty announced that the four converted destroyers were to form a new 20th Flotilla, Cowie stating that, '. . . the name being chosen in view of its sentimental associations with the destroyer minelayers of World War 1'.[50] *Express* (flotilla leader) and *Esk* were to form the 39th Division and *Intrepid* (divisional leader) and *Ivanhoe* the 40th Division. The *Icarus* and *Impulsive* were also to be converted again, to further reinforce the flotilla in due course.

[49] Mack, George, *H M.S Intrepid, op. cit.,* pp 91–5.
[50] Cowie, *Mines, Minelayers and Minelaying, op. cit.*

The newly formed flotilla carried out its first offensive mission on the night of 17/28 December. This was Operation 'IB' and the four destroyers successfully laid 240 mines off the mouth of the Ems Estuary. In conjunction with their dangerous work, an anti-submarine sweep was mounted by the 1st Destroyer Flotilla from Harwich, with three 'G' class destroyers and a Polish ship, Operation 'JG2'. This was conducted to the westward of the German declared mine area, where, it was believed, the U-boats passed through their own minefields to commence operations. However, there was no result and all eight destroyers returned to harbour without incident.

This proved to be the last offensive operation conducted by *Express* and *Esk* in 1939. On its completion, these two ships sailed to carry out a refit and alterations at Portsmouth. *Intrepid* and *Ivanhoe* carried on, however, despite some accounts to the contrary. They also sailed to Portsmouth, but here they embarked mines once more on 22 December, although the actual lay was postponed until the 28th. On that date they sailed through the Dover Strait and, on reaching the vicinity of the Cromer Light, they streamed paravanes and started taunt wire gear before turning east. George Mack gave this account:

> About 01.00 we started to slow down as we reached the laying position, with everyone fully on the alert. Suddenly we felt our skins creep as a loud clicking started to come from the bridge. This was our 'ZAC' signalling device, which worked on ultra-violet rays, and could pick up invisible rays from the signal lamp of our chummy ship, who had a special screen over their searchlight. But this was no signal, as the buzzer was just giving out random noise! We soon worked out that it was picking up faulty blackout from the enemy coast which must be within the five-miles radius of this detector.
>
> Then came the order 'commence laying' followed twenty minutes later by the report 'all mines laid' and waited till the *Ivanhoe* had laid hers.
>
> When all the mines were laid, we turned westwards

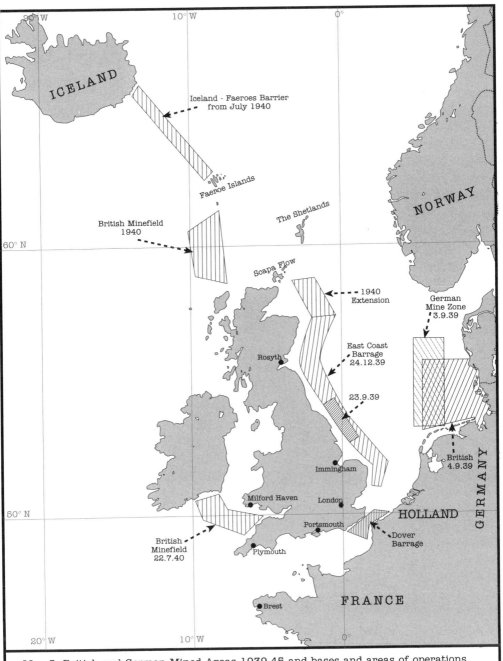

Map.5: British and German Mined Areas 1939-45 and bases and areas of operations of XXth Destroyer Flotilla.

for home and started to work up to twenty-eight knots. As the wind started to blow harder, with the increased speed, we took shelter inside the gun-shield. We were talking of our leave, which was already a pleasant memory, and looking forward to our next run ashore, when a loud thrumming was felt through the bow! Our hearts dropped as we recognised the sound we had last heard in the dummy minefield, and we knew at once we were cutting mines, though these were not dummies! Even now I can recall my thoughts: was it better to stop inside the gun shield and avoid being thrown overboard by the spring steel decks if there was an explosion, or was it better to be outside the gun shield and avoid being smashed up against the roof? I decided to get out and hang on the guardrails, and made sure that my lifebelt was blown up under my overcoat!

Then came an almighty crash and a splintering of wood; our wooden derrick which stuck out on the starboard side had broken its forward stay, jerked round and smashed to smithereens against the side of the bridge! As we could not pull up the point of tow of our paravanes, we had a picking-up wire permanently fitted to the paravanes under water and led up through a block at the top of the derrick ready for recovery. What had happened was that the paravane towing wire had parted; the full weight of the paravane had come on to the picking-up wire, which had broken the guy on the derrick. This had swung round with such force that the foot-thick, twenty foot long derrick had smashed to pieces, then the 'picking-up' wire broke and we no long had a starboard paravanes. The problems of being in an enemy minefield did not bear thinking about too long, but now we could occupy our minds by pulling what was left of our starboard derrick and then we were clear of the area.[51]

Despite this unpleasant experience, all returned safely to Immingham, which now became their main base. A further

[51] Mack, George, *HMS* Intrepid, *op. cit.*, pp 96–7.

offensive field was laid early in the new year, Operation 'EW'. *Intrepid* and *Ivanhoe* laid their mines for this field on the night of 2/3 January 1940. Seven destroyers of to the 1st Flotilla were out in support, operating to the westward of the mine zone.

This lay was followed by a series of planned anti-submarine sweeps, organised in the same area as to the previous operation of this type and again conducted in support of laying runs by *Intrepid* and *Ivanhoe*. These lays were Operations ID1, ID2 and ID3. The two minelayers sailed from the Humber to carry out the first of these three operations on 9 January. On 14 January, the second of the lays was completed, but ID3 had a less happy outcome.

Bad weather had caused the cancellation of the 20th Flotilla's part in this operation and, instead, the two minelayers were ordered to Chatham on the 19 January. Unfortunately, the flotilla leader *Grenville*, while returning from the anti-U-boat sweep leading the 1st Flotilla, was herself mined near the North Hinder Light Vessel, and sank with heavy loss of life. While *Intrepid* and *Ivanhoe* operated with the Home Fleet on normal destroyer duties for a further short period (which included the interception of the German prison ship *Altmark*), their sisters *Icarus* and *Impulsive* arrived at Portsmouth dockyard to convert to minelayers. The *Express* and *Esk* had completed their modernisations and were engaged on further tests and trials.

In order to close the gaps in the declared East Coast Barrage at its extremities, a series of defensive anti-U-boat minefields were laid early in February. Standard contact mines were laid deep to catch the submarines while they were submerged and trying to penetrate British shipping lanes via these gaps. In order to ensure that none of the mines had been laid too shallow, whereby they might endanger friendly surface ships, a skimming sweep was passed over them by minesweepers once they were down. The *Express* and *Esk* sailed from Rosyth on 6 February in company with the large converted minelayer *Princess Victoria*, to lay the first part of this field, LD1. This lay was completed the following day. The two destroyers arrived at Aberdeen on 8 February, but the second part of this operation was delayed by thick fog.

Having blocked the northern end of the barrage, the *Princess Victoria*, *Esk* and *Express*, sailed again on 10 February to carry out similar operations, LD2 and LD3 further south, off Great Yarmouth. These defensive fields were laid without incident the following day.

As a further temporary measure, for the declared East Coast Barrage existed more on paper than in fact at this period of the war, a series of dummy minefields were laid by the same vessels, working under the auspices of Nore Command. Dummy mines were used initially, in order to avoid the need to sweep them up later on when the real minefields could be laid. Until that time, it was thought that the dummies would serve to keep the enemy out of our restricted area. These mines were specially laid so that they appeared on the surface at odd intervals at half-tide, when it was hoped that they would be sighted by the enemy or by neutral fishing boats who would report them. The appearance of a few of these 'floaters' would give the impression that more of the same were just under the surface and that the barrage was really substantial and to be avoided. Bluff always plays a large part in mine warfare.

These two fields were therefore laid along the eastern edge of the declared mine barrier in tow operations, code-named Operation LD3. Part one of this consisted of fifty-two dummy mines put down from position 53°53'N, 01°52'4"E, on a line of 135.5° for a length of 47.1 miles. Part two consisted of thirty-eight dummy mines laid from a point 52°48'N, 03°09'5"E, on a line 202° for a length of 34.2 miles. Both fields were laid in bitterly cold winter weather by the *Princess Victoria*, *Esk* and *Express*, on the nights of 11 and 13 February.

Although Captain Roskill in *The War at Sea*, states that the destroyer minelayers, '...did not return to minelaying until 3rd March,'[52] this is not the case. As we have shown, they were actively employed through the intervening period. In fact, a further operation of a similar defensive nature took place that month, Operation DML, with the *Esk*, *Express* and *Teviot Bank* being employed on the night of 18/19 February. Following the

---

[52] Roskill, Captain S W, *The War at Sea, Vol 1*, HMSO, London, 1954.

completion of this lay, the two destroyers joined the escort of convoy FS100 to take passage to Portsmouth, where they joined their newly converted brethren, *Icarus* and *Impulsive*, to prepare for yet another offensive sortie.

This sortie was Operation IE1, and the four minelaying destroyers conducted the lay on the night of 2/3 March. Some 240 mines, set to shallow depths, were laid in suspected enemy channels inside the German declared area, again without incident. Once more, all the ships returned to the Humber the following morning. The *Icarus* and *Impulsive* continued to assist in the laying of yet further defensive minefields. This pair sailed from the Humber for Invergordon on 7 March along with *Teviot Bank*. On 11 March, along with the minesweepers *Seagull* and *Sharpshooter* operating the skimming sweeps, they put down further deep anti-submarine fields, in Operation PA3. They returned to the Humber on 14 March and reloaded for the next mission.

On 16 March, *Princess Victoria, Teviot Bank, Esk, Express, Icarus* and *Impulsive* sailed to carry out Operation PA4, which was of a similar nature. This force left Invergordon on 20 March, each of the larger minelayers with two of the destroyers. On completion of the lay, all were to return to Immingham once more. However, after the mines were laid, these orders were changed. *Esk* and *Express* were diverted to hunt a suspected submarine contact, while the two big minelayers returned independently to Rosyth with *Icarus* and *Impulsive*, which later continued on to Scapa Flow.

The *Esk* picked up survivors from the sunken neutral Danish vessel, *Minsk*. However, the *Express* was involved in a collision with the Grimsby trawler *Manx Admiral* some ten miles off Kinnard Head on the morning of 23 March and sustained considerable damage to her stem. The *Express* was forced to put into Aberdeen for temporary repairs and was then sent south for more lasting work to be carried out at Hartlepool. She duly arrived here on 28 March. Meanwhile, *Icarus, Esk* and *Impulsive* returned to the Humber on 29 March and were joined by the *Ivanhoe* from Sheerness on 1 April. Momentous events were now in the offing.

The background to the ill-fated Norwegian Campaign has

been described often enough before. With regard to our story, the initial British response to the continued (and quite illegal) use by German ore-carrying ships of Norwegian territorial waters, the 'Inner Leads', had aroused the greatest indignation. The Norwegian Government were too frightened of upsetting the Germans, or losing their exports, to halt this traffic themselves. Churchill therefore took it upon himself to mine these waters and so force the enemy ships out into the open sea, where they could be intercepted by the Royal Navy. This minelaying campaign, Operation 'Wilfred', was expected to arouse retaliation from the Germans, and so troops were embarked aboard some of the cruisers of the Home Fleet in readiness to forestall any such counter-moves against Norwegian ports. Unknown to the British, the Germans had already decided to invade and occupy Norway themselves, to secure these vital supplies and provide air bases on Britain's flank. Both operations came to fruition almost simultaneously. We are only concerned here with the minelaying part of the complex story that resulted, for all the minelaying destroyers (save the damaged *Express*) were to be involved in its ramifications.

In brief, three separate minelaying forces were involved. Force 'WB' comprised the destroyers *Ivanhoe* and *Hostile*, which were to simulate the laying of one minefield off Bud (62°54'N, 6°55'E), but no mines were to be actually put into the water (*Hostile* was incapable of doing so of course). Force 'WS' comprised the *Teviot Bank*, escorted by the destroyers *Inglefield*, *Ilex*, *Imogen* and *Isis*. Force 'Ws' was to lay mines off Stadtlandet (62°N, 5°E) and Force 'WV', which consisted of the *Esk, Icarus, Impulsive* and *Ivanhoe*, escorted by the destroyers *Hardy, Hunter, Havock* and *Hotspur* was to lay mines off Hovden in Vestfiord. When it was reported that four Norwegian coast defence ships were concentrated at Narvik, the C-in-C, Home Fleet, despatched the battle-cruiser *Renown* (flying the flag of Vice-Admiral W J Whitworth), escorted by the destroyers *Hero, Hyperion, Glowworm* and *Greyhound*, to act in their support.

The original date for the operation to commence was 5 April, but a vacillating Government postponed it until the 8th, by which time the German invasion convoys were already at sea.

Force 'WV' had actually set sail from Scapa Flow for Sullom Voe in the Shetlands on 3 April. It was not until 6 April that they finally left that anchorage and headed north-east toward the Norwegian coast.

Table 9
Operation Wilfred. Area mined by Force 'WV'
8 April 1940

Area: Vestfiord. The area enclosed by the Norwegian coast and lines joining the following positions.

1	67° 24'40"N	14°34'00"E
2	67°27'30"N	14°24'00"E
3	67°28'55"N	14°06'45"E
4	67°33'55"N	13°51'30"E
5	67°37'55"N	14°02'15"E
6	67°26'20"N	14°38'30"E

12

LONG ODDS

Even before the 20th Flotilla had sailed, the Admiralty was made aware through intelligence reports that the Germans were already on the move. Even the fact that Norway was to be invaded reached them on 4 April. However, despite further reports of shipping movements, little was done to alter the limited British plan to encompass these new events. The minelaying destroyers duly joined company with the *Renown* and her escort in appalling weather early on 7 April. Save for the detachment of *Glowworm* from the squadron, in order to search for a man lost overboard in the heavy seas, nothing untoward took place to mar their progress.

The southern approaches to Vestfiord were reached on the same evening and the four minelayers were detached to carry out their task. Captain Cowie recorded:

> It was decided to invoke the 'military exigencies' clause of the Eight Hague Convention on account of the difficulty of predicting the conditions off the Norwegian coast with any accuracy. It would have been most un-desirable to issue the warning statement on the assumption that everything had gone according to plan, only to find that the minelaying had, in fact, been post-poned due to bad weather. The most elaborate arrangements were therefore made to inform the Admiralty that the first mine had been laid, and to pass this information on to our Legation in Oslo.[53]

[53] Cowie, *op. cit.*, p 144.

At dawn on 8 April, in the relatively sheltered waters of Vestfiord, Captain Bickford started to carry out his orders and the first mine was put down by the *Esk* at 04.30. Laying continued without interruption from the Norwegians. The Admiralty received the signal notifying the successful commencement of the lay at 04.45 and it was broadcast on the radio by 05.00. This remarkably efficient piece of work, unfortunately was not matched by events elsewhere. With the field laid, the 20th Flotilla commenced patrolling its perimeter to warn neutral shipping of its location. Meanwhile, *Renown* and her three remaining destroyers stayed out of sight, in case they were required to back them up.

All had so far proceeded according to plan, but this relatively peaceful situation was soon interrupted as events close by developed with alarming speed. The *Glowworm's* suicidal clash with the German heavy cruiser *Admiral Hipper;* the sailing of the Home Fleet to prevent an incorrectly assumed break-out by German heavy ships into the Atlantic; the sending of the battle-cruiser *Renown* and light cruiser *Penelope* to reinforce Admiral Whitworth; the first German landings ashore and the destruction of the surprised Norwegian defences; all followed with bewildering rapidity. It is no part of this volume to describe the events that followed in this ill-conducted campaign. Churchill was at his worst, and battles were fought, orders issued, countermanded and re-issued, troops disembarked, re-embarked and sent to the wrong ports and many opportunities to destroy virtually the whole German fleet, though fleeting, were generally lost. Suffice it to say that the minelaying destroyers had done their job well enough in the midst of this bedlam and confusion. Again, Captain Cowie recorded that, incredibly, '. . . in a statement published in the Press, the Germans saw fit to praise its technical excellence'.[54]

When the damaged *Admiral Hipper* and her accompanying destroyers (with troops aboard bound for Trondheim) parted company with the ten further destroyers also laden with

[54] *Ibid.*

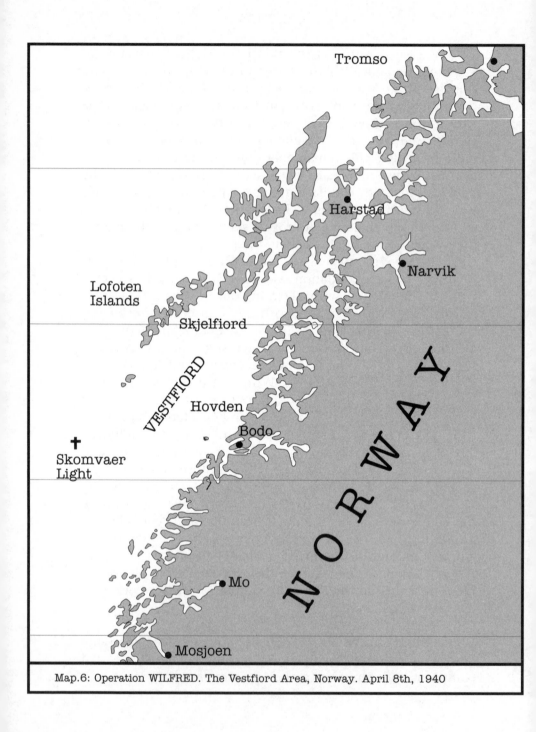

Tromso

Harstad

Narvik

Lofoten
Islands

Skjelfiord

VESTFIORD

Hovden

Bodo

NORWAY

✝
Skomvaer
Light

Mo

Mosjoen

Map.6: Operation WILFRED. The Vestfiord Area, Norway. April 8th, 1940

soldiers, and heading for Narvik via Vestfiord itself, it would seem that the enemy was steaming straight into the arms of the patrolling destroyers of the 2nd and 20th Flotillas. Of course, both sides were totally unaware of each others presence at the time. Instead, Admiral Whitworth had turned south with the *Renown* and three destroyers on receipt of *Glowworm*'s last brief signals before she was sunk, and Admiral Sir Charles Forbes sent *Repulse, Penelope* and four further destroyers to assist. However, the C-in-C was himself bypassed totally by Churchill, who took the unheard-of step of direct intervention over his head. The 2nd and 20th Flotillas were instructed to join Whitworth's flag, and the latter turned back north to meet them. Thus, the approaches to the vital port of Narvik were left totally unguarded at this critical juncture.

The minelayers and Captain Warburton-Lee's destroyers duly rendezvoused with *Renown*, which by now only had a single destroyer left in company, off the Skomvaer Light at 17.15 in filthy weather and a rising gale. An incorrect report had meanwhile placed the *Admiral Hipper* and her force steering westward, away from Trondheim, when in truth, the *exact reverse* was the case. Admiral Whitworth had insufficient evidence in front of him at that time to be certain that the invasion of Norway was indeed taking place. He therefore decided, as Admiral Forbes had done earlier, to head out to sea in case the enemy fleet was breaking out into the Atlantic, as they had done once before. Thus a second chance of effecting a concentration of British warships to bar the port of Narvik to the enemy, was abandoned and the minelaying destroyers found themselves clawing out to sea once more in terrible conditions, during the darkness (in more ways than one) of the evening of 8 April.

In the absence of any British force to prevent them, the ten German destroyers steamed through Vestfiord unscathed. They overwhelmed the Norwegian coast defence ships defending Narvik, and landed their troops unopposed. Out at sea, a full gale had developed from the NNW, in which just keeping in contact with each other was a more than sufficient task for the little destroyers. At 03.37 the next morning, the *Renown* sighted the German battle-cruisers *Gneisenau* and

Scharnhorst. Despite the odds being two to one against her, she unhesitatingly engaged them. She hit the German flagship as the Germans fled the scene, driving them before her into the storm. The British destroyers attempted to join in the action with their 4.7-inch guns, but had nothing like the range to be of any use. However, the flashes from their puny weapons added additional speed to the German battle-cruisers' hasty flight and all three heavy ships were soon lost to sight in the spray, spindrift and half-light. In the interim, the Admiralty had decided that the invasion of Norway was, after all, on the cards, and signalled Admiral Whitworth: 'Most Immediate. Concentrate on preventing any German force proceeding to Narvik.' Whitworth was fully engaged with the enemy big ships and the Admiralty signal was merely a classic case of shutting the stable door that it had opened, well after the horse had cantered out!

Already, the 2nd and 20th Flotillas had been ordered to do just this by Admiral Whitworth, as they clearly had no hope of keeping up with the running battle in the prevailing weather and sea conditions. Thankfully, all nine destroyers reversed their helms and headed back eastward to their former patrol positions. *En route,* Captain Warburton-Lee received orders from the C-in-C that he was to send some of his destroyers, '. . . to Narvik to make certain that no enemy troops land', but of course, they were already ashore. Further direct intervention from the First Lord followed at noon, when Captain Warburton-Lee was ordered to sink or capture German transports now lying at Narvik.

Given these quite clear instructions by his superiors (who did not have the slightest idea of the actual strength of the enemy force at that time), the commander of the 2nd Flotilla decided to take his four ships, *Hardy, Hotspur, Havock* and *Hunter,* later providentially joined by *Hostile,* up to Narvik to investigate the situation. Captain Bickford was left with the 20th Flotilla vessels to continue the watch on the approaches to the minefield and the patrolling of the entrance to Vestfiord. They applied themselves to this task throughout 9 April in poor visibility and continual snow storms, while the 2nd Flotilla steamed into history at the First Battle of Narvik. Only three of the five British destroyers were fated to return. None of the minelayers was engaged in this battle, but the 20th Flotilla was represented when, on 13 April, the battleship *Warspite* with nine destroyers, one of them the *Icarus*, returned to the fiords and totally wiped out the eight remaining enemy destroyers and a skulking U-boat. For this engagement, the Second Battle of Narvik, *Icarus* made good use of her bow para-vanes to clear a passage for the battleship in case the Germans had used the time in-between to mine the fiord, but no such initiative had occurred to them.

So, with her solitary 'B' gun mounting forward in action as she went, *Icarus* led the British force to victory. For the remainder of the 20th Flotilla, however, more prosaic duties awaited. The confused events that followed, saw them thrown into action as conventional destroyers wherever they were required and no further minelaying duties occupied them during the campaign. The *Icarus* herself was to arrive back at Scapa Flow on 17 April with *Esk*, *Ivanhoe* and *Greyhound* as escort to the battleship *Rodney*. The three minelaying destroyers then sailed the following day for Immingham, arriving on 19 April. The next day, *Icarus* and *Ivanhoe* were back at Rosyth. From that port, with the destroyers *Impulsive*, *Campbell*, *Witch* and *Witherington* they sailed on 22 April, escorting the light cruisers *Glasgow* and *Sheffield* to carry out Operation Sickle 2, the evacuation of British troops from Aandalsnes. This showed the way the land campaign was going wrong. This duty done, again the three minelayers sailed for Immingham, arriving on 25 April, but sailing again the next day.

Meanwhile the *Intrepid* had completed her repairs (after the collision with the trawler *Ocean Drift* on 17 March) and left Middlesborough for Immingham. Here, she joined *Express*, her own collision repairs completed, and *Esk*, and the three ships sailed for Scapa Flow on 29 April. The two sections of minelaying destroyers now interchanged continually. 'Bernard' Brotheridge, serving aboard *Impulsive* at this time, recalls laying mines off Trondheim on the night of 29/30 April. On 1 May, *Express*, *Esk* and *Intrepid* left Scapa Flow again, to replace *Icarus*, *Impulsive* and *Ivanhoe*, and, on the 5 May, once more sailed from Immingham to Scapa Flow. Next day these same three ships left Scapa Flow to return to Immingham once more, under orders to carry out boiler cleaning and await further orders on completion. They arrived at their home base on 7 May and were joined by *Princess Victoria* and *Teviot Bank*.

The news from Norway continued to be uniformly bad. However, it was overtaken by the first of many even greater disasters, which began to overtake Western Europe as the Germans opened their *Blitzkrieg* against Denmark, Holland, Belgium, Luxembourg and France on 10 May. Urgent work was now at hand for the 20th Flotilla. A plan was already in existence for laying a minefield off the Dutch coast in the event of a German occupation of that country. This was to give the evacuating ships some additional protection in such an eventuality. The *Princess Victoria* was held in reserve but, when the expected invasion did take place while half the destroyer force was boiler cleaning, she was at once pressed into service.

The *Express, Esk* and *Intrepid* were, in fact, already at sea on a minelaying mission, Operation XMO, which had taken them back to their old haunts in the Heligoland Bight. Here, on the night of 9/10 May, they laid 180 mines in the enemy-swept channel once more. While on their way back to the Humber, they received orders to take over the escort of the *Princess Victoria* from the coastal corvettes *Puffin, Sheldrake* and *Widgeon*, and escort her back to the coast of Holland immediately. This was complied with, and during the forenoon, *Princess Victoria* reported her intended movements and that she expected to commence her lay at 21.15 that same night. This information was duly passed on by the Admiralty to all ships and the British Naval Attaché at The Hague, which prevented her being engaged by the Dutch coastal batteries. She actually commenced laying at 21.07 and there were no interruptions. The whole force returned safely to Immingham at 09.30 on 11 May after a perfect operation. A total of 236 mines were laid off Egmond that night.

With the Low Countries falling to the Panzer / Stuka combination in quick succession, it was obvious that further stern work lay ahead of the 20th Flotilla in these same waters. On 12 May the three destroyers were out again, returning the same night. Operation 'BS4' was carried out on the 14 May, again with the same three ships, and the *Princess Victoria*. By this date, *Impulsive* and *Ivanhoe* were once more ready for duty. Bernard Brotheridge gave the Author this eyewitness account of events:

I joined HMS *Impulsive* in early May 1940. Three of us left Portsmouth Barracks and after travelling to Scapa, we were told the *Impulsive* was now at Immingham near Grimsby and we retraced our steps and eventually arrived at Immingham Dock. HMS *Impulsive* was lying alongside the jetty being loaded on her upper deck with sea mines, and we found on going aboard that *Impulsive* was engaged in laying mines anywhere in the North Sea. We were the first 'Hostilities Only' ratings to join the ship, the rest of the crew being regulars. Our Commanding Officer at that time was Lieutenant Commander Thomas and with his black beard and his undoubted qualities he reminded me of Sir Francis Drake and *Impulsive* was a happy and efficient ship.

Immingham Dock seemed a desolate place, all the ships berthed in the inner basin which was connected to the Humber by a lock. The sheds were full of mines, for apart from the six destroyers of the 20th Flotilla, there were two large converted merchant ships, HMS *Princess Victoria* and HMS *Teviot Bank*, who we were to escort at various times to lay the East Coast Mine Barrier and other fields.

We sailed next day on my first trip to lay mines at night on the other side of the North Sea, and this pattern continued during the next three weeks. Usually the destroyers left the Humber in daylight, at times we were delayed because the Humber Estuary had been subjected to German air minelaying operations and we had to wait for the minesweepers to perform their functions. There were a few wrecks at the mouth of the Humber where previous German mines had proved effective. We were always alert during daylight hours and it was quite unnerving to come across lone German aircraft as nobody looked forward to a bombing attack when carrying sixty mines!

As we approached our dropping zone at night, 'Action Stations' were sounded as there was always the chance of coming across German E-boats. The mining party unshackled the mines and they were dropped one by one by each destroyer; five destroyers usually operated together as one often remained behind each week for boiler cleaning.

For our own defence we had our 'B' and 'X' guns only, two .05 machine-guns, a Lewis gun on the searchlight platform and, after July 1940, a 3-inch anti-aircraft gun amidships in place of one of our sets of torpedo tubes. I remember at times helping to unshackle the mines as we approached the dropping area; it seemed to me to be quietly done and I cannot recall any undue noise, the mines seemed to glide down the rails very easily. We concentrated on our own minelaying and the other ships with us, as far as I was concerned, seemed very remote. During all the minelaying I did from *Impulsive*, we never once encountered any German opposition. We had no radar at that time and probably the Germans hadn't either so I guess we were lucky not to have been suddenly discovered.[55]

On 15 May the *Express, Esk, Intrepid, Impulsive* and *Ivanhoe* sailed from Immingham for the coast of Holland once again. While *Intrepid* added her sixty mines to the Egmond field, guarded by *Impulsive*, the three other destroyers laid a new field of 164 mines off the Hook of Holland. All the ships returned safely to port the next morning. It is now known that the German Navy lost no fewer than three modern minesweepers on this particular minefield, the *M61, M89* and *M136* on 26 July, a most happy outcome for one night's work.

Their next sortie to Holland was less fortunate. The flotilla was again accompanying the *Princess Victoria* for this job,

[55] Mr T E Brotheridge to the Author on 26 November 1979 and 2 December 1979.

Operation 'BS5', *and Express, Esk, Intrepid, Impulsive* and *Ivanhoe* sailed with that ship on 18 May. George Mack described the operation, and the outcome:

> At dawn we found ourselves almost alongside the sea wall which runs along the coast of Holland and watched the *Princess Victoria* steam almost up to the wall before turning westward. As she started to lay her mines one of our flotilla turned with her and laid a parallel line. As each destroyer completed her quota, another took her place so we finished up with two long lines of mines from the sea wall out to sea for several miles.
>
> When it was all completed and the mines laid, the destroyers formed a screen round the *PV* and we hurried to get back to safer waters before the German Air Force came after us; but in fact, they were very busy with the invasion of the Low Countries and battering the Allied armies. When we reached the Cromer light and swung round to steam northward up the swept channel, it was decided to send two of the escorts on ahead so that we could get through the locks at Immingham before the rest arrived.
>
> So *Impulsive* and *Intrepid* increased to thirty knots and soon reached the Humber and were through the lock and in the basin by 06.30. No sooner had we completed securing alongside, than the call came for 'All hands to stations for leaving harbour!', and the buzz went round that the *Princess Victoria* had blown up! Within five minutes the order was cancelled and we heard that the *Princess Victoria* had indeed sunk.[56]

The unfortunate ship had, in fact, herself been mined in a position one mile south-east of the Humber Light Vessel, and was resting on the bottom. She lost four officers, including her captain, and thirty-three men. The rest were picked up by her accompanying destroyers and landed safely. But this loss caused no slackening of effort on the part of the 20th Flotilla.

---

[56] Mack, *HMS Intrepid, op cit*, pps 109–10.

Europe was rapidly collapsing in chaos and as the friendly shoreline shrank day-by-day, so did the calls to lay minefields off the newly conceded territory facing the British coast increase.

A whole further series of minelaying operations was undertaken in the following week. For these, *Express, Esk, Intrepid, Impulsive* and *Ivanhoe* were once more joined by *Icarus*. These destroyers carried out Operation BS6 on the night of 21/22 May, followed on the night of 23/24 May by BS7, on 25/26 May by BS8 and, finally, on the night of 27/28 May by BS9. These operations were all mine lays off the Dutch coast.

This intense work was interrupted by a much larger disaster ashore. With the utter rout and collapse of the Dutch, Belgian and then French armies, the small British Expeditionary Force (BEF) was left trapped around Dunkirk. Every available destroyer was called upon to take part in their rescue. The evacuation from Dunkirk has since become legend. Every one of the 20th Flotilla destroyers took part in Operation *Dynamo*, despite Admiralty reservations about using such relatively modern ships in so risky a venture. Their fears were justified, for all the minelaying destroyers, save the *Esk*, were damaged to some degree or other by the German dive-bombers operating almost unhindered over the beaches and embarkation points. Fortunately, none of these valuable vessels was seriously damaged, but it was some time before all rejoined the flotilla at Immingham after repairs and refits. During this period, the opportunity was taken to equip them all with a single 3-inch HA gun and other light weapons as some small measure of protection against air attack. Meanwhile, limited mining operations were gradually resumed and increased in scope as the flotilla built up to full strength once more.

With the surrender of the French, the whole of the European coastline, from the North Cape of Norway to the Spanish border, lay open to their nocturnal ventures. The most pressing need was to lay minefields, both offensive and defensive, to counter the expected German invasion of England, which most people (but *not* Admiral Forbes) expected would follow within a few weeks.

Naturally, the incomplete East Coast Barrage, was now seen

as one of the first lines of defence against such invasion fleets, and not just as a handy protection for our coastal convoys. Work began in May in earnest to try to make this barrage more of a reality than it had hitherto been. To replaced the large *Princess Victoria*, the smaller coastal minelayer *Plover* arrived at Immingham. She was later joined by the Dutch minelayer *Willem van de Zaan*, which had escaped the carnage and had been fitted with British broad-gauge mine rails in a British port. The destroyers of the 20th Flotilla took part in many operations with these two ships on the Barrage reinforcement, laying a whole series of BS fields in conjunction with them during June, July and August 1940. These defensive lays were interspaced with the odd foray futher afield into more dangerous waters for offensive lays on their own.

These operations were numerous. On 15 June, *Teviot Bank* and *Plover* laid minefield BS15 with *Express* and *Intrepid*, arriving back at Immingham the following day. The same two minelayers, escorted this time by *Esk* and *Intrepid*, laid BS16 on the night of 18/19 June, while *Intrepid* and *Icarus*, escorted by *Esk* and *Express*, laid 'BS17' on 21/22. These same four destroyers escorted *Teviot Bank* and *Plover* on the night of 24/25 June to carry out BS18. Many of these fields were laid to close the 'gates' in the East Coast Barrage, with short-term sinkers that opened them again after a brief interval. Mainly, however, they were desperately attempting to fill in the many holes that still remained in the largely paper plan of the Barrage.

On the night of 28/29 June, *Express*, *Icarus* and *Intrepid* carried out Operation BS19 and the destroyers *Javelin* and *Jupiter* of Lord Louis Mountbatten's 5th Flotilla were withdrawn from their anti-invasion patrols to provide an escort into hostile waters. These ships always kept to the westward of the danger zones, while the 20th Flotilla ships passed through to carry out their dangerous work. June gave way to July and the pace quickened as the German hold on the Continent tightened. Across the narrow English Channel, massed *Stuka* attacks were pounding the coastal convoys in the Dover Straits, hitting one ship in every three that attempted to run the gauntlet. These dive-bombers also decimated the 4th Destroyer Flotilla based at Dover as the first line of defence against invasion convoys. However, off the east coast the 5th and 20th Flotillas were comparatively undisturbed, although the *Luftwaffe* was a constant threat.

On 1 July, *Express, Icarus* and *Intrepid* escorted *Plover* and *Teviot Bank* to lay minefield BS20. On 6 July, the latter ship, this time with *Esk* and *Intrepid*, carried out the laying of BS22, returning to Immingham on 8 July. And so it continued with little respite. Minefield BS23 was put down by *Teviot Bank, Express* and *Esk* between 10 and 11 July; BS24 by *Express* and *Impulsive* on 18/19 July and BS25 by *Esk, Icarus,* and *Intrepid* on 19 July.

There was little to occupy the ships' companies at Immingham dock during the brief free moments between returning from one sortie, loading and preparing for the next one, as Bernard Brotheridge recalled later:

> There was nothing much to do on our days in Immingham and we used to spend our off-duty hours 'enjoying' the somewhat tawdry flesh-pots of Grimsby![57]

George Mack has similar memories.

> Immingham was a fine, modern port, built mainly to handle ships bringing timber from Scandinavia and the Baltic. The basin was almost square, with rows of cranes standing like flamingos along each wall. This made it such an ideal base for the minelayers as these cranes could quickly load a ship, using up to as many as four cranes simultaneously.
>
> In taking over this dock, we also took over the superb railway canteen, which not only had the longest bar I've ever seen, but was stocked with a remarkable variety of beers from all their previous customers' countries.
>
> Every night in harbour, the 'non-duty' half of the watch aboard was allowed Canteen Leave from when they had completed loading mines, or from 18.30 to 22.00 hours. In this time one could sample beers from

[57] Brotheridge to the Author, *op. cit.*

half-a-dozen different countries. I never tasted every type but made a valiant effort.[58]

On 20 July, *Express*, *Esk*, *Icarus*, *Intrepid* and *Impulsive* laid minefield BS26. On 24/25 July BS27 was laid by *Icarus*, *Intrepid* and *Impulsive*, while, two days later, the whole flotilla, less *Ivanhoe*, laid BS28. *Plover* and *Willem Van de Zaan* joined *Esk*, *Intrepid* and *Impulsive* for the laying of BS29 on 29/30 July. On 1 August, all six destroyers were present, with both minelayers, in the laying of BS32, sailing from Immingham at 22.00 that night. Smaller fields were laid in connection with the East Coast Barrage later in August – BS34 by *Esk*, *Icarus* and *Impulsive* on 24/25 August; BS35 by *Express*, *Esk* and *Icarus* on 26/27 August; and BS36 by *Intrepid* and *Icarus* on 28/29 August. An unexpected hazard was encountered on their homeward voyage from one of these missions, as George Mack was to relate:

By now at Immingham, we knew every part of the dock area. First, there was the small pier, which stuck out into the River Humber to allow small ships to unload without needing to enter the lock. Mostly these were the ferry boats, which brought dock workers, or passengers, from Hull on the other side, and a bit further up-river. This pier was not solid masonry but built of wooden piles driven into the riverbed, on which was built a wooden deck, which was about fifteen feet above the water at high tide. On it were also built a couple of shelters for passengers and a hut for the railway Pier Master. The River Humber is a very fast-flowing river when in full ebb tide, and can ebb at about seven knots. We got to know all about this pier and the current, due to a very close inspection we once gave it, under conditions which could easily have led to one of the major disasters of the war.

We had left Immingham with a full load of mines with one other ship of the flotilla [*Icarus*], but when we reached the other side of the North Sea we found that it

[58] Mack, *HMS* Intrepid, *op. cit.*, pp 125–26.

was too rough to lay the mines, as the waves were too high. We had to abandon the operation and bring them back to Immingham. We came up the Humber in the later afternoon, and though the tide was ebbing fast, it was decided that we could enter the lock and unload the mines which were of a special type.

As we came level with the lock gate, which had the outer gate open, we turned towards the entrance and started to enter the lock. Unfortunately, we made a slight miscalculation of course so that while the bow was in the still water of the lock our stern was swinging rapidly downstream. The Captain decided to have another go, and rang down for 'Half Astern' so to pull back into the river and try again. But something went wrong and we found our stern swinging into the jetty! When the ship started to go ahead it was too late and we were too much out of line to get into the lock, and too late to miss the jetty.

Our experienced eyes soon realised that we were in a very shaky position, as unless there was an instant reversal of the tide, nothing was going to stop us hitting the jetty. We also realised that when we hit the jetty that the deck was well above our hull and we were going to smash the very rotten looking piles and the stern would almost certainly pass under the pier.

It did not take a lot of working out that when we hit the piles the weakest part, which was underwater, would break at the bottom, but still be fixed at the top. This meant that as we drove under the pier the piles would overhang the mines, and knock them over, and mines are not keen on that sort of treatment!

I was up on the forecastle, looking at, and like every one else, holding my breath wondering what was going to happen in about two minutes time, as an explosion of one mine would almost certainly cause a sympathy explosion in the next, and if the whole sixty went off so close to the mine sheds ashore, they might also go off, which would make a mighty big hole where Immingham was now and probably Hull as well.

31. Disaster in the 'Bight. *Jupiter* with the damaged *Express* in tow and surrounded by
    tugs, with a *Hunt* class destroyer astern, as seen from the *Kelvin* during the long
    voyage to safety. *(Imperial War Museum, London)*.
32. Disaster in the 'Bight. *Ivanhoe*: listing to port and low in the water after her mine
    damage, with the destroyer *Garth* (*right*) standing by her.
    (Imperial War Museum, London).

32a. The body of Captain J.G. Bickford, DSO, RN, who died aboard HMS *Express* after the disaster in the Bight, aboard the auxilliary vessel that took him to sea for burial. The armed guard at the ceremony. *(Imperial War Museum, London)*.

33. *Impulsive*: a 1941 photograph showing her as she appeared during her final days as a minelaying destroyer before joining the Home Fleet in a conventional role. She has now shipped her full main armament, but her mine traps aft are readily evident, as is the boom abreast her bridge structure and the davit amidships. *(Imperial War Museum, London).*

34. *Icarus*: this photograph shows her in 1942, after being fully reconverted back to conventional destroyer configuration. Full gun armament is shipped as are also one set of torpedo tubes, a 3-inch HA gun in place of the after bank of tubes plus light AA weapons. All mine rails, booms and winches have now been discarded and put ashore into depots, and TSDS minesweeping equipment replaces her minelaying gear aft, only her tell-tale sponsons remain to indicate her former duties.

(Ministry of Defence, Navy).

35. *Opportune*: this 1951 photograph shows her serving in her training role. Her minelaying sponsons aft are clearly shown, as is Taunt Wire Measuring Gear on a drum in front of the 40-mm Bofors AA gun on her quarterdeck. She carries a highly unconventional armament for training purposes, with, in addition to the Bofors in 'Y' position, another in place of the after bank of torpedo tubes (with totally restricted sky arcs both fore and aft) and a quadruple pom-pom abaft the funnel.

(Ministry of Defence, Navy).

36. *Obedient*: featured here post-war (1952) but still carrying her destroyer pendants. She is fitted out for minelaying with all torpedo tubes landed, a 40-mm Bofors in 'Y' position and the mine sponsons aft, together with winches and associated gear.
(Ministry of Defence, Navy).

37. *Orwell*: a 1953 photograph after she had been reduced to a frigate (F98), with a mainly anti-submarine role, but still retaining her original classic destroyer lines and the mine chutes aft.
(Ministry of Defence, Navy).

38. *Contest*: this photograph was taken during a visit to Hamburg in the late 1950s and shows her in her minelaying configuration. Both banks of torpedo tubes and both after guns have been put ashore and a large deckhouse has been fitted aft, together with extra winches fitted either side of the iron deck abaft the funnel.

(Schiffsfotos C. Jeske, Hamburg).

39. *Comet*: as a minelayer in 1957, she still retains her anti-submarine capability unimpaired with the twin Squid mortar and handling deckhouse. Her light AA armament has been much reduced and both after gun mountings and torpedo tubes have gone. In this aerial view her mine rails can be clearly seen and she has had four mines visible on their sinkers. *(Ministry of Defence, Navy).*

40. *Chaplet*: in her later days but still with her minelaying potential in evidence as this photograph taken of her in 1957 illustrates.   *(Ministry of Defence, Navy).*

41. *Comet*: also in her later days.   *(Ministry of Defence, Navy).*

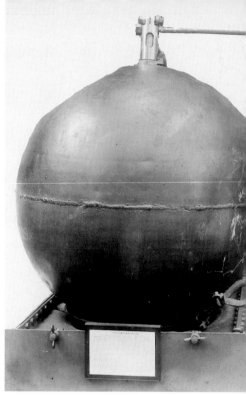

42 & 43. British *Elia* mine. *(Imperial War Museum, London)*.

44 & 45. Mk XIV mine on trolley. *(Imperial War Museum, London)*.

There was nothing we could do except to whisper a fervent prayer, as the jetty steadily got closer. But things could get worse, and when we were about ten feet off, the Pier Master came out of his little hut and shouted, 'Captain, whatever you do, don't hit the jetty, we've just mined it!'

This was the final straw for while we had some faith in the safety devices built into the Naval mines we were far from sure of all the amateurs who were fitting 'Anti-invasion' devices to anywhere they thought might be harmful to an invader.

Finally we hit. The ship went under the jetty, with wooden piles splintering and hitting our mines, knocking them off their sinkers. Eventually we ground to a standstill and remained jammed under the jetty until the tide changed and a tug managed to pull us out. Most of us collected a few more grey hairs that day, and the canteen sold a record amount of beer that night.[59]

The *Impulsive* was due for a boiler clean at Hull at this time. The flotilla's next major operation, the laying of an offensive minefield off the Dutch coast, Operation CBX5, was scheduled to take place with the remaining five destroyers only, on the night of 31 August / 1 September. Events were now moving to a climax, with the invasion scares reaching a peak and the Battle of Britain dominating the air over south-east England. By now, the 20th Flotilla was reaching the peak of its performance. Hopes were high that this operation would play as equally a valuable role in defence of the homeland, as the exploits of the RAF fighter pilots, albeit even if it were unsung and unknown to all but a handful of people in Whitehall.

[59] Mack, *HMS* Intrepid, *op. cit.*, pp 123–4.

13

A TRAGEDY RE-ENACTED

The 20th Flotilla sailed to carry out Operation CBX5 on the evening of 31 August. Their laying zone was close to the Dutch coast in the heart of enemy-controlled waters. Tension was high in Britain, with the expected German invasion appearing to be imminent, and this fact was to have the most tragic results for the destroyers. Captain Bickford in the *Express*, had in company for this mission the *Intrepid, Ivanhoe, Esk* and *Icarus*. All these ships commenced streaming their paravanes just before they reached the vicinity of the Cromer Light, in readiness for crossing over to the Texel.

Acting in support of the minelaying destroyers on this operation was the 5th Flotilla under Captain Lord Louis Mountbatten. He was embarked aboard the *Jupiter* and had *Kelvin* and *Vortigern* in company. These three destroyers also sailed from the Humber at 19.45; their job was to mark Gap 'D' for the minelayers and act in direct support if required. The 5th Flotilla reached the area between the Outer Dowsing Light Float and the 62E buoy at 22.00 and commenced patrolling. Mountbatten planned to carry out a searchlight exercise but the constant presence of German aircraft overhead in the darkness, prevented this. It was also planned that the 5th Flotilla would pass the Outer Dowsing Light Float at 02.20/1 and then proceed at high speed to be in position to mark the eastern end of Gap 'D' by 04.30 to help the minelayers locate it on their return.

Meanwhile, the 20th Flotilla was experiencing some difficulties of their own. The *Intrepid's* paravanes fouled up early on and she fell behind while her companions pressed on. Eventually, after some considerable effort, Commander Gordon ordered them to be cut free. With this done, and unprotected, the *Intrepid* steamed at maximum speed to catch up with her flotilla mates.

However, German minelayers were also astir in those water that night. A large operation had been planned for the laying of an extensive minefield to guard the seaward approaches to the Dutch coast in order to protect this area and the German convoys that now regularly plied it. The German Officer Commanding, Minelayers, Captain Bentlage, therefore put to sea that evening to conduct the first phase of this operation, SW3, his force sailing from Cuxhaven to Rotterdam to commence preparations. He had under his command the minelayers *Cobra*, *Roland* and *Tannenberg*. They were escorted by the 2nd Torpedo Boat (small destroyers) Flotilla, under Commander Riede with the *T-5*, *T-6*, *T-7* and *T-8*, and the 5th Torpedo Boat Flotilla, *Falke*, *Greif*, *Iltis* and *Jaguar*. These ships were joined in the actual laying operations by the large destroyers *Erich Steinbrinck*, *Karl Galster* and *Paul Jacobi*, all of which had conducted a whole series of successful minelaying operations off the British coast in exactly the same manner as had the 20th Flotilla off their own, during the previous ten months.

It is ironic that much of the work of the German destroyer-minelayers earlier in the war, had gone undetected and they had accounted for a large number of British ships without themselves being located or identified. This movement on 31 August however, *was* detected very early on by patrolling British aircraft. The sighting reports were received between 21.52 and 22.22 through the Whitehall W/T station and also by the *Kelvin*, which was keeping W/T watch for the British forces at sea. No. 206 Squadron, RAF, had aircraft in the area on watch for any enemy surface forces that might indicate the long-awaited invasion was underway. These reports of several large mercantile-like ships with a very powerful destroyer escort, naturally raised some alarm at the Admiralty.

Aboard the *Jupiter*, Mountbatten was, for a time, worried lest the RAF was in fact reporting not an enemy force, but the 20th Flotilla, a not uncommon occurrence! The course reported in these sightings appeared to be reciprocal but he later reported:

I considered the possibility of closing the 20th Destroyer Flotilla, in case these reports turned out to be of a separate enemy force, after all, but as they were about 100 miles from me, and steaming away from me at a speed probably greater than *Vortigern* [an old 'V & W' class ship] could keep station at, I decided to adhere to the arrangement whereby I was to mark Gap 'D' for their return. Your 22.11/31 (received at 22.40/1) was incorrectly received as indication to me that No. 206 Squadron (RAF) was endeavouring to locate and make a night attack on this enemy force, and caused some concern at the time in case our own minelayers might be attacked by them.[60]

By now, the Admiralty had convinced itself that what was taking place over on the other side of the North Sea was some sort of invasion convoy sailing. They decided it must be intercepted as the highest priority. Accordingly, at 23.13 Captain Bickford was instructed to jettison his mines at once and take the 20th Flotilla immediately to attack the enemy force. However, events had already overtaken this signal. At this time the flotilla was some forty miles north-west of the Texel.

The *Intrepid* had managed to catch up with the rest of the flotilla, but had not yet resumed her normal place as second ship in the line. At 23.00, the flotilla was running at a speed of 24 knots on a course 189°. The *Express*, as usual, was leading the line and running her taunt wire gear, while the *Ivanhoe* and *Esk*, fine of her port quarter, ran clear of the wire. *Intrepid*, also running her taunt wire gear, and *Icarus*, were following these leading ships some four cables astern.

At 23.05 the port paravane of the *Ivanhoe* fouled an obstruction and was carried away. Almost immediately, a heavy explosion occurred off her port quarter, resembling that of a mine. Almost at once another explosion rocked the line; at 23.07 *Express* struck another mine. It was clear that the flotilla had run into an unknown German defensive minefield.

---

[60] Captain (D) 5 and 20th Flotilla Report of Proceedings, 31 August – 2 September 1940, dated 20 September 1940.

Events now took place with confusing rapidity. The explosion in *Express* warned *Intrepid* and *Icarus* of the grave danger ahead of them. Orders for this much-feared type of incident were explicit; no danger should be courted by any other ship of the flotilla unnecessarily. *Ivanhoe* and *Esk* were close to their leader and appeared to be standing by her, so *Intrepid* and *Icarus* at once reduced speed and turned violently away to starboard. Commander Gordon now faced the same dilemma that his First World War predecessor had faced. Reluctant to leave his stricken companions, but aware that it was the correct course of action, he called to *Esk*, who was closing the *Express*, but failed to get a reply. He therefore took *Icarus* under his command and both destroyers retired at 24 knots through position 53°30'N, 3°25'E at 00.01 on 1 September.

It will be convenient here to follow their subsequent movements before returning to the scene of the tragedy. *Intrepid* had got away a report, at 23.59, that the *Express* had been mined and that *Ivanhoe* and *Esk* were standing by her. At 01.15, while retiring westward, *Intrepid* picked up further signals from *Ivanhoe*, timed at 00.50, reporting the mining both of herself and of the *Esk*. Again, Commander Gordon was faced with an appalling decision. Should he endeavour to regain contact with the mined ships or should he continue to extract his undamaged destroyers to safety, as per standing orders. At 01.37, any doubts were happily resolved for he received a further Admiralty signal, which stated that nine MTBs were on their way to rescue survivors. This information was reinforced by the Admiralty signal timed at 01.31, which warned that no ships were to enter the mined area. *Intrepid* and *Icarus* therefore continued their retirement to the Humber, proceeding via Flamborough Head, and duly arrived back at Immingham safely.

Captain Mountbatten with his three destroyers, had also been in receipt of these, and other, signals. The Admiralty signal timed at 00.05/1, which corrected the earlier 22.11/31, was taken in by *Jupiter* at 00.13. It was then realised that the Admiralty intention was for the 5th Flotilla to join the 20th Flotilla in the attack on the suspected invasion force. Mountbatten reported:

At this time, I was in the vicinity of 62 Buoy, and I
immediately made for Gap 'D' at the maximum speed at
which *Vortigern* could keep station, twenty-three knots.
On the way, some very large flashes were seen to the
southward, but clear of the land. As it was now clear that
enemy forces were active, the possibility that invading
forces might be the cause of these flashes could not be
discounted, so I decided to 'march to the sound of the
guns'. As no further sign of gunfire was observed, I
turned northward on reaching 59 Buoy, still main-
taining my speed, and set course for the Gap via the
Outer Dowsing Light Float.[61]

The true and grim meaning of those 'large flashes' became only
too apparent when, at 00.35, the *Intrepid*'s 23.59 signal was
received, reporting that the *Express* had been mined in position
53°25'N, 03°48'E. Thirty-five minutes later, *Ivanhoe*'s signal of
00.50 was also received, reporting that the same fate had
befallen her and *Esk* in the same position.

Although it was now obvious that the three minelayers were
in a bad state, the *Intrepid*'s signal seemed to Captain
Mountbatten to indicate that she and *Icarus* were retiring. He
considered his first action must be to mark the Gap in case
these two ships wished to use that route. Therefore, the 5th
Flotilla continued in that direction. His decision not to venture
further in beyond the Gap was confirmed by the same
Admiralty signals received by *Intrepid*, with their unambiguous
instructions not to do so.

The rest of the night was not completely uneventful for the
5th Flotilla, however. At 02.10, they sighted a darkened ship
and illuminated it. The *Jupiter*'s searchlight attracted the attention of another cripple. A Fleet Air Arm Fairey Swordfish had
been bombing Rotterdam that night. The crew, Lieutenant (A)
H Shaw and Sub-Lieutenant Phillips, RNVR, from No. 812
Squadron based at North Coates, were in grave trouble. Their
compass was defective and they had run out of fuel. Seeing the
light in the middle of the black North Sea must have seemed

---

[61] *Ibid.*

miraculous. They ditched close alongside *Jupiter* and were quickly taken aboard. As Captain Mountbatten later recalled: 'They reported to me on the bridge, in monkey jacket and stiff collar, quite unperturbed.' On a night that brought sudden death to so many, their survival was a tiny bonus.

At 02.53, the 5th Flotilla passed the Outer Dowsing Light Float. At 05.05, they arrived in position 53°38'N, 02°23'E, at the eastern end of Gap 'D'. Here, they laid a dan buoy to guide the *Intrepid* and *Icarus* home. The three destroyers then patrolled in the vicinity of this buoy. An Admiralty signal timed at 01.57 ordering them to return to base, was not received until 08.46, but merely confirmed Mountbatten's decision to do just that if no ships had appeared by 07.00. But, before this order could be complied with, further events involved them in mercy work and yet more danger.

We will now return to the stricken *Express* and her ill-fated companions. Immediately after the first explosion, her whaler was lowered into the water and was quickly filled with men. Nonetheless, the boat stayed in the vicinity of the ship to ascertain whether any more men could be taken off. Once they observed that Carley floats were being lowered, they decided to make for the nearest destroyer, *Esk*, in the hope of boarding her.

The mining and stopping of *Express* immediately in front of her, coupled with her own explosion close by, caused *Ivanhoe* to pass up her leader's port side at some speed. She then checked, and passed under the stern of the *Express* in order to go alongside her starboard side. The *Esk* was then observed stopped close astern of *Express*. She hailed the *Ivanhoe*, reporting that there were men in the water. While the two ships were alongside, a few ratings transferred from the *Express* to the *Ivanhoe*, before the two destroyers drifted apart again. *Ivanhoe* put her whaler into the water and also dropped Carley floats in order to rescue some of the men swimming.

Some five minutes after the initial explosion in *Express*, at 23.12, the *Esk* detonated a mine right forward. She stopped at once. Things were now desperate, for the minefield appeared to be a thickly sown one, and the three destroyers, two of them now crippled, were right in the midst of it. To emphasise this, almost before this second blow had been taken in, yet another disaster took place.

The *Ivanhoe*, after drifting away from the starboard side of *Express*, turned round her bows, then passed down her port side and lay alongside the *Express*, with her stern opposite the latter's 3-inch gun. They once more drifted apart and, at approximately 23.17 *Ivanhoe* struck a mine under the bows, when the bows were one hundred yards away from the port quarter of *Express*. The *Ivanhoe* was then sent astern out of it. Some of her crew took to their boats after the explosion, but they were subsequently recalled when it was realised that the ship was still floating. Owing to the presence of water in her tanks, all steam was lost until 01.45.

On the bridge of the *Esk*, Yeoman of Signals Sears was talking to his captain when, at about 23.20, there was a second explosion, larger than the first, amidships in the *Esk*. The ship appeared to break in halves immediately. Sears later reported that he then, 'Jumped for it' and that the captain, 'just seemed to have vanished' after the second explosion. This sudden destruction of the flotilla mate was witnessed by the survivors aboard the *Express* whaler. They had got within forty yards of her when she blew up amidships with a shocking explosion. They then made their way towards the *Ivanhoe*, which was giving off flames forward from her own mine damage. However, an officer in one of *Ivanhoe*'s own lowered boats told them to 'keep on rowing' so they lay off until about 03.00. We shall return to their adventures later.

By this time *Ivanhoe* had got underway, albeit astern only, at a speed of 7 knots. Even then, on occasion, she had to halt owing to loss of steam pressure. At 02.45, she stopped to pick up a Carley float full of survivors and lowered her motor boat to pick up others seen in the water. As the wind had been from the north-west, force 2–3, it would appear that, after drifting while stopped, she had by this time regained the position of the bulk of the survivors in the water. The prevailing tide stream was recorded as being approximately 000° at 1½ knots.

The damage to the destroyer was extensive, despite her apparently stable state. Her position was made worse when, at about 04.00, either both the propellers fell off or both propeller shafts fractured, and she was unable to proceed any further. In addition to these woes, the paravane boom was anchoring the ship. Fortunately for *Ivanhoe*, her W/T was still fully functional. However, she was dangerously exposed, with the sky growing steadily lighter, still deep within enemy waters, and helpless to extradite herself. The threat of more mines was also haunting the crew. Black though things looked, far away, help was on the way.

The first sign of activity was, fortunately, friendly. An RAF Lockheed Hudson aircraft appeared overhead at about 05.00. Two hours later, an escort of long-range Bristol Blenheims appeared and these remained in the vicinity until noon. Unfortunately, after the RAF had abandoned them once more, the *Luftwaffe* took over. A Dornier flying boat put in an unwelcome appearance at 12.30, and continued to circle the crippled ship outside effective gun range.

Meanwhile, the survivors from *Express* aboard the whaler, had an equally lonely night. They had pulled steadily westward throughout the day without sighting anything, friendly or hostile, on the sea or in the sky. It appeared as if they were alone in the whole of the North Sea. Taking rests and turns at the oars, they made their way slowly west throughout the following day until 19.00, when they sighted a buoy to which they made secure as they were making little or no headway against the tidal stream. It was marked 'TS' and was conical in shape, painted with red and white horizontal stripes. It was the only indication they had that day that man existed in these wastes. Here they lay until the tide turned once more, when they slipped and continued their painfully slow westerly progression.

In the interim, the 5th Flotilla had been preparing to return to the Humber. The *Jupiter* hoisted the dan marker back aboardwhen it was obvious that *Intrepid* and *Icarus* had found another route to safety. The time was 07.00. Just as they were preparing to leave, they received the sighting report from the Hudson of two damaged destroyers [*Ivanhoe* and *Express*], still afloat about twenty-five miles to the east of their position.

At once, Mountbatten abandoned his earlier plan. Leaving

Vortigern to lay another buoy for his own guidance, and to remain on patrol in the area as long as she was able, Captain D5 took *Jupiter* and *Kelvin* at high speed in the direction of the reported cripples. *Kelvin* was prudently stationed four miles on *Jupiter's* port beam in such deadly waters as these had proved to be. On reaching position QZY26, a turn together to the north-west was made, followed later by another turn to the north-east and again, at 08.35, to the south-east. The aircraft on patrol over the two damaged ships made numerous reports of the position of their charges before they left for good, but these positions proved to be conflicting for a long while and caused much confusion.

Thus it was that, at 08.00, it was not the 5th Flotilla that first made contact with the two damaged destroyers, but nine of the MTBs sent out earlier by the Admiralty. Four of these little craft, *MTB-14*, *MTB-15*, *MTB-16* and *MTB-17*, arrived from the eastward at this time to join the *Ivanhoe*; the other five went to the aid of the *Express*. The *Ivanhoe* retained *MTB-15* while the others embarked all but thirty-seven of the destroyers' ships' company and then proceeded back to their home base.

At 08.40 the *Kelvin* finally sighted *Express* and her five small consorts in position 53°37'N, 03°25'E, steering a course of 315°. As they closed the cripple, her shortage of feed water finally brought to a halt her painful journey west under her own steam. Her bows had disappeared right up to the fore end of her bridge structure, but she was otherwise in perfect trim and on an even keel. By 09.01, *Kelvin* had a tow passed into her and had sent her doctor aboard the *Express*. Unfortunately, at 09.38, the tow fouled *Kelvin's* starboard propeller and it proved impossible to clear it. Meanwhile, with the help of the MTBs, twelve of the most seriously wounded, including Captain Bickford himself, were transferred to *Kelvin*. This transfer was completed by 10.30 and, at 11.12, *Kelvin* turned her screws to clear the tow and it parted.

While this was going on, Mountbatten aboard *Jupiter* was searching vainly for *Ivanhoe*, returning at 11.15, whereupon *Jupiter* took over the tow of *Express* and set a course toward *Vortigern* and Gap 'D' at the best speed possible. Mountbatten expressed his appreciation of the fine seamanship displayed by

Jupiter's captain, Captain D B Wyburd, in getting *Express* underway so quickly. As they began to leave the scene, *Kelvin*, with *MTB-30*, set off on another hunt for *Ivanhoe*, whose last reported position, by her own signal of 09.46, was 53°43'N, 03°34'E. This signal had been received by *Jupiter* at 11.40.

The reason for this signal was clear enough. By 10.30, *Ivanhoe* was settling slowly but remorselessly, and listing to port. It was becoming increasingly difficult to keep steam to the pumps. In short, the destroyer was sinking and was certainly not salvageable. Help was needed fast. By 13.45, steam pressure could no longer be kept up and, as a consequence, the engine-room could not be kept from flooding further. At 14.15, the ship was clearly settling further with an ever-increasing list. Orders were reluctantly given for her to be abandoned. The captain and the remaining thirty-six members of her crew were transferred to *MTB-15*, and *Ivanhoe* was scuttled. The blow-down valves, air compressors and diesel weed traps of the circulators in the engine-room were removed. Her captain estimated that his ship would sink within thirty minutes. So confident was he of this, that he did not consider it necessary to take any further steps to ensure her sinking. The long fight throughout a night and a day had ended in defeat. But, for the moment, *Ivanhoe* was still afloat.

Of the mined trio, it seemed that only the *Express* remained. Would she share the fate of her sisters? At 13.00, the tow was continuing slowly when further reinforcements arrived in the lithe and welcome shapes of the destroyers *Hambledon* and *Garth*. The *Hambledon* was retained to carry out an anti-submarine patrol around *Jupiter* and *Express*, while *Garth* was sent off to help in the search of *Ivanhoe*, joining *Kelvin* at 13.30. Six Blenheim aircraft arrived overhead at 14.16 to resume air cover. *Jupiter* signalled to them that, '. . . the damaged destroyer had been reported being bombed fifteen miles to the eastward of us.' What damaged destroyer was this? It turned out to be none other than the *Ivanhoe*! Taking in water, crippled, abandoned by her crew, the little destroyer was still fighting for her life.

The *Kelvin* had received a reported position for the *Ivanhoe* from an aircraft signal timed at 08.41, giving her position as

53°33'N, 03°34'E, and she later also took in *Ivanhoe*'s own last signal, which corrected this. The *Ivanhoe* had been last underway steering 315° at 5 knots. *Kelvin* therefore initially searched to the north, according to a signal from C-in-C, Nore, timed at 05.13. But, at 13.44, *Kelvin* received *Ivanhoe*'s signal asking for fighter protection when the Dornier aircraft had first appeared overhead. At 15.00, *MTB-30* had to be sent home, due to shortage of fuel. Half an hour later, *Kelvin* twice requested *Ivanhoe* to report her position on low power in order to get a D/F (Direction Finding) bearing, but of course by now there was nobody aboard her to hear or comply.

It was therefore not until 16.19 that *Garth* finally sighted the abandoned destroyer. Stepping her speed up to 28 knots, her maximum, *Garth* closed her and, while so doing, the Dornier was observed carrying out bombing attacks on the abandoned wreck. Gunfire from *Garth*'s high-angled 4-inch main armament soon drove this vulture off, however. The *Kelvin* circled slowly round the wallowing wreck, but could see no sign of life aboard her. Nor was any reply received to hails. All the ship's boats and rafts had gone, save for the motor boat hanging in the starboard davits. *Ivanhoe* was listing heavily to port, there was a large hole through the forecastle starboard side and she was eight feet down by the stern. There was yet more damage amidships, between her two funnels, possibly caused by the Dornier's bombs, and it appeared that her back was broken. She was still defiantly refusing all the attempts of the enemy and the elements to send her under, although her end could not now be far away.

The captain of *Kelvin* considered that, even if she could have been taken in tow, it was not likely that she would ever reach port. Also, as she lay so close to an enemy minefield, it was not justifiable to risk ships in the area longer than necessary to save life. He therefore decided to sink her without more ado, and a torpedo was fired at 1500 yards, which struck *Ivanhoe* below her after superstructure.

After all her efforts to remain afloat, this final blow from her own side finished off this tough little ship and *Ivanhoe* sank in about one minute of receiving the blow. At 17.00, *Kelvin* and

Garth proceeded at 27 knots for Gap 'D', being all the while shadowed by enemy aircraft flying low at six miles distance astern. By 17.45, they had joined company with *Vortigern* and, at 18.30, all sighted *Jupiter* and *Express* and they struggled out of the minefield to safety.

In the interim, there had been further additions to the flotilla attempting to save the *Express*, during the afternoon. At 15.30 the minesweepers *Leda* and *Saltash* were sighted. *Saltash* was ordered to relieve *Vortigern* in marking the Gap, while she was despatched at 16.15 to assist in the search for *Ivanhoe*, joining *Garth* and *Kelvin* later. Mountbatten had refrained from breaking radio silence up to then, as no enemy force or aircraft had sighted him, but he now felt that it was time that those ashore were put fully in the picture. *Leda* closed, and a signal was passed by Coston line gun to her. She was then sent clear, to the vicinity of the Outer Dowsing Light Float at her best speed, with orders not to transmit it until she had reached that area.

At 17.15, three tugs arrived, the *St Cyrus*, *Irishman* and *Wheeldon*. But now sadly there were not three, but just one destroyer left afloat to tow to safety. *Jupiter* continued with the tow for the time being, with the tugs following in case they were required. The tow was being conducted with *Jupiter* setting revolutions for 8½ knots, but making good about 6 knots. She was using three shackles of cable at her own end, tailed with 15 fathoms of 4-inch wire. The tow was most satisfactory through the day, but although it appeared possible safely to increase the speed, the risk was considered not justified until the arrival of the tugs. The tow passed through position 53°36'N, 02°27'E at 18.30, and at this point one of the tugs was ordered to play a hose on the bow of the *Express*, which was still on fire.

When *Kelvin*, *Garth* and *Vortigern* joined this group, *Kelvin* requested permission to return with all despatch to land seriously wounded men, and this was approved. *Saltash* was ordered to remain by the dan buoy until dusk to serve as a leading mark, and afterwards to proceed ahead to sight the Outer Dowsing Light Float in the same role. D/F bearings of Cleethorpes also proved invaluable as a lead for the Gap.

The *Luftwaffe* were still in distant but respectful attendance. The only serious attempt they made to intervene was a solitary attack conducted by a Junker Ju 88 upon *Kelvin* at 19.45. One small 100-lb bomb was also dropped by a Blohm und Voss HA140 seaplane against *Vortigern*, *Hambledon* and *Garth* that night, around 20.32, while they were sweeping well astern to cover the towing party.

It was due to the possibility of further air attack, that *Jupiter* finally slipped her tow to join in the gun defence of the squadron at 19.45 and allowed *St Cyrus* to take over this duty. Although she reported that she managed 8 knots, in practice the tug only managed to achieve 4 knots, and so the *Irishman* was sent in to assist her at 22.30. Having kept the two Hunt class destroyers in company for as long as their limited fuel supplies allowed, in order to take advantage of their superior AA firepower, Mountbatten was forced to release *Hambledon* and *Garth* at 21.20.

Another long night followed for the ships that remained, but nothing untoward hindered their slow progression to safety. The Outer Dowsing was passed at 05.40 on 2 September and the MTBs were also released to refuel shortly after. The *Wheeldon* was added to the tow, as was later a fourth tug, the *Norman*. Under the protection of the guns of *Vortigern*, the *Express* finally arrived at Hull safely at 17.30 that evening. It had been a long tow.

What of the rest of the survivors? It may be recalled that her whaler had spent the night of 1/2 September huddled to a lonely buoy in the middle of the North Sea. All through the morning of 2 September they rowed with exhausted bodies to westward. At about 12.30, two Dornier floatplanes arrived over them, taking photographs and circling. They did nothing more until 16.30, when one left for the Dutch coast. The other aircraft fired off two red flares, apparently to indicate their position to searching ships, and soon afterwards *MTB-29* and *MTB-31* arrived. After they had picked up the whaler's crew, the second Dornier also left. This act of mercy was given no publicity at the time, or indeed, since, but is recorded here for posterity. As the report stated at the time, it showed that, '. . . not all Germans are Nazis.'[62] Fifty-three other survivors were rescued by the Germans, and taken into captivity.

And so, history repeated itself for the 20th Flotilla. Apart from the loss of two fine destroyers, casualties were grievous among their skilled personnel, most of them regulars and irreplaceable. The bare facts are recorded in Table 10.

Table 10
20th Flotilla – Casualty figures for 1 September 1940

Destroyer	Officers		Ratings	
	Killed or missing	POWs	Killed or missing	POWs
Esk	7	2	127	24
Ivanhoe	–	1	8	22
Express	4	1	54	7
Total	**11**	**4**	**189**	**53**

If there is any consolation to be found from this disaster, it is in the bearing of the survivors. The flotilla may have been broken, but the spirit of the flotilla survived this tragedy. As Mountbatten himself was to record:

> The Senior Officer of the 20th Destroyer Flotilla is forwarding recommendations for awards and decorations for personnel of the damaged ships, some of whom undoubtedly behaved with great gallantry. The spirit on board the *Express* was particularly good. When I went alongside in the *Jupiter* to take her in tow, she piped the 'Still' and all men still capable of doing so, stood to attention.

An inadequate epitaph perhaps, in the present age of cynicism, but a sincere one. Regrettably, the gallant Captain Bickford was later to die of his injuries.

---

[62] Not a sentiment shared by Winston Churchill, who at this time, ordered all German floatplanes engaged in rescuing ditched airman of *both* combatants in the English Channel, to be shot down!

14

LOST OPPORTUNITIES

Some distinguished historians dismissed the 20th Minelaying Flotilla in a few short sentences after the disaster of 1 September 1940. Captain Cowie wrote:

> Thus were the events of 1918 repeated, and it is a fair assumption that the activities of the flotilla in the Heligoland Bight had driven the enemy to take retaliatory measures.

He added:

> In April 1941 the surviving destroyers of the 20th Flotilla returned to Fleet duties. They had done excellent work in laying nearly 7000 mines in various areas.[63]

The author of the Official Naval History, Captain S W Roskill, was even more dismissive:

> The surviving ships continued to serve as minelayers for a short time, but the shortage of destroyers in the fleet for escort work was so acute that they reverted to those duties in April 1941.[64]

In actuality, although the flotilla had its strength halved by the events of 1 September, the three surviving ships of the 20th Flotilla continued to lead a very active minelaying life. The view that none of their subsequent missions are thought

[63] Cowie, *op. cit.*, p 147.
[64] Roskill, *War at Sea, Vol1*, p 334.

worthy of record in any other volume of naval warfare, does them and their crews a grave disservice. Let us put the record straight here.

The 20th Flotilla was, in fact, back in action within a very short time. Its offensive functions were actually *increased* in scope, even if, perforce, reduced in size. During the seven months that followed 1 September, the minelaying destroyers operated both off the coasts of Occupied France and Norway, as well as around our own shores. Further, even when the three destroyers did cease to lay mines, the work of the 'S' and 'T' class destroyers continued in the Far East. Finally, at the end of the Second World War, the newer ships of the 'O' class destroyers took up the mantle.

One survivor told me that, naturally enough, the loss of so many of their flotilla mates cast a deep gloom over them all. Nevertheless, the *Intrepid*, *Icarus* and *Impulsive* carried on without a break in their minelaying duties. On 3 September, all three sailed from the Humber and laid defensive minefield 'MSA', returning without incident the following day. Loading again took place swiftly, and, on 5 September the three ships left Immingham once again to lay minefield 'MSB', also a defensive field, on the same night, returning to base the next day.

With the apparent threat of imminent invasion, and the existing destroyer force at full stretch after the heavy losses sustained off Norway and along the Channel including the evacuation from Dunkirk, there was clearly a demand for these three modern destroyers to utilise their in-built adaptability to the full. So, they alternately loaded their guns and torpedo tubes when required, and then quickly landed them back ashore once more to carry on with their mining missions. They quickly became highly proficient at this metamorphosis. For example, on 25 September, *Icarus* arrived at Immingham, embarked her guns and forward bank of torpedo tubes and sailed for Sheerness, where she arrived on 26 September. Her two sisters followed her example, *Intrepid* on 26 September and *Impulsive* on the 27th. But, with the immediate alarm over, all three ships had arrived back at Immingham ready for minelaying duty once more as early as 1 October.

George Mack again provides a unique insight into the vicissitudes of these frequent conversions, and just what it actually involved.

> The *Intrepid* was now being used as was originally conceived, that is, using her own crew temporarily to take off two guns and the torpedo tubes; load the mines; lay them then replace the guns and tubes to become a normal destroyer again!
>
> Each gun weighed about nine tons and I suppose the tubes were around that same weight, so as long as a crane capable of lifting about ten tons was available, they were in business! Soon it became a first class manoeuvre in which guns and tubes were removed, the mine rails brought up from the racks in the boiler room and bolted down; then sixty-four mines loaded in eight hours of really concentrated effort.
>
> The Ordinance Artificer, OA Scott, Gunner's Mate, Tim McCoy and gun sweepers, would undo about thirty one-inch bolts which held the gun to the deck, which with being regularly washed with salt water, would be stiff and rusty, while PO Howting, the torpedo gunner's mate, and the electrical artificer, disconnected the numerous electrical connections. While this was happening, seamen were removing four brass studs from each of about 150 plates welded to the deck, then bolting the rails to these same number of plates by steel bolts! Once more these were constantly swept by salt water and very rapidly rusted![65]

The work of adding to the, now extended, East Coast Barrage preoccupied the flotilla during the autumn and winter of 1940. It was during one such operation, on 2 November, that *Intrepid* herself was damaged by a mine off Hartlepool. Her hull was not breached by the explosion, but her delicate machinery suffered much from the concussion, which cracked engine and boiler mountings, and she spent the next seven weeks in dock-

---

[65] Mack, *op. cit.*, pp 131–2.

yard hands. During her enforced absence, *Icarus* and *Impulsive* continued the work by themselves.

As the New Year came in, the 20th Flotilla, although still utilising Immingham as its home base, shifted its scene of operations northward as far as the east coast of Scotland part of the barrage until that had been completed. Then it undertook a series of lays off the coast of southern Norway, in an effort to try to catch the abundant German coastwise traffic in this region.

In commencement of one such operation, the flotilla sailed from Scapa Flow on 1 January 1941. However, soon after leaving harbour, it encountered very heavy weather and the mine rails aboard *Icarus* were damaged. Rather than lay an incomplete field, the destroyers put about and returned to base to enable repairs to be effected. The next day, *Icarus* and *Intrepid* sailed again, each with a full cargo of mines embarked. The object was to lay a small, but strategically important, minefield along the 100-fathom line off Jaedens and Obrestad, a channel much used by German convoys passing south into the Skagerrak. To cover this audacious intrusion deep into hostile waters, the Home Fleet provided a strong covering squadron, which comprised the 6-inch cruisers *Arethusa* and *Aurora* and the 'Tribal' class destroyers *Bedouin*, *Mashona*, *Matabele*, and *Tartar* of the 6th Destroyer Flotilla. The whole force put to sea on 2 January.

As far as the minelaying destroyers were concerned, the operation went without hitch and the minefield was duly laid in the correct position. One report talks of co-operation from ashore, with a flashing light from an agent placed there to indicate that they were in the correct position before the lay commenced, but there is no confirmation of this in the Reports of Proceedings. Be that as it may, the minefield was put down precisely and the two destroyers returned to Scapa Flow without further ado. Not so their escort! Navigation aboard some of the Tribals appeared to be a trifle shaky. The host of small islands that lay off this part of the Norwegian coast, was reported by one of them as being a convoy of enemy merchant ships! Fire was opened by some of the 6th Flotilla before their mistake was discovered and the 'battle' called off. Fortunately, the pitch-black night hid some red faces, and it did not affect the minelaying itself. The *Icarus* and *Intrepid* were back in the Scapa Flow by 3 January. From here, they both sailed south to the Humber the next day, *Icarus* to carry out a boiler clean. She was relieved by *Impulsive* for another lay off southern Norway, which was scheduled for 21 January. Complete with full mine load, the two destroyers returned to Scapa Flow to carry out this operation. But, again, atrocious weather forced the postponement of this lay until 2 February.

Conditions had improved slightly by that date, and the two ships sailed at 08.30 that morning with a reduced covering force, *Arethusa*, *Aurora*, *Matabele* and *Tartar*. The minefield was to be laid off FroHavet, but once at sea, conditions again deteriorated alarmingly during the afternoon. The seas grew very heavy and the minelayers, rather unstable in such weather with their extra top hamper, continually had to reduced their speed. By 21.00, they could only steam at 10 knots without risking bad weather damage, and the lay was therefore abandoned as impracticable, the whole force returning to Scapa Flow on 3 January.

The combination of appalling weather and the period of the moon, thereafter caused the operation to be aborted completely and the two minelayers returned to the Humber on 4 January. The *Icarus* completed her boiler clean shortly afterwards. The three destroyers were lying at Immingham, having all embarked a mixed mine load, on 8 January, when they received a hurried summons to sail once more for Scapa Flow, complete with their mines.

What had prompted this hurried recall ready for immediate action, was the sighting by the battleship *Ramillies* at dawn that day, of a single enemy heavy unit approaching the convoy she was protecting, HX106. The British battleship reported the sighting as 'A possible Hipper class heavy cruiser'. At that time the Admiralty was daily expecting either the *Admiral Hipper* herself, or the pocket battleship *Admiral Scheer*, to make a breakout into the North Atlantic. The C-in-C, Home Fleet, therefore immediately made his dispositions in order to try and intercept her. The suspected enemy vessel had sheered off

Table 11
Typical record of mines embarked – HMS *Intrepid*, 8 February 1941

Mines (Mk XVIIA (Phd))		Sinker	
Serial No.	Mech. Plt.	Serial No.	Mark
376	IVA	17586	XVII^{x}B
4495	"	17120	"
708	"	17572	"
242	"	17122	"
11385	"	7815	XVB
9225	"	8050	"
9556	"	8099	"
333	"	8512	"
9554	"	8060	"
11396	"	16995	XVII^{x}B
3644	"	17631	"
9336	"	7822	XVB
3362	"	17121	XVII^{x}B
297	"	16852	"
168	"	17565	"
9447	"	16857	"
9473	"	17076	"
298	"	17627	"
3094	"	17344	"
2706	"	16860	"
9312	"	8524	XVB
705	"	17390	XVII^{x}B
335	"	8101	XVB
61	"	7869	"
167	"	8517	"
3643	"	8053	"
3622	"	17635	XVII^{x}B
5130	"	17610	"
90	"	8289	XVB
4488	"	17505	XVII^{x}B
9255	"	7875	XVB
9226	"	8771	"

immediately upon sighting *Ramillies,* and so the report remained vague. In fact, the German squadron actual comprised the two powerful battle-cruisers *Gneisenau* and *Scharnhorst,* which had left Kiel on 23 January, and had since passed into the Atlantic hitherto undetected by British aerial reconnaissance.

The two German heavy ships were much-sought targets at that time, but following their turn away, strenuous searches failed to re-locate them. They both vanished into the wastes of that vast area very quickly. It now seems that Admiralty Intelligence had deduced from intercepted W/T traffic, that the two German battle-cruisers were to sortie out at this time and had already warned the C-in-C. When the Germans had sailed through the Great Belt, an agent ashore had reported the fact, and the Home Fleet had sailed on 23 January. However, the same bad weather, which had prevented the minelaying destroyers from putting a trap in the homeward path, enabled the enemy to evade our patrols. Save for an earlier brief sighting by the cruiser *Naiad* on 28 January, the enemy had made good their evasion.

Thus, when the *Ramillies'* sighting of a Hipper class cruiser came in, there was some confusion about which German ships were now loosed on the convoy routes. It remained the case, however, that, whatever ships were out, their likeliest haven or bolt-hole would be the French port of Brest. The three minelaying destroyers remained at Scapa Flow awaiting confirmation of whether they should lay their mines off Norway or France until 15 January. They then sailed for Plymouth, the decision having been made. By now, the clever money was on *Scharnhorst* and *Gneisenau* as being the targets.

Although the German ships remained at large and their position unknown, it was felt that Brest would indeed be the most probable port, with sufficient dockyard facilities to look after them. It was decided that the 20th Flotilla should try and block this port as quickly as possible. Accordingly, Operation GS [*Gneisenau/Scharnhorst*] was put into effect.

At 16.30 on Wednesday 19 February, the *Intrepid* (Commander R C Gordon), *Icarus* (Lieutenant-Commander L C Maud) and *Impulsive* (Lieutenant-Commander M S Thomas), sailed from Plymouth to carry out Operation GS forthwith.

It was a calm night, especially welcome after those wild hours off Norway earlier, with the wind from the north-west backing slowly to the west, and steadily lessening in force from 5 to 2. There was only a slight sea and a moderate westerly swell, which also decreased as they neared the coast of France. The sky was clear, with between 1 to 4 tenths cloud. Visibility started off as good, improving to very good. It was ideal weather for cruising, but *not* for laying mines off a heavily guarded enemy-occupied harbour!

At 19.30, *Intrepid* streamed her taunt wire measuring gear (TWMG) and, just over half an hour later, she began registering at 000,000 with the Lizard Lighthouse bearing 352° at a distance of 7.2 miles. The course was set to 188° to make good 190° and the speed was increased to 25 knots. The tidal stream between 19.30 and 21.30 was estimated as a set of 315°, 1.4 miles, and due allowance was made. The log reading was set at 000,000 at this time to check, and the four ships of the 5th Destroyer Flotilla, *Javelin*, *Jersey*, *Jupiter* and *Kashmir*, joined company as their escort. These four ships took station on the starboard quarter of the minelaying trio.

There was an early upset to their careful calculations when, at 19.41, the TWMG wire parted. The measurement at the time of the breakage was 003,982, the log was 003,8. By 19.55, the taunt wire was again streamed. At 20.00, the reading was recommenced at zero, with the log reading of 010,9, the distance being run in the interim being estimated as 11.3 miles. As Commander Gordon was later to record in his report:

> It was satisfactory to note that after one early failure the taunt wire ran correctly at twenty-five knots and the comparison of taunt wire and log readings indicated accurate recordings.[66]

At 21.30, the force was making fast progress across the Channel, logging 71,3, and they altered course 192° to make good 188°, the tidal stream between 21.30 and 23.30 later

---

[66] Report of Proceeding, *Operation GS*, dated 22 February 1941 – ADM1/11327. The TWMG had never been streamed at speeds in excess of 20 knots before this operation.

being estimated as a set of 53°, 2.7 miles. By 23.30, the total distance run was ninety-seven miles and they had reached a position 48°15'N, 05°35'W. At this time they altered course once more to 120° and reduced speed to 15½ knots in preparation for the lay. The four destroyers of the 5th Flotilla passed them and proceeded to their covering position, two miles to the westward of position 'F'. Commander Gordon later reported that the support given by these ships was 'most encouraging', and:

> . . . the position taken up by them during the approach and operation appeared to give the best possible cover and, had surface patrols been encountered by them during the lay, it might well have been possible to continue without detection.[67]

It should be remembered that the approaches to Brest, one of the major ports in Occupied France, and recently a safe haven for the *Admiral Hipper*, would be among the most heavily patrolled along the whole European coastline. In addition, German radar stations were expected to have been established in the area. However, the Germans were known to have only four large destroyers of their own on hand, so the protection of the four ships of the 5th Flotilla would have been quite sufficient to deal with any surface intervention, other than the heavy ships themselves.

Midnight came and went, however, without any such unwelcome interruptions. At 00.30 on 20 February, position 'P' was reached and the taunt wire cut. The course was altered to 73° and, two minutes later, in position 48°07'6"N, 05°14'8'W the lay was commenced. Three minutes after the first mine slid into the dark water a white light, which flashed every five seconds, was sighted at 00.35. This was not some clandestine agent furtively signalling to the flotilla, as lower-deck rumour later would have it, but simply the Les Pierres Noire Light. The flotilla took bearings from this marker, which confirmed the accuracy of their lay, and it proved quite useful.

[67] *Ibid.*

Table 12
Typical mining report of operation – HMS *Icarus*,
20 February 1941

1	Date of operation	20 Feb 1941
2	Title of peration	GS
3	Type of mine and sinker used	Mines XVII: Sinkers Mk XVII^{x}B & XVB
4	Number of mines laid	26
5	Special fittings for arrangements	4 sinkers fitted grapnels 4 sinkers fitted sprockets Mines fitted with flooders Mk IA
6	Identification marks painted on mines	–
7	Depth set (plummet sinkers)	23 feet
8	Depth set (hydrostatic sinkers)	–
9	Depth of tops of mines below chart datum	6 feet
10	Charted depth of water where mines are laid	51 fathoms
11	Height of tide at time of laying	17 feet
12	Strength and direction of current when laying	See remarks of senior officer
13	State of sea	Moderate
14	Visibility	7 miles
15	Time began laying	00.58.06
16	Time finished laying	01.08.34
17	Speed of ship	15 knots
18	Position of first mine of line	48°10'N 48°11'48'N 5°8'39'N 5°7'0'W
19	Direction of line	015-1/2° 000-1/2°
20	Number of groups in line	2
21	Number of mines in each group	7 6 6 7
22	Spacing of mines in groups	150 feet
23	Interval between groups in line	650 yards
24	Date and time at which flooders or delayed release devices are set to operate	Flooders operate at 14.00 on 21 March 1941
25	Date mines were embarked	9 Feb 1941
26	Test carried out on board	As laid down in OU 5302 Chapt 'X'
27	Number of mines remaining on surface	–
28	Number of premature locks	–
29	** Remarks on failures, delays, accidents, etc.	–
30	Number of units observed	–

** Full report of failures, etc., to be rendered, vide *Mining Drill Book*, para 78(v).

The mines were laid in a complicated pattern in groups in the rough form of a many-angled salient to make detection and regular pattern sweeping impossible. However, with a mixed mine load various combinations were also utilised to make life yet harder for the enemy. Grapnels were fitted to one in five of the mines laid, and sprocket-wheel evaders, a device invented in 1911 by Assistant-Paymaster C Bucknell but not adopted until the 1920s, which allowed the minesweepers' sweep to pass through the mine mooring rope without disclosing the presence of the mine. Sinkers and Mark 1 flooders were also utilised to make the amatol-loaded Mk XVIIIa mines yet more potent. The flooders were set to operate at 14.00 on 21 March.

Four to seven mines were laid in each of the groups along the complex line at spacing intervals of 150 feet, *Intrepid* and *Impulsive* laying thirty-two mines each and the *Icarus* twenty-six in all. The mines were laid at depths of between fifty and sixty fathoms, and the set depth was twenty-three feet. *Intrepid* commenced laying at 01.12 and completed at 01.30. *Icarus* started at 00.58 and finished at 01.08 and *Impulsive* commenced at 00.32 and terminated at 00.52. *Impulsive's* group spacings were 400 feet to further cause confusion among the enemy sweepers.

By 01.32, the field had been completed, and the flotilla altered course to 315° increasing speed to 25 knots. The 5th Flotilla rejoined them, and all seven destroyers sped back undetected across the Channel, the Lizard Light coming in sight at 06.19 and Plymouth Sound being reached at 09.30. Commander Gordon reported that the fitting of ASV[68] in *Icarus* was a boon and recommended that *Intrepid* should be so fitted, '. . . at the earliest opportunity'.

Captain Cowie, for DDOD(M)[69] noted, 'This has the appearance of a successful operation.' He added, '*Intrepid* is now boiler cleaning at Portsmouth and opportunity is being taken to fit ASV gear'. It was indeed a remarkable operation by the 20th Flotilla, which makes its omission from Cowie's own

[68] ASV – Aircraft/Surface Vessel, radar.
[69] DDOD(M) = Deputy Director Ordnance Department (Mines).

book, as in all other naval histories, all the more bizarre.

The 20th Flotilla's three remaining ships continued to be usefully employed for some weeks after this audacious sortie. T Brotheridge recalled:

> We loaded mines at Portsmouth and proceeded from there to either Dartmouth or Plymouth to await darkness for laying mines on the other side of the Channel, off Brest and the Channel Islands. Dartmouth seemed quiet, but often when leaving Plymouth at night we would hear the German bombers overhead and see the flames of the city in our wake. We were now supplied with moored magnetic mines and were the first to lay them off Cap d'Antifer. Another source of supply for our mines was Milford Haven and we used to go there often and then back to Plymouth for our operations.
>
> In April 1941, we were transferred to Scapa Flow again and from there we laid mines north of the Faeroes. In early May we were withdrawn from minelaying duties and together with HMS *Intrepid* and HMS *Icarus* we were transferred to fleet duties, and were attached to the Home Fleet. After that the only minelaying duties we took part in were to go south to the Kyle's of Lochalsh where we picked up large minelayers and escorted them on their operations into the Denmark Strait.[70]

Another veteran has memories of a similar nature:

> The *Intrepid* loaded mines in Sheerness, Portsmouth, possibly Southampton, the mouth of the River Dart and finally at Milford Haven. After this, we laid mines off Norway and Iceland, completing that phase by about late spring 1941. There was no more minelaying after this as they reverted us to normal destroyer duties.[71]

[70] T Brotheridge to the Author, 26 November 1979.
[71] George Mack to the Author 10 August 1978.

So finally, and more than eight months after the disaster of 1 September, the 20th Flotilla passed into history. Their work had been brief, but very valuable and worthwhile. Indeed, the ships and men themselves did not fail or falter. The sole reason for the disbandment was the dreadful lack of destroyers following heavy losses off Norway, the Low Countries and in the Channel, which compounded the shortage brought about by myopic politicians in the 1920s and 1930s. But that decision did not mean the end of destroyer minelaying, far from it.

15

DESTROYER MINELAYERS
IN THE FAR EAST

The paucity of British naval resources in the Far East had already been the cause of much concern to the Admiralty. The strict adherence to the terms of the various naval treaties the British Government had saddled the country with since 1921, had so cut the size of the fleet that, by 1940, with both Germany and Italy combined against us, and Vichy France openly hostile, there was little or nothing to spare against Japanese aggression. The situation had been foreseen, and the vulnerability of the Empire in the east was acknowledged[72], but little could be done. Indeed, the highly trained naval forces originally available, which included the fast minelayer *Adventure* and the minelaying submarines *Seal, Grampus* and *Rorqual,* had all been withdrawn from the area to operate in Home Waters. Enemy mines in the Channel damaged the *Adventure* very early on, while off Norway and in the Mediterranean, the three submarines had quickly been lost to enemy attacks along with the *Narwhal.*

What remained to offer even a token resistance to the

---

[72] Other than by Winston Churchill, who had, and who continually retained, a wilful blind spot (or, more likely, a stubborn refusal to face facts), with regard to the menace posed by the Imperial Japanese Navy (IJN). This fleet, the third largest in the world, and mainly modern, Churchill continually under-estimated, while over-estimating the power and strength of the United States Navy in the Pacific, and, more importantly, the willingness of that force to be used to protect the British Empire! Even a cursory reading of Churchill's account of the Second World War reveals his vast ignorance, or disbelief in Intelligence Reports, on this issue, whose ultimate expression was the loss of the *Prince of Wales* and *Repulse,* sent out on their own, and against sound naval advice, to deal with the whole might of the IJN.

Japanese threat in 1939? In truth, there was very little, just the five small 'S' class destroyers of the Hong Kong and Singapore Local Defence Flotillas. These ships, *Scout*, *Tenedos*, *Thanet* and *Thracian*, reinforced by the *Stronghold*,which was *en route* from the UK, had already all been earmarked for adapting as destroyer minelayers in anticipation. Each was fitted with rails to carry forty broad gauge mines and in August 1939, all four were based at Hong Kong.

Plans were drawn up in the event of Japanese aggression, to offer just a token resistance at Hong Kong, but for the main base of Singapore to be defended to the utmost, pending re-inforcement from the UK. Accordingly, two of the minelaying destroyers, *Scout* and *Tenedos* left Hong Kong on 24 August 1939, to be based at Singapore, where the fifth ship, *Stronghold*, arrived on 22 September[73].

No time was lost in utilising these destroyers in laying defensive minefields, although the destruction of the detailed records makes precise reconstruction impossible. Regrettably, unthinking Civil Servants who 'weeded' such material prior its transfer to the Public Record Office destroyed both the original plans and the individual ships' laying records. The historian is therefore restricted to the Area War Diaries and such individual Ships' Logs that did survive. There are also bare outline details and some charts, contained in a letter from the C-in-C, Eastern Theatre to the Admiralty, dated 10 November 1943[74]. From this, the following reconstruction of the minelaying conducted by the flotilla from September 1939 to February 1942 can be recorded.

Singapore Defensive Minefields – September 1939

Three main defensive minefields were envisaged for the protection of the seaward approaches to Singapore. The first field was designed to bar the western approach routes to the Johore Strait and the entrances to Selat Sembilan. The second

---

[73] For details of the plans in the event of the Japanese joining the Axis, see BR 1736 (50) – *War with Japan*.
[74] See MO13129/43.

minefield closed off the southern approaches to Keppel Harbour between Palau Sebarok and St. John Island West, while the third covered the eastern approaches to the harbour, between St John Island East and Siglap.

Immediately the *Scout* and *Tenedos* reached Singapore from Hong Kong, on 28 August 1939, they were taken in hand for conversion to minelayers. This was quickly accomplished. By 2 September, the day before the declaration of war against Germany, both destroyers were able to embark a full outfit of Mk XIV mines from the Armament Depot. Thus, by 4 September, the two destroyers were able to commence work on Minefield No. 1, and this continued until 8 September. During this five-day period, the destroyers laid 544 mines in fifteen separate lines. The mooring depth of the Mk XIV was four feet. The *Scout* made eight lays in this period, laying 278 mines in all, while the *Tenedos* laid 266 mines in seven lays.

The *Scout* took no further part in the proceedings after this date. She was reconverted to an anti-submarine role on completion of the first series of minelaying, with her mine rails removed once more and ASDICs fitted. This done, on 1 November, the *Scout* returned to Hong Kong at the request of the C-in-C, China. The *Tenedos* therefore had to carry on the good work on her own.

This intensive work enabled the Admiralty to declare the dangerous area covered by Minefield No. 1 on 16 September[75], and those covering Minefields 2 and 3 on 3 October.[76] Instructions to shipping entering Singapore were also broadcast locally, but this failed to prevent the masters of two vessels from ignoring the warnings, and resulted in the loss of both ships.[77] This led to the Admiralty to further declare, on 2 December, that the sole entrance to the harbour was now Selat Sinki.[78]

[75] Admiralty Notice to Mariners No. 2081.
[76] Admiralty Notice to Mariners No. 2217.
[77] The Norwegian *Hoeg Transporter* (4914 Gross Registered Tonnage (GRT)) was mined and sunk off the Outer Shoal Beacon on 3 October, with no loss of life. Incredibly, the British *Sirdhana* (7745 GRT) followed exactly the same route and was mined and sunk at almost the same spot on 13 November, with the loss of twenty of her crew.
[78] Admiralty Notice to Mariners No. 2713 (T).

Her work done, the *Tenedos* was reconverted to her patrol destroyer status, like the *Scout*, and never again employed as a minelayer, although she remained at Singapore. The minelayer *Redstart*, which had meanwhile been despatched from Hong Kong to Singapore, in order to carry out the laying of a controlled minefield, took the destroyers' places.

Hong Kong Defensive Minefields – October 1939

A similar dearth of detailed information appertains to the minefields laid off Hong Kong in this period, although, thankfully, the Port War Orders have survived the various culls.[79] The overall plan called for the laying of two separate and independent minefields, one in the North Lantau Channel, to cover the northern approaches to the harbour, and a second, which would totally close the West Lantau Channel. In addition, controlled minefields were to be laid in the two remaining entrances with eight loops guarding all the southern and eastern approaches. No work was carried out in August or September, as the Commodore, Hong Kong, felt it unnecessary while there was no U-boat activity in that area, although the destroyers *Thanet* and *Thracian* were held at short notice to commence the task once ordered.

Meanwhile, an auxiliary minelayer, the converted *Mao Lee* (1900 GRT – Gross Registered Tonnage) was requisitioned in August, as there was, astoundingly, no provision for shore loading facilities for minelayers at Hong Kong at this time. Another conversion was that of the ferryboat *Man Yeung*, with a capacity for one hundred mines. She was readied, and commissioned on 28 August, with a crew drawn from the river gunboat *Robin*. However, the laying of the Tathong controlled minefield was undertaken by the coastal minelayer *Redstart*, commencing on 3 September, and this was completed by 18 October. The same vessel then laid the East Lamma Channel controlled minefield, prior to her transfer to Singapore for similar work, as previously related.

The enforced idleness of the two minelaying destroyers came

[79] Hong Kong Port War Orders, M.05687/41 contained in WHC 7988.

to an abrupt end following an Admiralty warning that Far Eastern waters required vigilance in anti-submarine precautions. This prompted the C-in-C, China, to order the Commodore, Hong Kong, to initiate the laying of the Hong Kong independent minefields without further delay. The aim was to bar surfaced U-boats entering either the North Lantau or West Lamma Channels. Accordingly, *Thanet* and *Thracian*, with the assistance of the *Man Yeung*, were prepared for this work.

Thus, between 25 and 27 October, the two minefields were laid according to plan.[80] The *Thanet* and *Thracian* conducted six separate lays in the West Lamma Channel, laying two lines on each of the three days – a total of 240 Mk XIV mines. The destroyers reloaded after each run from the *Man Yeung*. These mines were laid at depths varying between four and sixteen feet. The *Thracian* then continued the work alone, laying a line of forty mines, at a depth of four feet, across the entrance to Shap Long (Silver Mine) Bay on 28 October and twenty more in the same area on 31 October. That same day she laid twenty more mines in the North Lantau field, which had already been commenced by the *Man Yeung*, before that vessel was decommissioned and returned to civil operations.

Again, on completion of this work, both destroyers were reconverted back to normal destroyers, and the *Thanet* took part in no further minelaying operations at all. The Admiralty issued a declaration notice of these fields on 10 November 1939,[81] and replaced it with a further declaration once the *Redstart* had finished her work, on 22 November.[82] This limited entry to the port to the Tathong Channel, which was continuously patrolled.

Reinforcement of Singapore Minefields – January to March 1941

The natural active life of the minefields laid off Singapore was not expected to be high, due to a combination of rough weather, corrosion and fast currents. By September 1940, a trial examination was called for and only 60 per cent of the mines were

---

[80] Signal, Commodore, Hong Kong to Admiralty, 1350/3/11/39.
[81] Admiralty Notice to Mariners No. 2523.
[82] Admiralty Notice to Mariners No. 2604.

recovered from the inner line of Minefield No. 2. The condition of twenty of those mines was such that general replenishment and replacement was deemed essential if they were to be an effective shield. Accordingly, a request was made to London for one thousand new mines to be sent out. On the arrival of the first of these, Minefield No. 2 was completely cleared and re-laying took place between 2 and 5 February 1941.

The destroyer *Stronghold* carried out this work, and she laid a total of 186 mines in six new lines, which alternated between deep and shallow lays, all within the original declared area. Similar concern was expressed about the effectiveness of the other minefields. With time running out, it was decided not to raise the existing mines but to lay further lines to seaward of them. The *Stronghold* had to await the arrival of a fresh load of mines, which finally reached Singapore in early March. She then resumed work on Minefield No. 3 between 3 and 8 March. In total, the destroyer laid eleven new deep and shallow lines, totalling 418 mines, either Mk XIV or Mk XVII types. Minefield No. 1 was similarly reinforced by another auxiliary minesweeper, the *Kung Wo* (4636 GRT) which had a capacity of 248 mines and had been commissioned on 7 March. The *Stronghold*'s work is summarised Table 13:

Again, although every precaution was taken, including a new Admiralty declaration issued on 20 March 1941,[83] further loss of friendly life was the initial result of this work. This came about when an RAF Bristol Blenheim light bomber crashed into the sea just south of Siglap Obelisk at about midday on 4 April. The RAF's Air Headquarters, Far East, requested the captain of the dockyard to salvage this machine. The mooring vessel *Buffalo* was therefore despatched at 06.00 the following morning.

Aboard the *Buffalo* was a nineteen-strong dockyard mooring party, a twenty-five strong RAF salvage party and an officer and signalman from the cruiser *Dauntless*.[84] In order to make a safe approach to the wreck, a senior surveying officer was separately embarked in a surveying motor boat. He directed

[83] Admiralty Notice to Mariners No. 658.
[84] Board of Inquiry Report, NL 520/43.

the *Buffalo*, but, due to faulty navigation, he led her over a corner of the original north-easterly line of Minefield No. 3 and she struck one of the mines. The resulting explosion broke the *Buffalo* in half, the stern part sinking at once, but the forepart remained afloat for another seventeen minutes, raising hopes of survivors being rescued. Unfortunately, this section suddenly capsized, taking down with it many of the RAF and dockyard personnel, several injured and a number of those trying to rescue them. This tragedy left thirty men dead and twenty-five more injured.

Table 13
HMS *Stronghold* minelaying record off Singapore, January – March 1941

Minefield	Line	Date laid	Number of mines	Depth laid	Total
	L 1	4-1-41	38	6 ft	
	L 2	4-1-41	38	⅓ charted depth	
	L 3	5-1-41	38	6 ft	186
No. 2	L 4	3-1-41	29	6 ft	
	L 5	2-1-41	18	⅓ charted depth	
	L 6	3-1-41	25	6 ft	
	L 1	3-3-41	38	6 ft	
	L 2	4-3-41	38	6 ft	
	L 3	7-3-41	38	⅓ charted depth	
	L 4	4-3-41	38	6 ft	
	L 5	7-3-41	38	⅓ charted depth	
No. 3	L 6	3-3-41	38	6 ft	418
	L 7	5-3-41	38	⅓ charted depth	
	L 8	4-3-41	38	6 ft	
	L 9	5-3-41	38	⅓ charted depth	
	L 10	6-3-41	38	6 ft	
	L 11	8-3-41	38	⅓ charted depth	

Reinforcement of Hong Kong minefields –
January to February 1941

In a similar manner to above, the numbers of drifting mines from the Hong Kong minefields reported from December 1939 onward, caused concern about their continued effectiveness. Rough seas were in part to blame for this wastage, which steadily increased throughout 1940. It was calculated by September of that year that the strength of the North Lantau field had been reduced to 87 per cent and the West Lamma field to just 43.5 per cent. The reinforcing of these fields was therefore considered essential. The civilian *Man Yeung* was again taken into service to assist the *Thracian* in this work, and the auxiliary minelayer made two lays in conjunction with the destroyer in January and February 1941.

On 23 January, the *Thracian* laid forty Mk XIV/XVII mines along a line at a uniform depth of four feet, along a line joining 22°14'21"N, 114°02'03"E and 22°13'38"N, 114°03'12"E. The second lay took place on 11 February, when the destroyer put down forty more mines of the same types, again at four feet depth, along a line that joined positions 22°14'00"N, 114°01'06"E and 22°13'40"N, 114°2'11"E. These news lines, south of the originally declared area, plus the *Man Yeung*'s lays, were duly announced by the Admiralty on 18 February 1941.[85] The declared area also included a northern extension, which was reserved for mining at a future date.

Defensive minefield off eastern coast of Johore – February and July 1941

Anglo-Japanese relations continued to deteriorate sharply during 1941, following the granting of air bases in northern Indo-China to Japan by the Vichy Government on 22 September 1940. This was followed shortly afterwards by Japan signing a mutual assistance pact with Germany and Italy on 26 September 1940. The granting of air bases, when further extended to southern Indo-China in July 1941, would bring Singapore and Malaya into land-based air strike range of Japanese long-range naval aircraft. The pact gave Japan a free hand in the Far East in return for the recognition of the Axis New Order in Europe. The threat was growing, but attempts by the concerned parties to make some mutual defence preparations were thwarted by the isolationist attitude of the United States, who refused to take part in the conference held at

---

[85] Admiralty Notice to Mariners No. 408.

Singapore in February. Discussions were limited to the British, Australian and Dutch authorities. Among the defensive measures taken was the planning of new protective minefields.

Already, on 17 January 1941, the C-in-C, Far East, had independently voiced concerns of the possibility of the Singapore naval base being outflanked from the north by Japanese amphibious landings on the eastern coast of Johore in the event of conflict. The announcement of a protective minefield was considered desirable, covering the most vulnerable approaches, roughly contained in a triangular area extending from Palau Tioman, Seribuat Island a position out to sea at 01°50'N, 104°20'E. The C-in-C proposed that a token lay of mines take place in the area to give the announcement some credence.[86]

The Foreign Office was consulted due to a view that the laying of the minefield beyond territorial waters, might further antagonise Japan, but the feeling in Whitehall was that the new field could hardly be considered anything other than defensive in nature. The Plans Division of the Admiralty added a further rider to the original plan, stressing the need to increase the actual area of the field; the need to achieve a high density of mines in the declared area; and the need to commence laying of the field as soon as possible,[87] and while the very few minelayers on station were still available to carry out the work. Extra stocks of mines had already been despatched to Singapore so there was no shortage, but the number of ships capable of conducting the lays remained minimal. In fact, the work, such as it was, had to be carried out by just one minelaying destroyer, the *Stronghold*. This meant that both the first two requirements were never met. The third, an early start, was complied with, however.

In February, the *Stronghold* laid six lines of mines, L1 to L 6. Each line was of about one mile in length, and consisted of 38 mines laid a uniform depth of six feet. There was a total of 456 mines. L1 and L2 were put down between Siribuat Island and Bara Rock; Lines L3 and L4, between Palau Tioman and Palau Permanggil; and L5 and L6 between Palau Permanngil and

[86] Signal, C-in-C China to Admiralty, dated 17 January 1941.
[87] Message, Admiralty to C-in-C, China, 14 February 1941.

Palau Aur. No further lays took place for several months, and it was not until July that the *Stronghold* recommenced her work, laying a further six lines of mines, of similar number, composition, length and depth. L7 and L8 were laid between Bara Rock and Gut Island; L9 and L10 just south of Pulo Aur; and L11 and L12 inshore, between Babai Island and Tingi Island. This gave a total lay by the destroyer of 456 mines, which proved to be a negligible obstruction when it came to the test.

The Admiralty, notwithstanding, announced the dangerous area as being within the following box parameters:

> North – the parallel of 02°44'N; East – the meridian of 104°30'E; South – the parallel of 01°35'N; the West – the Malayan coast.[88]

Any shipping that wanted to pass through that defined box, including local coasting craft, and Japanese ships still legitimately loading cargoes of ore from off the mouth of the River Endau, had first to apply to the British Naval Authorities, Singapore, for permission. Following the July lays by the *Stronghold*, again no further work was done to strengthen this minefield, other than a solitary lay by the minelayer *Teviot Bank* in December 1941. Plans to send out the fast minelayer *Latona* to help in the work came to nothing when she was sunk by Stuka aircraft in the Mediterranean on 25 October.

Final pre-war minelaying off Hong Kong October 1941

At Hong Kong, the *Thracian* and the auxiliary *Man Yeung* each made a final lay to extend the northern limits of the West Lamma minefield on 21 October 1941. The *Thracian* laid one line, 0.95 mile in length; laying forty Mk XIV mines, at a depth of four feet. The line started in position 22°15.3'N, 114°06.0'E in a direction 287°.

[88] Admiralty Notice to Mariners, No. 445, dated 21 February 1941.

Final pre-war minelaying off Singapore
November /December 1941

As the sands of time ran out, the *Stronghold* was involved in laying Minefield No. 5, a new field off the southern coast of Johore at the western end of the Lima Channel in November and December. The destroyer laid three lines, L1 to L3, each of thirty-eight Mk XIV or XVII mines, at a uniform depth of six feet on 30 November and 1 December, a total of 114 mines. The auxiliary minelayer *Kung Wo* had previously laid six lines extending existing minefields, 1A and 2A, on 9 September and 4 October respectively; Japan went to war with the Allies on 7 December 1941, attacking both Hong Kong and Singapore the following day, but *Stronghold*'s field was not declared by the Admiralty until 20 December.[89]

Hong Kong – wartime minelaying

The *Thracian* remained the only converted destroyer at Hong Kong. Both the *Scout* and the *Thanet* had been employed as conventional destroyers and they were both sent away immediately to the comparative safety of Singapore. As *Thracian* had her full outfit of mines already embarked, she was retained, and on 7 December sent to lay them at Port Shelter in the New Territories as a barrier to the invading Japanese forces. A further mine lay in Tolo Harbour was planned for 9 December, but was abandoned for it was feared the solitary destroyer would become cut off by the advancing enemy. Instead, on 10 December, *Thracian* was sent to lay her mines in Kap Shui Mun, in the north-west approaches. This proved to be her final minelaying sortie. By the morning of 12 December, the Japanese had largely overrun the New Territories defences and *Thracian* was employed in her conventional role in an attempt to stop enemy troop movements across the island itself.

On the night of 14/15 December, the *Thracian* intercepted and sank two river steamers carrying Japanese troops in

---

[89] Admiralty Notice to Mariners, No. 3037.

Kowloon Bay. During the course of this engagement, however, she unfortunately ran aground and sustained severe damage. The damaged destroyer was docked at Aberdeen Yard that morning, but she was clearly doomed. The Commodore, Hong Kong, ordered her to be undocked and beached. This was carried out and she was later disarmed and her crew joined the fighting ashore when the Japanese landed on the island on the night of the 18/19 December. Eventually, the Japanese salvaged the *Thracian*, patched her up and utilised her as a patrol ship. She survived the war, was repatriated and then scrapped.

Of the other 'S' and 'T' class destroyers used for minelaying, most also became war casualties in the weeks that followed. The *Thanet* was sunk in a heroic action against a superior force of modern Japanese destroyers off the eastern coast of Malaya on 27 January. The *Stronghold* was caught and destroyed after a gallant hour-long battle, by the Japanese heavy cruiser *Maya* and destroyers *Arashi* and *Nowake* south of Java on 4 March. Finally, the *Tenedos* was sunk by Japanese carrier bombers while at anchor in Colombo harbour on 5 April. Only the *Scout* survived the carnage to return safely to the UK. Between them, these little ships had laid 2198 mines.

The final destroyer minelaying off Singapore – December 1941

The local defence destroyers at Singapore were utilised in the conventional roles during the period of the Japanese invasion. This included acting as escorts to the British minelayers *Teviot Bank*, *Kung Wo*, and the Dutch *Willem Van de Zaan* in the numerous lays these ships conducted between 8 December 1941 and 9 January 1942. Following the sinking of the *Prince of Wales* and the *Repulse* on 10 December, one of the surviving destroyers of their escort, the *Express*, was pressed into service in her old minelaying role on just one occasion. On Christmas Eve, she embarked eighteen Mk I–IV ground mines, which she laid in the southern approaches to the port of Penang. The Japanese were known to have laid their own ground mines in the northern channel there and the *Express* lay closed the other entrance, blocking its use to the many small boats abandoned there and which it was feared the Japanese would use to bypass British defences. This operation was to be the final destroyer minelaying operation by British ships in the Far East.

16

FINAL DAYS

Following the heavy loss of minelaying destroyers in the Far Eastern debacle, other than *Scout*, none of the surviving destroyers capable of minelaying were again used in that role after April 1941. The potential remained but the ships were used as conventional fleet destroyers. Even the potential was steadily reduced, the *Intrepid* being sunk by German dive-bombers in Leros harbour on 27 September 1943, and the *Express*, although rebuilt as good as new, was transferred from the Royal Navy to Canada the same year. The three remaining destroyer minelayers all survived the war, only to be sent to the breakers' yards immediately afterwards.

This reduction of potential was offset, however, by the arrival of the four ships of the Onslow class, which had been constructed with the capability of being converted into minelayers, with a maximum carrying capacity of sixty Mk XIV mines. These were 1540-ton destroyers of the First Emergency Flotilla and were armed with such weapons as could be made available in the desperate days of their construction. Four of the eight destroyers of this class were fitted as fleet destroyers and armed with the standard pre-war 4.7-inch LA (low-angle) single guns as were the pre-war destroyers. Even these guns were in short supply, and so four others, *Obedient*, *Obdurate*, *Opportune* and *Orwell*, were equipped with old 4-inch single HA guns. In the event, these weapons were to prove more valuable than the standard 4.7-inch gun, which could not engage enemy aircraft. Subsequently, the 4-inch gun ships were much in demand to provide AA cover for convoys to Russia, spending most of their first years at sea with the Home Fleet in this role.

Strange as it now seems, it had been in March 1941, just as

the pre-war ships were being withdrawn from their minelaying duties, that the decision to construct these four new destroyers with the potential for minelaying had been taken and approved! As before, the quartet was to be capable of fast conversion to and from minelayers. This involved the landing of the after 4-inch mounting and torpedo tubes and converting within 48 hours. These ships used the stored minelaying sets and conveyor gears that had been manufactured for the twenty unconverted ships of the 'G', 'H' and 'I' classes that had never used them, and were now destined never to do so. Although these sets were in store in the dockyard depots, the minelaying capstans allocated to them, were not. Indeed, one had been destroyed by an enemy air raid, thus delaying the ships' completion by eight months.

Although small ships by the then prevailing standard destroyer classes, their construction was painfully slow. All four were not even launched until 1942 (*Obedient* and *Obdurate* by Denny in February and April of that year respectively, and *Opportune* and *Orwell* in January and April from the Thornycroft yard). By the time they had joined the Royal Navy's destroyer force, the pre-war ships had reconverted and there were no plans for destroyer minelayer operations as the needs of the anti-submarine and anti-aircraft duties overrode all other considerations as Britain fought for her survival.

Just two months after the initial decision to build four of the 'O' Class vessels with minelaying potential, and while they were still on the stocks, further conclusions were reached that affected their role. The Admiralty was belatedly learning the power of the Stuka dive-bomber at this time (May 1941, and during the battle for Crete). Some concern was expressed that, because minelaying was a nocturnal operation, these four destroyers had not been allocated any of the new 20-mm Oerlikon cannon then coming into favour in other modern destroyers as defence against the Stuka. This lack, in view of events taking place in the Mediterranean, plus the fact that these four vessels would only rarely be employed as minelayers in the foreseeable future, could not be accepted. However, when an inclining experiment was conducted with *Oribi* (one of the 'conventional' 'O' class ships and the first to complete), it was found that she had no margin for additional top-weight, even of such a vital nature as the Oerlikon cannon.

This presented the designers with a cruel dilemma. The minelaying 'O' class had to have the Oerlikons for their own survival, but it was calculated that their mine load, with sixty mines embarked, amounted to some 74½ tons. The TWMG added a further 1¾ tons, and this combined total had to be reduced by at least 10 tons to enable the destroyers to ship the weapon. Basic mathematics meant that their maximum mine load had to be reduced to just fifty Mk IV mines.

The Director of Torpedoes and Mines then pointed out that these calculations were all very well, but according to the type of mine shipped, the weight could vary from 1150 lb to 4090 lb. He suggested it would simplify matters if the mine load for all minelaying destroyers was defined by total weight rather than numbers of mines. This common-sense idea was agreed to, and became the standard practice thereafter, the number of units being adjusted accordingly. In fact, as A&As[90] were loaded into these destroyers as the years passed (such as radars and the like), the four minelaying 'O' class ships were reduced to a working practical capacity of just forty sea mines.

By the time all four ships were nearing final completion, they were clearly not going to be presented with much opportunity to carry out minelaying for a considerable time. However, in order to assess their capability in this respect, should it again become a requirement of the war at sea, the practice of conversion from destroyer to minelayer had to be conducted as one of their trials. Accordingly, in May 1942, the order went out that *Obedient, Obdurate, Opportune* and *Orwell* were to complete as normal destroyers, with all four guns and both sets of torpedo tubes, two Oerlikons, a four-barrelled 2-pdr pom-pom and two 0.5-inch machine-guns on twin Mk V power-mountings. The four ships were to work up in that configuration and then sail to Immingham to carry out the conversion trial, embarking mines and carrying out a practice lay. They were then to immediately reconvert and commission for service in the Home Fleet.

[90] A&As = Additions and Amendments

This was how it turned out and all four saw much hard service in both the Arctic and the North Atlantic, their most famous engagement being against the *Lutzow, Admiral Hipper* and six big destroyers on New Year's Eve 1942. Later in the war, in 1944, the *Obdurate* was mined and repairs took over a year to complete. Hard worked in their main role, they saw no minelaying until very late in the war and then they took part in two special operations of interest to our story.

Starting as early as June 1941, the Royal Navy had been charged with escorting huge convoys of war material to Soviet Russia, who had been Germany's very willing ally until that date. Although, in theory, the Russian Northern Fleet was supposed to provide the cover for the last stage of the long journey, in fact their forces proved largely ineffective, particularly so against German U-boats. All these convoys had to pass through the bottleneck of the Kola Inlet in order to reach their destination ports of Murmansk and Archangel. Naturally, this choke point proved an irresistible ambush point for German submarine commanders seeking easy pickings, once the bulk of the Royal Navy escort had turned back. An obvious solution was to lay a deep anti-submarine minefield in the area. However, although the Russians were supposedly the experts at this type of naval warfare, they proved either unwilling or incapable of laying such a field, to protect the Allied merchantmen bringing them aid.

The Admiralty therefore offered to do the job for them with our own ships, but the suspicious ally put a whole series of objections in the path of even this. Negotiations dragged on for months without permission being granted. It was not until the war in Europe was almost at an end that the Soviets finally gave way. Even then, they insisted that the British vessels sailed from Scapa Flow to carry out the operation and not from their own adjacent ports.

The intensifying of U-boat attacks in the North-Western Approaches had also led to a call for the renewal of deep mining operations in the northern part of the Irish Sea and other focal points. Both the fast minelayer *Apollo* and her sister ship *Ariadne* took part in these operations, supplemented by the *Plover* and the *Willem van de Zaan*. But in this, and the Arctic lay, minelaying destroyers were required as well.

Accordingly, *Obedient, Opportune* and *Orwell* converted to their minelaying role for the first time in earnest at Immingham. Each destroyer embarked a full outfit of forty mines in March 1945. Practice at laying deep fields was carried out by adding to the Irish Sea fields, *Opportune* making three such runs and the other pair two apiece. In total, three U-boats were sunk on these minefields, *U-275, U-260* and *U-1169* during the closing stages of the war, an excellent outcome. This duty completed, the three destroyers reloaded and joined the *Apollo* at Scapa Flow. The squadron sailed from Scapa, and on 22 April they commenced their work. They laid some 276 deep mines, between Syet Navolok and Kildin Island, most successfully. In truth, it proved too late to be of much practical help and no German submarine was lost in this minefield in the short period of its existence. However, as the last wartime operation lay conducted by destroyers it is of some interest and, fortunately, two of the commanding officers of those destroyers were interviewed by the author. They provided posterity with a very interesting commentary on this unique operation.

Captain John Gower, who at that time was commander of HMS *Orwell*, recalled:

> . . . we were with *Obedient* and we picked up our mines at Immingham. I think we carried about forty normally released aft manually by order of a buzzer on the bridge. All I can say is when detailed to do this lay so close to the finale, we were not very keen to stick out our necks just once more on the enemy's doorstep![91]

Captain Ryder, VC, commanding HMS *Opportune* at that date, provided this comprehensive and amusing account of the operation, which is well worth reproducing in full.

> We had been on Russia convoys since shortly after the Normandy landings and had done about three convoys

[91] Captain John Gower, RN, to the author, 10 November 1980.

to Murmansk or, more accurately, Polyarnoe. The
trouble arose because our asdics were hopelessly
impeded by the layering of the warm and cold water
right in the approaches to Polyarnoe and Murmansk,
and the German U-boats took advantage of this and each
time they picked off one, two or three ships or escorts,
just as they were entering these enclosed waters. The
Russians appeared unable, or unwilling, to do anything
about it. Their attitude was that this was just inefficiency
on our part. While they were driving back the forces of
Nazi Germany on land, it was the responsibility of the
Royal Navy to make sure that war supplies promised
were duly delivered safely into their hands, and we were
not doing it very well.

In fact, this was all a bit cynical because these cargoes
brought through at such risk were piling up at Murmansk,
delayed because all evidence of American manufacture
had to be painted out or otherwise obliterated.

In view of all this, it was decided to lay a deep minefield right in the Polyarnoe inlet, just before the next
convoy arrived, in the hope that the close escort would
force the U-boats deep and thus destroy them.

Four of the 'O' Class destroyers were fitted to take
mine rails and thus it was at very short notice we were
diverted to Hull to fit rails. This was completed in something like thirty-six hours and we were sent over to
Immingham to load. At this stage I rang up the
Admiralty over a scramble telephone and was put
through to the Underwater Division. I asked if I might
have some expert assistance with the mines – 'No need,
it's all in the mining manual' – 'But I've never seen
a ruddy mine in my life' – 'Oh yes you have, you did a
two-day mining course at *Vernon* as a Sub-Lieutenant.'

I must have slept through it – I certainly couldn't
remember anything about the inside of a mine.
However, it was obvious that true to the best naval tradi-
tions I was expected to learn on the job.

As a practice run I was ordered to fill in the gap in the
East Coast Mine Barrage opposite the Humber, some

thirty-five miles off Spurn Head. I was conscious that this required precise navigation. We had to steam thirty-five miles from our last fix to exactly one side of the channel and then turn at right angles; dropping our full load of eggs by the time we reached the far side. Then turn smartly back home.

Our Taunt Wire Measuring Gear was a great comfort as distance was concerned but apart from compass and steering errors, the normal uncertainties of the tidal stream flowing athwartships opened up all sorts of possible inaccuracies as far as our course was concerned.

I must say that my misgivings at finding myself in command of a minelayer were not shared by the ship's company. The two imposing rows of mines down the full length of the deck clearly boosted their morale. All sorts of ribald slogans were chalked on them, and had to be rubbed off – and sailors were photographed leaning nonchantly on these great beasts.

We set out boldly and had not gone far when there was a cry from aft – 'Taunt Wire Measuring Gear carried away.' A stop-watch, ready for just such an emergency, was started to time accurately the interval before it was re-started. It lasted for only about ten minutes and parted again, and again and again. The useless coil of piano wire had obviously rusted through in many places – so not for the first or last occasion it boiled down to ordinary dead reckoning.

The fact that we didn't blow ourselves up could hardly, in the circumstances, be attributed to the accuracy of our navigation – but more as evidence that the East Coast barrier was no longer a hazard to shipping.

We then reloaded and proceeded round to the Clyde still not knowing, of course, what all this was 'in aid of'. On arrival at the Clyde we were ordered to lay a deep field to the north of Rathlin Island and then loaded up again at, I think, Milford Haven.

The minelaying destroyers then proceeded under my command to Scapa Flow where we joined HMS *Apollo*, a fast minelayer, who became Senior Officer of this minelaying force. We were carefully briefed – each ship being allocated a line on which it was to make its lay in the Polyanroe inlet. After this, we sailed, the destroyers forming a screen for the *Apollo*. We proceeded at fairly high speed both for our own safety and in order to arrive at first light – undetected we hoped, and so make our lay before the awaiting U-boats woke up to what we were doing. In order to lay we had to reduce the speed of the destroyers to eight-to-ten knots and remain on a steady course throughout the lay. During the critical period therefore we were very vulnerable to torpedo attack.

It was therefore with some indignation that, a few hours before we were due to commence, a coded signal was received – 'Do not lay but enter harbour and embark Russian liaison officers prior to carrying out the operation previously planned.' This was maddening. It transpired that the Russian authorities, nothing if not paranoid, thought that, with the approaching defeat of Germany, this was all a sinister plot by the wicked British to mine them in before transferring hostilities to Russian soil. The fact that there was nothing much to 'mine in' except perhaps an odd water boat, fuel barge or harbour launch, made it all the more ludicrous.

Acting on our orders, therefore, we steamed in, in full view of any lurking U-boats thereby giving them ample warning of what was afoot. We each embarked a Russian officer and an interpreter and then carried out our lay independently. The Russian request that we lay the mines ten miles further to seaward was ignored, it would have made the whole operation valueless.

They also wanted to know details of the mines we were laying. This was easily answered, as they were exact copies of Russian mines of the First World War! [*sic*]

Lining up on a selected shore mark we steadied on the appropriate course and reduced to ten knots. At the precise moment I gave the crisp order – 'Commence Laying' – Nothing happened! The mines were frozen

solidly to the rails. 'Stop Laying.' We circled round. The
idea of applying a blow-torch to the situation didn't
seem to meet with much enthusiasm. Then the Chief
Buffer came up to the bridge and said, 'Sir. If we get
enough of the lads and give 'em a shove I think they will
go.' Thinking the whole U-boat fleet was watching our
predicament I replied rather testily, 'Yes. For God's Sake
do just that!'

I blessed the Chief Buffer, he was plumb right – over
they went one-by-one and just to give the Russians a
fright I said to him, 'Now we will steam back over the
mines just to make sure they work all right.' This had to
be reinterpreted and caused some dismay, especially
when we produced a lifebelt for him to put on! No one
had told him that they were laid very deep.[92]

Thus, the minelaying destroyers ended the Second World
War as they had ended the First, at sea and working against
the enemy to the last. As before, the true results of their
efforts could never be known precisely, but during the war
the fast minelayers and destroyers laid a total of 11,100 mines
in enemy waters, 15.5 per cent of the total laid, the
destroyers' contribution to this being just 2.8 per cent of
the total mines laid in *all* areas. Although this percentage was
tiny, the areas in which the destroyers had sown their deadly
cargoes were exceptionally relevant. A total of 228 enemy
ships were lost to mines in the Heligoland Bight and 168
more in the Texel to Brest region. Of the total enemy losses,
mines laid by the fast minelayers and destroyers amounted to
43 ships, or 3 per cent, a ratio of mines laid to ships sunk of
231 to 1.

This was a not inconsiderable achievement, when added to
the extra work they created for the German defending and
minesweeping forces. There is also considerable evidence that
the submarine *U-54* was sunk by mines laid by the 20th Flotilla
at the end of February, although it is not conclusive.

[92] Captain Robert Ryder, VC, RN, to the author 7 November 1980.

Table 14
Individual totals of mines laid by British destroyer
minelayers 1939–45

Intrepid	1592
Express	1210
Icarus	1196
Stronghold	1174
Esk	1110
Impulsive	892
Ivanhoe	754
Tenedos	484
Scout	278
Thanet	200
Opportune	170
Thracian	160
Orwell	120
Obedient	120
Total	**9460**

Post-war operations

That destroyer minelayers were considered still to have a valid
future role was made evident when the 1st Emergency Flotilla
(originated in 1941) and the 12th Emergency Flotilla
(launched 1944–5) joined the much reduced post-war fleet.

The founding of the North Atlantic Treaty Organisation
(NATO), which replaced the Western Union, in the face of
what seemed an imminent Soviet threat to overrun Western
Europe, provided a catalyst for a limited reappraisal and re-
armament. Whereas Great Britain and the United States had
disarmed quickly and with relief, post-1945, Stalin's empire
had energetically increased arming. Stalin had imposed
Communist rule on Poland, Czechoslovakia, Romania and
Bulgaria in the space of three short years; and had supported
the Communist takeover of Yugoslavia, as well as the failed
Red uprising in Greece. NATO's policy was to attempt to
contain the southern expansion of the Soviet Union further
into the Mediterranean.

Thus, once again as so often before, the strategical importance of the Dardanelles in such a policy was obvious from our

own experience in the First World War, as was the importance of minefields to enforce the blocking of this vital link from the Soviet Black Sea Fleet in the event of war.

With Turkey joining NATO, the Royal Navy's Mediterranean Fleet had an obviously important part to play in this policy. Early in 1948, the C-in-C Mediterranean called for the conversion of two of his destroyers, *Chaplet* and *Comet*, to a minelaying capability to enable such a high-speed operation to be carried out, if, as expected, Russia marched south and west. These 1710-ton destroyers had an estimated capacity for fifty 'T' mines once the after 4.5-inch gun, both sets of torpedo tubes and the anti-submarine 'Squid' mortar were landed. Two sister ships, *Chieftain* and *Contest*, were also considered suitable for such a conversion, giving a full squadron of four such destroyers. Until that could be done, the *Obdurate* was retained in commission in a series of ongoing tests and experiments in high-speed minelaying.

The *Comet* finally refitted as a minelayer as late as 1953, the work being carried out by Chatham Dockyard. The *Chaplet* followed early in 1954 and finally *Contest* converted at Portsmouth during 1954–5. I have been unable to verify whether the proposed further modification of *Chieftain* was ever undertaken. All three converted ships were given an interim modification, fitted for minelaying and also for cold-weather service, perhaps with a view to repeating the minelaying operations off Murmansk as carried out by the 'O' class ships at the end of the war, described earlier. To compensate for the top weight of the mine load, this trio dropped the after 4.5-inch gun permanently and shipped thirty tons of ballast, but they retained one set of torpedo tubes, a twin 40-mm Bofors and two single Bofors as AA protection, plus their 'Squid' mortar, which gave them a somewhat unique profile. The total mine load for the 'C' class was fifty tons. All three were equipped with the hydraulic conveyor belt with variable speed gear and capstan bogie lay. TWMG was also fitted as standard. The squared-off sterns of the 'C' class destroyers proved more suitable for minelaying than the rounded sterns of the 'O' class ships in practice. The loading plane for the entry port was aft in these ships, but in

Contest it was abreast the forward torpedo tubes and the mines were loaded straight off flat rail cars by the destroyers themselves.

Lieutenant-Commander 'Robbie' Robertson, the commanding officer of HMS *Contest* in the Mediterranean during 1958–9, and Lieutenant-Commander Richard Reynolds, her first lieutenant, described some of the last destroyer minelaying operations ever conducted by British destroyers, during an interview with the author held at HMS *Vernon* on 6 June 1978.

Minelaying was carried out several times as part-and-parcel of the standard NATO exercises in the Mediterranean Fleet, being considered a prime strategical function. The *Contest* conducted the last ever destroyer mine lay in November 1959. She loaded straight from rail cars at Messina, Sicily, as she had done on at least one earlier occasion that spring, and the dummy field was laid off the coast of Sicily. Both men emphasised the role of the Gunner (T) in the smooth running of these lays. No specialised course had ever been taken by any officer or man aboard in minelaying, (echoes of Ryder's wartime experience) but, despite this everything went strictly according to plan and the fields were accurately placed.

Table 15
British Destroyer equipped as minelayers 1953–60

Ship	Tonnage	Mine capacity	Year of original completion	Speed in knots
Chaplet			1945	
Comet	1710	50 tons	1944	35
Contest			1945	

This again reflected the high standard of the destroyer's navigation officer, who obtained precise fixes with consummate ease. The TWMG was exactly the same as that used during the war. The wire itself was wound on the reel at the manufacturing factory, dipped in hot grease throughout the process to prevent rust at sea and then allowed to cool. These reels were estimated to have a shelf life of at least ten years in such condition. One thing that went to the heart of her officers, commanding a destroyer in the crack Mediterranean Fleet in peacetime, was the after effects of using this device. As can be imagined, the spinning reel cascaded the after part of the ship liberally with oil, and the gleaming white paintwork suffered accordingly!

The mine runs always involved the laying of non-contact mines, such as acoustic and magnetic – all had rendered the old traditional horned mine largely obsolete by this period, at least as far as the destroyer trio was concerned. The laying itself took place at night to simulate real war conditions as closely as possible, sometimes when within sight of the Sicilian coast. I asked about the noise and whether this would have compromised the operation in real conditions by giving away to the enemy the approximate position of the minefield. Both officers agreed that, in the still of a Mediterranean night, the noise of the capstan and bogie chain seemed to be very loud indeed up on the bridge. However, both also stated that such noise at sea, is very often 'lost' across the water in and would not be picked up ashore at the distance they were laying.

After 1959, British destroyers appeared to have ceased conducting such exercises. The traditional Fleet destroyer was itself fading away from the ever-dwindling strength of the Royal Navy, as it sank from a first class fleet to a second and then third or fourth rank force in numbers. The fast, lithe, well-armed, all-purpose destroyer was steadily replaced by the slower, bulkier and more specialised frigate, which had no provision whatsoever for minelaying, despite their enormously increased size and cost. In truth, the shrinking fleet made it increasingly necessary to concentrate only on essentials, of which anti-submarine and anti-aircraft capabilities were by far the most important overall. The sweeping of enemy mines also carried a high priority, owing to Britain's own vulnerability in this respect. Many small minesweepers of the coastal and inshore types were constructed (the Ton, Ham and Ley classes) but offensive minelaying took more and more of a back role in the Royal Navy's war plans.

Engineering Officer Ray Schofield served aboard the destroyer *Orwell* for a couple of weeks in 1955, while she was still a fully operational unit based at Plymouth training artificers. He recalled:

She did no minelaying exercises at all during this period, although she still had the trolley rails leading to the stern, on the iron deck, and I believe she was still capable of performing this duty.[93]

So, throughout the 1950s and early 1960s the last of the destroyer minelayers followed the sad example of their forebears of the 20th Flotilla. They were towed away, one by one, to the breaker's yard. The *Opportune* was scrapped at the old minelaying base of Milford Haven in November 1955; *Obdurate* at Rosyth in April 1959; *Contest* at Grays in February 1960; *Chieftain* was broken up at Sunderland in 1961; *Comet* at Troon in November 1962 and *Chaplet* followed shortly after. By May 1961, 'Geiger', writing in *The Navy* magazine, was lamenting that surface minelayers were fast becoming an extinct breed of warship. By this time, all the destroyer minelayers had gone, save one. The survivor was the *Orwell*, which remained the last of her type to serve in the Royal Navy. But all too soon her day was also done. She was broken up in 1965. Thus passed an era in naval history.

And so, with the passing of the destroyer minelayer, came the end of the fast surface minelayer story. Their exploits were always secretive. Their achievements were little known outside a restricted circle and ignored by historians recording the main sweep of Royal Navy operations. Indeed, little record remains anywhere on their operations or methods. If nothing else, it is hoped that this first complete account of their actions will finally set things straight on this little-lauded facet of the destroyer story.

[93] Letter to Mr Walter Watkin, dated 23 October 1980, quoted with his permission.

INDEX

Abdiel, HMS 16, 19, 20, 21, 24–25, 26, 27, 29, 31, 32, 33, 34, 35, 36, 38, 39, 40, 44, 47, 51–52, 53, 54, 56, 57–58, 59, 63, 64, 65, 66, 67, 68, 69, 70, 72, 74, 76, 77, 78, 82, 83, 89, 90, 92, 93, 99, 101
Acasta class ships 103
Admiral Hipper 137, 139, 170, 174, 195
Admiral Scheer 170
Adventure, HMS 179
aircraft *see also* Zeppelin airships
  Blohm und Voss HA140 164
  Bristol Blenheim 159, 161, 184
  Curtiss Large America flying boats 52
  Dornier floatplanes/flying boats 159, 162, 164
  Fairey Swordfish 156–157
  Junkers Ju 88: 164
  Junkers *Stuka* 147, 188, 193
  Lockheed Hudson 159
Albatross 7
Altmark 131
Amazon, HMS 103
Ambuscade, HMS 103
American Civil War 4
Amphion, HMS 7
Angora 13
Apollo, HMS 195, 198–199
Apollo class cruisers 5, 11
Arashi 190
Arethusa, HMS 169, 170
Ariadne, HMS 195
Ariel, HMS 22, 23, 26, 29, 31, 33, 35, 36, 39, 40, 44, 47, 48, 51, 52, 53, 57, 59, 64, 68, 70, 74, 79–81, 88
Audacious, HMS 1, 13
Aurora, HMS 23, 32, 33, 34, 35, 36, 169, 170

Baltic Sea 32, 98
Beagle class ships 103
Beardmore 14
Beattie, Lieutenant-Commander K A 39
Beatty, Admiral Sir David 32, 38
Bedouin, HMS 169
Bellona, HMS 23, 33, 34, 36, 37
Bentlage, Captain 153
Biarritz 13

Bickford, Captain J G, DSO, DSC 124, 137, 140, 152, 154, 160, 165
Blanche, HMS 23, 33, 34, 36, 37
Blonde, HMS 23
Boadicea, HMS 23, 32, 33, 34, 36
Bowles, Lieutenant-Commander G P 39
Bremse 7–8
Brest 172, 174
British Expeditionary Force 146
British Government 4, 10, 13, 111
Brotheridge, T E 'Bernard' 141, 143–144, 148, 177
Brummer 7–8
Bucknell, Assistant-Paymaster C 176
Buffalo 184–185
Bullen, Chief ERA Alfred James 79–81
Burney, Lieutenant D 62

Cammell Laird 16, 19
Campbell, HMS 141
Chaplet, HMS 202, 203, 205
Chatfield, First Sea Lord 111
Chatham 126, 131, 202
Chieftain, HMS 202, 205
Childers, Erskine 55
Churchill, Winston 10, 11, 12, 15, 23, 98, 103, 134, 137, 139, 165, 179
Clutterbuck, Commander (later Captain) Francis A 39, 52, 68, 70
Clyde, River 198
Cobra 153
Comet, HMS 202, 203, 205
Conquest, HMS 36
Contest, HMS 202–203, 205
convoy FS100 133
convoy HX106 170
Cooper, Duff 111
Courageous, HMS 23
Cowie, Captain J S, CBE 3, 32, 50–51, 62, 84–85, 100, 104, 124, 127, 136, 137, 166, 176–177
Crimean War 4
Cromer Light 128–129, 145
Crusader class ships 103
Curtis, Captain Berwick 'Budge', DSO 19–20, 21, 34, 39, 40–41, 43, 44, 46, 47–48, 53–54, 55–56, 57–58, 59–60, 65, 67, 70, 72, 77, 84, 89, 90–91, 93

Dardanelles 13, 23, 201–202
Dartmouth 101
Dauglish, Lieutenant-Commander E H,
    RIM 39
De Winton, Captain F S 100–101
Defender class ships 103
Denmark 27
destroyer minelayers 8–12
    fates of, 1919–39 101
    genesis of 16–18
    mines laid, 1916–18 95
    mines laid, 1939–45 201
destroyer minelaying first conducted 19–21
destroyer minelaying potential on outbreak
    of Second World War 115
destroyers converted or built for
    minelaying, 1939–45 122, 126–127
destroyers equipped as minelayers,
    1953–60 203
Dogger Bank 20
Dogger Bank Noord Light Vessel 35, 43,
    56, 70, 84
Dogger Bank Zuid Light Vessel 33, 34, 36,
    40, 46, 53, 54, 56, 66, 67, 73, 90
Dorling, Captain Taprell, DSO see 'Taffrail'
Dover 29, 87, 106, 147–148
Dover Straits 10, 27, 147
Dresden class ships 7
Dunkirk 29, 30, 86, 87, 146, 167
Dutch Free Channel 42, 43, 54, 73–74

E-24 14, 15
E-29 68
E-34 15
E-41 14
E-45, E-46 and E-51 15
East Coast Barrage 131–132, 143, 146–147,
    149, 168, 197–198
Eclipse class ships 103, 104, 107
Elbing class ships 7
Ems Estuary 128
Erich Steinbrinck 153
Esk, HMS 105–106, 107, 108, 109, 114,
    118, 122, 124, 125, 127, 128, 131–133,
    134, 137, 141–142, 143, 144–145, 146,
    147, 148, 149, 201
    Operation CBX5 152, 154, 155, 156,
    157–158, 165
exploders, 'O' 44
Express, HMS 105–106, 107, 108, 109–110,
    114, 122, 124, 125, 127, 128, 131–133,
    141–142, 143, 144, 146, 147, 148, 149,
    190–191, 192, 201
    Operation CBX5 152, 154, 155, 156,
    157–158, 159, 160–161, 163, 164, 165

Falke 153
Fearless class destroyers 107, 108
Ferret, HMS 22, 24, 26, 29, 31, 32, 33, 35,
    36, 39, 40, 44, 47, 49, 51, 53, 57, 60,
    64, 65, 66, 68, 70, 74, 87–88, 90, 93,
    99, 101, 114
First World War, situation at outbreak 4–5

Fisher, Admiral Sir John 3, 11
Fleet Air Arm, No. 812 Squadron 156–157
Forbes, Admiral Sir Charles 124, 139, 146
Forth, Firth of 28, 37
Frankfurt class ships 7
Frater mine depot 106
Freemantle, Commander C A 34, 36
French Navy 6
Fulton, Robert 2, 3

G-37 class destroyer minelayers 9
G-96 9
Gabriel, HMS 19, 25, 26, 63, 64, 88, 90, 93,
    99, 101
Galatea, HMS 23
Galloper Shoal 125
Garth, HMS 161, 162–163, 164
Gazelle 13
Geddes, Sir Eric 94
German Navy 1, 7–9, 10, 144
    2nd and 5th Torpedo Boat Flotillas 153
    High Seas Fleet 11, 20, 98
Glasgow, HMS 141
Glowworm, HMS 134, 136, 137, 139
Gneisenau 139–140, 172
Goito 8
Goodwin Sands 10, 86
Gordon, Commander R C 152, 155, 172,
    173, 174, 176
Gower, Captain John 196
Grampus, HMS 179
Grangemouth 28
Graudenz 7
Greif 153
Grenville, HMS 131
Greyhound, HMS 134, 141
Greyhound class destroyers 107, 108, 109,
    111, 114

H26 70
Hambledon, HMS 161, 164
Hammersley-Heenan, Lieutenant-
    Commander Vernon 39, 75, 78–79
Hardy, HMS 134, 140
Hartlepool 133
Harwich 125
Hatch, Lieutenant George 84
Havock, HMS 134, 140
Heligoland Bight 10, 11, 14, 15, 17, 19, 20,
    27–28, 31, 38, 42, 70, 94, 95, 124, 142,
    166, 200
Hero, HMS 134
Hero class destroyers 107, 109, 111
Hillier, Gunner (T) E G 79, 80
Hipper class cruiser 170, 172
Hitler, Adolf 111
Hoeg Transporter 181
Holland 27, 52, 142, 144, 145, 146, 151,
    152, 153
Hong Kong 106, 180, 181, 182, 189–190
    defensive minefields 182–183, 185–186,
    188
Hook of Holland 144

horn firing gear, Herz 7, 14
Horns Reef 19, 20
Hostile, HMS 134, 140
Hotspur, HMS 134, 140
Hotspur class destroyers 114
Howting, PO 168
Humber, River 35, 36, 37, 54, 65, 67, 73, 84, 90, 125, 131, 133, 143, 149
Hunter, HMS 134, 140
Huxley, Chief ERA Harry 76–77, 78, 81, 83
Hyperion, HMS 134

Icarus, HMS 113, 122, 127, 131, 133, 134, 141, 146, 147, 148, 149, 167, 169, 170, 172, 176, 175, 201
  Operation CBX5 152, 154, 155, 156, 157, 159
Ilex, HMS 134
Iltis 153
Immingham 38, 40, 42, 44, 48, 51, 52, 60, 66, 68, 89, 93, 106, 124, 125, 130, 141, 142, 145, 167, 170, 196
  description 143, 148–149, 150–151
Imogen, HMS 134
Impulsive, HMS 113, 122, 127, 131, 133, 134, 141, 143–145, 146, 148, 149, 151, 167, 169, 170, 172, 176, 177, 201
Inconstant, HMS 23
Inglefield, HMS 134
Intrepid, HMS 112–113, 122, 125–127, 128, 130, 131, 141–142, 143, 144–145, 146, 147, 148, 149–151, 167, 168–169, 170, 177, 192, 201
  mines embarked, 8 February 1941 171
  Operation CBX5 152–153, 154, 155, 156, 157, 159
  Operation GS 172, 173, 176
Intrepid class destroyers 111, 112, 114–116
Invergordon 133
Irish Sea 195, 196
Irishman 163, 164
Isis, HMS 134
Italian Navy 6, 8, 9
Ivanhoe, HMS 113, 122, 125–126, 127, 128, 131, 133, 134, 141, 143, 144–145, 146, 201
  Operation CBX5 152, 154, 155, 156, 157–159, 160, 161–162, 163, 165

Jackson, Sir H 16
Jaguar 153
Jantine Fenegine 51
Japan 186, 189
Japanese Navy, Imperial 6, 179
Javelin, HMS 147, 173
Javelin class destroyers 113
Jellicoe, Admiral Sir John 11, 14, 19, 20, 21, 23–24, 27, 38
Jersey, HMS 173
Johore defensive minefield 186–188
Jupiter, HMS 147, 152, 153, 155–156, 157, 159, 160–161, 163, 164, 165, 173
Jutland, Battle of 20–21

Karl Galster 153
Kashmir, HMS 173
Kattegat 32, 51, 95
Kelly class destroyers 113
Kelvin, HMS 152, 153, 160, 161–163, 164
Kempenfelt, HMS 16–18, 19
King Edward VII, HMS 14
Kitchener, General 10–11
Knight, E F 52–53
Koenigin Luise 7
Koenigsberg class ships 7
Kola Inlet 195, 196
Kung Wo 184, 189, 190

Laforey class destroyers 9–10, 113
Latona, HMS 188
League of Nations 111
Leda, HMS 163
Legion, HMS 22, 24, 26, 29, 31, 33, 35, 36, 39, 44, 47–48, 51, 52, 53, 64, 65, 66, 68, 70, 93, 99, 101
London Navy Treaty 102–103
Lutzow 195

'M' class destroyers 16, 18, 22
M61, *M89* and *M136* 144
Mack, George 112–113, 126–127, 128, 130, 145, 148–151, 168, 177
Malta 106, 112–113
Man Yeung 182, 183, 186, 188
Manx Admiral 133
Mao Lee 182
Marder, Professor Arthur 5, 27–28
Mars 48
Marsala 8
Mashona, HMS 169
Mastiff, HMS 18
Matabele, HMS 169, 170
Maud, Lieutenant-Commander L C 172
Maya 190
McCoy, Gunner's Mate Tim 168
Messina 203
Meteor 7
Meteor, HMS 18, 22, 26, 29, 31, 64, 88, 99, 101
Milford Haven 106, 125, 177
Milne class destroyers 113
mine areas, declared, 1939–40 129
mine depots, specialised 106
minefields *see also* operations
  A21 31
  A23 31, 32
  A25 32
  A26 32–36
  A27 32–36
  A28 32–34, 36–37
  A29 32–34, 36–37
  A30 40
  A31 40–41
  A32 42–43
  A33 44, 45
  A34 44, 46

minefields *(continued)*
  A35 and A36 51
  A37 51–52
  A38 52–53, 54–55
  A40 and A41 53
  A43 53, 54
  A45 55
  A46 57–58, 59–60
  A48 65
  A51 66, 67, 68
  A57 68
  A58 68, 69
  A60 and A61 70
  A62 70, 71
  A63 70
  A64 70, 72
  A65 73
  A66 73–74
  A67 74
  A68 89
  A69 90
  A70 90–91, 92
  A71 93
  A72 93–94
  BS15–BS18 147
  BS20 148
  BS22–BS25 148
  BS26–BS29 149
  BS32 149
  BS34–BS36 149
  Hong kong defensive 182–183, 185–186, 188
  Johore defensive 186–188
  LD1 131
  'MSA' and 'MSB' 167
  Singapore defensive 180–182, 183–185, 189, 190–191
  W11 31
minelaying controls and instruments 116–120
  McKaffery-Klyne clock 102, 117, 120, 121–122
  mine dropping register 117
  minelaying instrument 117, 118
  order instrument 117
  sprocket-wheel evaders 176
  tachometer 117, 118–119
  Taunt wire measuring gear 62, 117, 119–120, 173, 198, 203–204
minelaying operations
  early British 10–12
  First World War 29–30
  hand laying 101–102
  by HMS *Icarus*, 20 February 1941 175
  measurement of extent of lay 15–16
  patterns 61
minelaying system, 'endless chain' design 104–105, 106, 120–123
Minerva 8
mines
  BE (British Elia) 5, 9, 13, 30, 37
  'contact' 2–3, 7
  'controlled' 2
  'DO' type 14, 31
  'Dummy' 39, 40, 52, 53, 132
  electro-contact net 14
  embarkation of 116
  embarked on HMS *Intrepid*, 8 February 1941 171
  'H' type 22, 24
  Herz horn-type 7, 13–14
  innovations 23
  Mk XIV 104, 107, 181, 183, 184, 186, 189
  Mk XIVa/b 119
  Mk XV 106
  Mk XVa/b 119
  Mk XVI 119
  Mk XVII 106, 184, 186, 189
  Mk XVIIa 171
  Mk XVIIIa 176
  Mk HII 16, 22, 28, 33, 44, 54, 65, 89, 104, 119
  moored acoustic 86
  moored magnetic (M-sinkers) 86–87
  'O' type 31, 32
  oscillating 5, 14, 31, 114
  Sauter-Harle 6
  Service 13, 16, 17
  'SO' type 31
  total laid by British destroyer minelayers 1916–18 95
  Vickers 5
  Vickers Elia, Mk IV 9
minesweepers, coastal and inshore 204
Minsk 133
Mitchell, Stoker Petty Officer Robert 80, 81
Motor Boats, Coastal (CMBs) 87
Mott, Stoker Petty Officer 79–80
Mountbatten, Captain Lord Louis 147, 152, 153–154, 155–156, 157, 159–161, 163, 164, 165
MTB-14 160
MTB-15 160, 161
MTB-16 and *MTB-17* 160
MTB-29 164
MTB-30 161, 162
MTB-31 164
Murmansk 195, 197, 202

Naiad, HMS 172
Napier class destroyers 113
Narvik 134, 139, 140
  Battles of 140–141
Narwhal, HMS 179
NATO (North Atlantic Treaty Organisation) 201, 203
Nautilus 7
navigation 56–57
Navy, The 205
Nino Bixio 8
Norman 164
North Dogger Bank Light Vessel 35, 43, 56, 70, 84

Norway 169–170
Norwegian Campaign 133–135, 136–141
Nowake 190

'O' class destroyers 167, 193, 194–195, 197, 202 *see also* Onslow class destroyers
Obdurate, HMS 192–193, 194–195, 202, 205
Obedient, HMS 122, 192–193, 194–195, 196, 201, 205
Ocean Drift 141
Ommaney, Admiral 18, 19
Onslow class destroyers 192–193 *see also* 'O' class destroyers
operations *see also* minefields
  BS4 143
  BS5 144–145
  BS6–BS9 146
  BS19 147
  CBX5 151, 152–165, 166
  DML 132–133
  Dynamo 146
  EW 131
  GS 172–177
  IB 128
  ID1, ID2 and ID3 131
  IE1 133
  JG2 128
  LD3 132
  PA3 and PA4 133
  RG 125
  Sickle 2: 141
  SW3 (German) 153
  'Wilfred' 134, 135, 138 *see also* Norwegian Campaign
  XMO 142
Opportune, HMS 122, 192–193, 194–195, 196–200, 201, 205
Oribi, HMS 193–194
Orvieto 13
Orwell, HMS 122, 192–193, 194–195, 196, 201, 204–205
Ostend 10, 29, 51, 88
Ostfriesland 21
Outer Dowsing Light Float 152, 156, 157, 163, 164

paravanes 62–63, 88, 126, 130
Paris 13, 88
Partenope 8
Paul Jacobi 153
Pawley, Leading Seaman 76
Pedita 15
pendant numbers 63–64
Penelope, HMS 32, 33, 34, 36, 137, 139
Persian Gulf 2
Phaeton, HMS 23
Phillips, Sub-Lieutenant, RNVR 156–157
'Piccadilly Circus' 52, 53, 66, 74
Pitt, William 3–4
Plover, HMS 147, 148, 149, 195
Plymouth 172, 177
Polarstern 48

Pollard, Chief ERA 83
Polyarnoe Inlet 197, 199–200
Port Arthur 6
Portsmouth 100, 101, 127, 128, 131, 133, 176, 202
Prince of Wales, HMS 179, 190
Princess Irene 11–12
Princess Margaret 11–12, 32, 33, 35, 36, 37
Princess Victoria, HMS 131, 132, 133, 142, 143, 144–145, 147
Puffin, HMS 142

Quarto 8

'R' class destroyers 23, 25, 89, 99, 114
Ramillies, HMS 170, 172
Redstart, HMS 182, 183
Regensburg 7
Renown, HMS 134, 136, 137, 139–140
Repulse, HMS 139, 179, 190
Reynolds, Lieutenant-Commander Richard 203
Richmond, Admiral Sir Herbert 10
Riddle of the Sands, The 55
Riede, Commander 153
Rival, HMS 34
Robertson, Lieutenant-Commander 'Robbie' 203
Rodney, HMS 141
Roland 153
Rorqual, HMS 179
Roskill, Captain Stephen W 125, 132, 166
Rosyth 28, 131, 133, 141
Rothera, Lieutenant F A 39, 79
Royal Air Force 159
  No. 206 Squadron 153, 154
Royal Navy
  1st Destroyer Flotilla 128, 131
  1st Emergency Flotilla 192, 201
  1st Light Cruiser Squadron 66–67
  2nd Destroyer Flotilla 139, 140–141
  3rd Destroyer Flotilla 9–10, 112, 113
  4th Destroyer Flotilla 147–148
  5th Destroyer Flotilla 147, 152, 155, 156, 157, 159–160, 173, 174, 176
  6th Destroyer Flotilla 169–170
  7th Light Cruiser squadron 72
  12th Emergency Flotilla 201
  20th (Minelaying) Flotilla 106
  39th and 40th Divisions 127
  areas of main activities 1918 and 1939–40 97
  bases and areas of operation 129
  First World War 38, 39–41, 42–44, 46–50, 51–56, 57–60, 61, 63, 65–72, 73–74, 77–78, 81, 83–85, 87–88, 89–94, 96
  Norwegian Campaign 134–135, 136–137, 139, 140, 141
  Operation CBX5 151, 152–165, 166
  Operation GS 172–174, 176–177
  pendant numbers 64

Royal Navy *(continued)*
  Second World War 122, 127–128,
    130–133, 142–146, 147, 148–151,
    166–167, 169, 170, 172–173, 178, 200
  Dover Patrol 22
  Grand Fleet 14, 19, 20–21, 32, 66
  Harwich Force 9–10, 52, 66, 91
  Home Fleet 134, 137, 169, 172, 177, 192,
    194
  Hong Kong Local Defence Flotilla 180
  Mediterranean Fleet 202, 203–204
  Mining School (HMS *Vernon*) 31
  Singapore Local Defence Flotilla 180
Royalist, HMS 23
Rushbridge, Leading Seaman Arthur 81
Russian convoys 195, 196–197
Russian Navy 6, 8, 9
  Black Sea Fleet 202
  Northern Fleet 195
Russo-Japanese conflict 4
Ryder, Captain Robert, VC 196–200

'S' class destroyers 105, 114, 167, 180, 190
S-13 class destroyer minelayers 8–9
S-31 and S-53 class destroyer minelayers 9
St Cyrus 163, 164
St Margaret 13
St. Vincent, Earl 3–4
Saltash, HMS 163
Sandfly, HMS 22, 26, 39, 53, 57, 58–59, 60,
  63, 64, 68, 70, 74, 90, 93, 99, 101
Sandford, Lieutenant 5, 14, 31
Scapa Flow 98, 135, 141, 142, 169, 170,
  172, 195, 196
Scharbentz 48
Scharnhorst 139–140, 172
Schofield, Engineering Officer Ray
  204–205
Scott, Ordinance Officer O A 168
Scott, Admiral Sir Percy 5
Scout, HMS 114, 122, 180, 181, 189, 190,
  192, 201
Seagull, HMS 133
Seal, HMS 179
Sears, Yeoman of Signals 158
Second World War statistics 200
Seymour, HMS 25, 26, 88–89, 99, 101
Sharpshooter, HMS 133
Shaw, Lieutenant (A) H 156–157
Sheerness 12, 126, 133, 167
Sheffield, HMS 141
Sheldrake, HMS 142
Singapore 106, 180, 181, 182, 186–187,
  189–190
  defensive minefields 180–182, 183–185,
    189, 190–191
sinkers (sinking plugs) 15
  delayed-release 39
  Mk VIII 22, 24, 33, 44, 65, 121
  Mk XII 54, 89
  Mk XIV 121
  Mk XV 115–116, 121
  Mk XVB 171

Mk XVI 121
Mk XVII*B 171
Sirdhana 181
Skate, HMS 25, 26, 89, 99, 101, 102, 114
South Dogger Bank Light Vessel 33, 34, 36,
  40, 46, 53, 54, 56, 66, 67, 73, 90
Stalin, Josef 201
Stronghold, HMS 114, 122, 180, 184, 185,
  187–188, 189, 190, 201
submarines, British minelaying 14, 15
Sullom Voe 135
Sutherland, Gunner (T) William 75–76, 77,
  82, 83

'T' class destroyers 167, 190
T-5 to *T-8* 153
'Taffrail' (Captain Taprell Dorling, DSO) 8,
  9, 19–20, 28–29, 39, 41, 43, 47, 48–49,
  56–57, 58–59, 60, 63, 66, 74, 81, 83, 84,
  87–88
Talbot, Leading Stoker 83
Tannenberg 153
Tarpon, HMS 23, 26, 27, 30, 31, 39, 53, 57,
  59, 64, 65, 66, 68, 74, 81, 83, 89, 90,
  93, 99, 101
Tartar, HMS 169, 170
Telemachus, HMS 23, 26, 27, 30, 31, 33, 35,
  36, 37, 39, 40, 44, 47, 51–52, 53, 57,
  58–59, 60, 64, 65, 68, 70, 74, 77–78, 82,
  83–84, 89, 93, 99, 101
Tenedos, HMS 114, 122, 180, 181, 182, 190,
  201
Terry, Lieutenant A H L 31, 32, 39
Terschelling Light Vessel 31, 32, 44, 51, 52,
  65, 68, 70, 90
Teviot Bank, HMS 132, 133, 134, 142, 143,
  147, 148, 188, 190
Thanet, HMS 114, 122, 180, 182–183, 189,
  190, 201
Thomas, Lieutenant-Commander M S 143,
  172
Thornycroft 'Special' design 18
Thracian, HMS 114, 122, 180, 182–183,
  186, 188, 189–190, 201
Tower, HMS 34, 36
Tribal class destroyers 113, 169
Tripoli 8
Trondheim 139, 141
Tudor, Commander E O 39
Turkish Navy 6, 13

U-54 200
U-260, *U-275* and *U-1169* 196
U-boats 8, 10, 28, 29, 36, 50, 65, 94–95,
  195, 197
UC I class submarines 8
Ulster, HMS 34
United States 186–187
United States Navy 2, 6, 179

'V' class destroyers 23–24, 25, 38, 99, 100,
  103, 105, 113

V-25, V-43 and V-67 class destroyer minelayers 9
Valentine, HMS 26, 34, 36, 88–89, 101, 113
Valorous, HMS 26, 88–89, 101, 113
Vanoc, HMS 23, 24, 26, 36, 39, 64, 65, 66, 68, 70, 74, 80, 83
Vanquisher, HMS 23, 24, 26, 33, 35, 36, 37, 39, 40, 44, 47, 48, 51–52, 53, 64, 66, 70, 74, 75, 78, 83–84, 89, 90, 93, 113
Vectis, HMS 34, 36
Vega, HMS 34, 36
Vehement, HMS 23, 24, 26, 39, 64, 66, 68, 70, 73, 74–79, 81–84, 88
Velox, HMS 24, 26, 113
Vendetta, HMS 36
Venetia, HMS 23, 24, 26
Venturous, HMS 23, 24, 26, 33, 35, 36, 39, 40, 53, 57, 59, 64, 65, 66, 67, 68, 70, 71, 89, 90, 93, 101, 113
Vernon, HMS 4, 31, 197, 203
Versatile, HMS 24, 26, 100–101, 113
Verulam, HMS 24, 26, 98, 101
Vesper, HMS 24, 26
Vestfiord 134, 135, 136, 137, 138, 139, 140
Vickers 5, 9
Vimiera, HMS 34, 36
Vimy, HMS 24, 26, 113
Violent, HMS 34
Vittoria, HMS 24, 26, 98, 101
Vivacious, HMS 23, 24, 26, 113
Vortigern, HMS 24, 26, 113, 152, 154, 156, 159–160, 163, 164

'W' class destroyers 24, 25, 38, 99, 100, 103, 105, 113
Wahine 15, 88
Walker, HMS 24, 26, 113
Walrus, HMS 24, 26, 101, 113
War at Sea, The 132, 166
Warburton-Lee, Captain 139, 140
Warspite, HMS 141
Warwick, HMS 24, 26
Washington Treaty 98, 99
Watchman, HMS 24, 26, 113
Wheeldon 163, 164
Whirlwind, HMS 24, 26, 100–101, 113
Whitworth, Vice-Admiral W J 134, 137, 139, 140
Widgeon, HMS 142
Willem van de Zaan 147, 149, 190, 195
Wilson, Admiral Sir Arthur 14
Wilson, Sub-Lieutenant David R 75, 76, 77, 78, 81, 83
Witch, HMS 141
Witherington, HMS 141
Wrabness mine depot 106
Wright, Lieutenant-Commander F E 39
Wyburd, Captain D B 161

Yorkshire coast 88, 125

Zeebrugge 10, 29, 51, 87
Zeppelin airships 64–65, 67